T0251652

Lightweight Enterprise Architectures

Fenix Theuerkorn

AUERBACH PUBLICATIONS

A CRC Press Company
Boca Raton   London   New York   Washington, D.C.

Library of Congress Cataloging-in-Publication Data

Theuerkorn, Fenix.
    Lightweight enterprise architectures / Fenix Theuerkorn.
        p. cm.
    Includes bibliographical references and index.
    ISBN 0-8493-2114-X
    1. Computer architecture. 2. Computer systems. 3. Business enterprises—Data processing. I. Title.

QA76.9.A73T49 2004
004.2′2—dc22   2004045086

Visit the Auerbach Publications Web site at www.auerbach-publications.com

CONTENTS

PREFACE

Simplicity is the ultimate sophistication.

— Leonardo DaVinci

Why This Book

For several years, it has been a goal of mine to write a book on enterprise architecture. While there are many good architectural books in circulation, they are either limited in scope or lack sufficient detail to be actionable. Early in my career, I found it difficult to translate the principles of these books into a logical flow of events that detail the purpose of the activities, the consumers of the outputs, and finally the control mechanisms for the enterprise. It is my intention to make these clear and easily referenced in this book.

"Lightweight Enterprise Architecture" (LEA) is an architectural approach that I have developed throughout my career to enable a quick alignment of technology to the business strategy. Similar to the popular lightweight programming approaches that have recently become popular, LEA has a simple and effective framework that facilitates the alignment of technology without a weighty methodology that typically makes architectures shelfware. In addition, LEA can reach a wider audience and hence become more effective within an enterprise.

In addition, architectural approaches of the past do not adapt well in today's environment, as systems are more complex and require tighter integration, shorter transaction cycles, and interoperability to trading communities. Hence, the days of large mainframes or ERP (enterprise resource planning) solutions providing the majority of an enterprise's needs have been replaced by diverse systems accumulated through merger and acquisition (M&A) activities, functionally divergent departments, geographic separation, and other factors. The bottom line is that the system landscapes in enterprises are becoming more complex and there is a need to control and manage the evolution of these complex environments.

Why a Diverse Audience Is Critical

The successful adoption of enterprise architecture in any organization requires the participation of many different stakeholders. The purpose of creating LEA was to reach a broad audience to ensure communication to all the key stakeholders required to adopt a technical approach. Hence, this book cannot cater to any single type of reader. The audience for this book includes, but is not limited to:

- Architects (technology)
- Senior management (CIO, CTO, VP, etc.)
- Managers in technology
- Engineers and programmers
- Technical operations staff
- Business management

In addition, the size of organizations for the above list of potential readers will range from the small technical firms to large corporations. The only criterion for a reader within an enterprise is that technology plays a key role. In today's environment, it is difficult to find an enterprise not shaped by its technology and, hence, most organizations require a proactive role in forming their technology. As more stakeholders from the different functions participate in the execution of the enterprise architecture, the more optimal technology is leveraged to realize the vision of the organization. The style of this book is in a clear and understandable language accessible by a diverse audience.

LEA will succeed if senior management can identify significant principles critical to the enterprise and use this approach in capturing the needs of key stakeholders that readily translates to technology. In addition, as technologists provide their solutions, business users should clearly understand where the technology fits within the enterprise. Hence, enterprise architecture needs to serve as a communication device to facilitate the coordination of technology resources to the requirements of the business and help set expectations for the optimal adoption of technology solutions.

What Is Architecture, and Why the Need?

Architecting is a discipline that is well understood and defined in the construction industry, but unfortunately is poorly understood and implemented in technology, thus resulting in systems that do not interoperate well and have difficulty in providing the required functionality for the enterprise. Technology is a complex and diverse industry that no individual can master in its entirety. Thus, implementing technology in the enterprise requires the coordination of many different resources to provide a successful environment in which to operate. Without an enterprise approach to guide technology, there is a large chance for continued failures that harm profitability.

There exists a variety of approaches for deploying architecture but they are often centric to a specific discipline. For example, there exists a good body of work around software architecture but this is only one facet of a technology solution and rarely do these approaches provide hooks to other disciplines to coordinate design, development, deployment, and ultimately support. In addition, a software architecture can be executed perfectly but, unfortunately, not provide the environment needed by the enterprise. Often, an argument is that diligent requirements gathering solves this problem, but there exist in organizations multiple influences outside the realm and control of software architecture. Hence, no amount of effort around the requirements effort can solve the demands for different stakeholders having different needs and expectations for technology.

Why Lightweight?

The success of enterprise architecture requires it to provide value to an organization but limit the amount of resources to design and maintain the architecture. This book provides a lightweight methodology and philosophy that is easily adopted by most organizations and quickly provides value. In addition, this approach avoids most of the pitfalls of traditional architectural styles, which tend to be over-engineered.

The use of the term "lightweight" proposes an approach that is easily executable and uses a streamlined approach to successfully implement architecture for the enterprise. LEA uses a simple set of architectural artifacts to address the needs of enterprise architecture. Most architectural approaches create far too many artifacts that far exceed the law of diminishing returns. In addition, some approaches create a set of artifacts that are too complex for most users to understand in today's corporate environment. In effect, the artifacts create an additional layer of abstraction for the deployment of technology and typically create issues in versioning or become shelved as developers create what they believe users need. LEA's premise is to keep it simple so that it is usable and adds value.

The intention of this book is not to introduce new jargon, but rather to base this approach on existing architectural artifacts that are successfully deployed in organizations. The true value of this methodology lies not in developing new terms or diagrams, but in developing a clear systematic approach that uses the right balance of tools and techniques to help an enterprise develop its architecture successfully.

What This Book Contains
Section 1: State of Architecture

The first section, entitled "State of Architecture," focuses on how enterprises currently deploy architecture and how architecture is an evolving discipline that will set the stage for why architecture is important.

Chapter 1: Architectural Chaos
The first chapter, "Architectural Chaos," introduces the reader to the current state of most enterprises and how there exists a large gap between business and IT. In addition, this chapter discusses how industry has led to multiple views of architecture for technology that further blurs the field of architecture.

Chapter 2: Architecture in the Enterprise
This chapter discusses where architecture needs to fit within the enterprise. In addition, this chapter discusses the benefits of architecture, which provide the reader with the necessary material to validate the need for architecture. This chapter then proposes a model for the reader that provides an understanding of the various domains of architecture.

Chapter 3: LEA Framework
This chapter covers the various industry methodologies and approaches toward architecture. In addition, it discusses how these various practices can work within LEA, since LEA is a framework. The reality of any organization is that there is no single means to accomplish architectural success, so the best practices are the identification of the best fits.

Section 2: Framework for LEA
This section builds upon the need for architecture identified in the previous section by introducing LEA. "Framework for LEA" is the heart of this book and provides a structure to support architecture in the enterprise through a well-defined lightweight approach from which all stakeholders in the enterprise can benefit.

Chapter 4: LEA Overview
This chapter introduces the framework of LEA, which sets the stage for the following chapters that describe the specific areas of LEA in more detail.

Chapter 5: Strategic Architecture
This chapter introduces the first section of the architectural framework: the "Strategic Architecture" that provides a set of guiding rules for a system

deployed or being developed. The strategic architecture provides the enterprise view of technology and sets the measures and guidelines for the successful stewardship of the systems.

Chapter 6: Conceptual Architecture

"Conceptual Architecture" provides the reader with a mechanism to capture high-level views to encapsulate key systems and subsystems, including their relationship to the enterprise and other systems. This system view helps decompose the enterprise into smaller systems that more readily help coordinate efforts between IT and business on technology.

Chapter 7: Execution Architecture

This chapter discusses the "execution architecture" that provides a view from a project perspective, giving an approach for the deployment and maintenance of technology. This chapter describes balancing the right amount of detail for increasing the chances for project success.

Section 3: Implementing Architecture

This final section, "Implementing Architecture," takes the framework discussed in the previous section and provides the reader with an approach to put the framework into practice.

Chapter 8: Philosophy of LEA

This chapter presents some of the beliefs of LEA that will assist the reader in implementing the framework. In addition, the architect is an interface to many different stakeholders in the enterprise and this requires different skills to interact successfully and is the subject of this chapter.

Chapter 9: Cycle of LEA

Implementing enterprise architecture is a complex endeavor for any organization. This chapter deals with the domains and perspectives of architecture observed in the enterprise. It presents to the reader some challenges to the introduction of architecture into the enterprise and how architecture is involved throughout the life cycle of technology projects and operational systems.

Chapter 10: Deploying LEA

This chapter provides a work plan for any practitioner who wants to implement LEA within an organization. The work plan begins with planning and assembling the core team and ends with the guidance of a pilot project.

Chapter 11: Dysfunctional Enterprise Architecture

This chapter illustrates some key symptoms observed in enterprises where architecture has been implemented improperly, including Ivory Tower, Tribal Lore, Diagrams are for Sissies, etc. This chapter contains descriptions of these common symptoms and includes key causes and potential solutions for such symptoms.

Section 4: Appendices

This section is supplemental to the book and provides material easily referenced by the reader.

Appendix A: LEA Artifacts Guide

This is a reference table for all the artifacts that LEA deems a minimum for successful enterprise architecture. The reference table provides a description, the relationship of the artifacts, and the primary audience. The relationship shows how these artifacts are interrelated by identifying each artifact's inputs (from other artifacts) and outputs (to other artifacts).

Appendix B: Reference Materials

Appendix C: Glossary

Reader Benefits

It is my hope that the reader will gain the following from this book:

- A simpler and easily executable enterprise architecture
- The ability to embrace a complex environment
- A framework to measure and control technology at an enterprise level
- A sense of purpose for architecture activities
- A resource tool (reference guide)

ACKNOWLEDGMENTS

I would like to thank both Stan Wakefield and John Wyzalek, who provided me with the opportunity to write this book. Special thanks go to my family; both Nikki and Ryan were very considerate in not disturbing Daddy during writing. However, my biggest gratitude goes to my wife and best friend, Chris. Without her support and editing skills, this book would not have happened.

ABOUT THE AUTHOR

Fenix Theuerkorn has over 20 years of technology background, including four years as a manager at Deloitte & Touche. His experience includes helping businesses of all sizes (Fortune 500 to start-ups) to identify key enabling technologies. Fenix is an expert at enterprise architecture, data warehousing, and Internet technologies.

Fenix developed LEA over the years to quickly and effectively align technology to the needs of his clients. In addition, he has taught at several major universities in North America, using his simple style of technology stewardship.

SECTION 1

STATE OF
ARCHITECTURE

Life is really simple, but we insist on making it complicated.

— Confucius

Chapter 1

ARCHITECTURAL CHAOS

RELATION OF TECHNOLOGY AND ARCHITECTURE

It is undisputed in today's corporate environment that the success of the enterprise depends on how effectively technology integrates within the organization. With recent advances in technology and more to follow, this becomes even more critical to corporations that want to survive in the marketplace. Competitors will not miss the opportunities to get new services or product offerings to market first by leveraging technology to gain market share and profit.

Unfortunately, many corporations still struggle with how to integrate technology, and failure is common today and often anticipated. Many organizations continue functioning with a large rift between their technology resources and their business resources. It is true that these two resources have a different lexicon and perceive the view of the organization from different perspectives; however, it is not healthy for the organization if these two resources do not interact efficiently. It should be unacceptable for an organization to continue to see technology resources as a separate entity and not as truly another business resource with different skills.

As technology advances, the need for new skills increases and specialization is more frequent. This results in the introduction of new languages to master these technology advances and the likelihood that such resource interactions will become more diverse. Not only does the jargon between technology increase, but also the rift between technology and the business users widens. Technology will only increase in complexity and this will increase the need to interpret communications between these resources.

One solution to this communication barrier would be the development of a common language for all the resources to use in organizational interactions. However, this would require a language that could adopt a very wide span of vocabulary to accommodate the various technology domains and the needs of the business community. This solution requires that business users understand technology nuances to best converse in this new language and this is a barrier, as now business users will need to learn a new skill. Most organization resources are already overburdened with their current responsibilities, so adding a new complex language is very likely an unsuccessful approach for many enterprises.

Another solution would require the creation of an independent third party to act as a mediator between these resources. The success of the mediator depends heavily on how well communications are facilitated between the groups and that the mediator does not provide a major obstruction for the organization. The architect is the best candidate for this role.

Architecture's primary responsibility is to serve as the conduit between various resources, as the languages between these resources will always remain different. However, architecture is a relatively new discipline and often has not provided the needed unification of these resources. Frequently, architectures in organizations create another abstraction layer that really is another language to contend with for resources and ultimately a barrier for efficient interactions between the diverse resources.

Lightweight Enterprise Architecture (LEA) combines the successful elements of architecture implemented in organizations today, provides a simple framework that does not burden the organization, and offers quicker results. LEA is not a rigid architecture that requires a long learning cycle, but provides a solid framework to more successfully evolve the technical landscape of most organizations today. LEA is a simpler set of responsibilities and deliverables for the architect to facilitate better communication between the resources in an organization.

In addition, the success of integrating technology is not simply building a technical masterpiece, as there are many other factors of success. First, technology needs to offer the organization the needed functionality to deliver a product or service to the marketplace with minimal effort. This means that technology needs alignment with the direction of the corporate strategy and fit within the current infrastructure of the organization. Technology is not just building a better technical solution, but understanding the processes, people, and goals of the organization — all within the limits of striving for profitability. This is the core goal of successful enterprise architecture and the force behind the development of LEA.

THE MANY FACES OF ARCHITECTURE

Let me start by saying that "architecture" is one of the most vague and abused terms in the industry. Often when I introduce myself as an "architect," I get puzzled looks from clients and am soon asked what type of architect. Expectations from me as an architect have ranged from helping develop a business strategy to process redesign to data center build-out and even programming code optimization. While I like to think of myself as talented, the breadth of expectations is staggering and over the course of my several decades in the industry, I have actually functioned in the various realms. Whether I have successfully been an optimal choice in these various roles is another matter.

Upon searching the Internet, there are many types of architects with plenty of material and groups to support these various domains, including:

- Computer architecture
- System architecture
- Network architecture
- Technical architecture
- Security architecture
- Application architecture
- Software architect
- Data architecture
- Information architecture
- Business architect
- Etc.

The difference these architectures place is within the scope of their domains versus understanding architecture from an enterprise perspective. To make matters worse, doing a search at a popular online bookstore[1] will reveal the following titles with architecture and enterprise in the title:

- Enterprise Information Architecture
- Enterprise System Architectures
- Enterprise Application Architecture
- Wireless Enterprise Application Architecture
- Enterprise Security Architecture
- Architectures for Enterprise Integration
- Enterprise IT Architecture
- Oracle Enterprise DBA Architecture
- Enterprise Reference Architecture

While all these are viable titles and are some great books, it does lend to confusion about how one defines "enterprise architecture" within an organization. Enterprise architecture as defined through LEA focuses on aligning all the systems in the organization to meet the needs of business from a holistic business perspective. It is the goal of enterprise architecture to deploy all the components of systems together as a whole, versus optimizing a particular aspect of technology. That is, it is more important to deliver a better total solution even through the sacrifice of one or more parts of the system. Specific architectures (e.g., application architecture, security architecture, etc.) are concerned with optimal design and evolution of their particular domain. These specific architectures in LEA play a support role and are critical to the successful execution of enterprise architecture but do not drive the enterprise architecture.

In addition, the confusion over enterprise architecture stems from the fact that this is relatively a new discipline, first identified in the 1980s by pioneers like John Zachman, Eberhardt Rechtin, and others. Even through their efforts, the benefit for organizations to pursue activities around enterprise architecture remains unclear; early enterprise architectures did not face the complex technical environments of today's organizations.

Even today there are limited resources on the subject of enterprise architecture (as identified here), and it is complicated by the fact that it is not a readily learnable career as the domain of knowledge is broad and can only be accomplished through years of industry experience. As technology evolves, it becomes more difficult for resources to readily gain the proficiency to practice enterprise architecture.

THE SCOPE OF ENTERPRISE ARCHITECTURE

First, let us get a clear understanding of what the definition of architecture is and then address the topic of how it fits in the enterprise. A standard definition of architecture is as follows:

> The manner in which the components of a computer or computer system are organized and integrated.[2]

In this definition, the idea of components is important for architecture to succeed. Essentially, an understanding of the components rather than the intricate detail of every element allows the architect to best understand the characteristics of this system and its relationship to other systems. There is an important balance to the level of abstraction that an architect focuses to best ensure the integrity of the systems across the enterprise. This also allows for a better communication vehicle for the resources of the organization to concentrate on usage at this level versus the details of implementation.

Similarly, an architect of a large building illustrates the primary architecture void of low-level detail such as using finishing nails in the cabinetry, because a competent carpenter will use the appropriate materials. However, the function of the cabinetry is important to architecture and its placement within the structure. As well, in technology and for enterprise architecture, it is important to understand the fundamental organization of the system and dictate how the components should work, but not expand to the details of how to construct the components.

Enterprise architecture provides the stewardship for the future of the technology within an organization. The architect looks at the fundamental structure of the system, its components and relationships, and then optimizes its design to meet the demands of the enterprise. Unfortunately, in organizations, there are many systems to contend with and the evolution of one system is not achievable without understanding its relationship to other systems. This is the domain of enterprise architecture.

How systems and their components interact and their relationships to other systems and their components, and the principles governing the design and evolution of all the systems, constitute the domain of enterprise architecture. To effectively manage the evolution of a single system requires an understanding of its relationship to all the systems and the needs of the organization.

Not understanding this relationship is like building a beautiful house without any concern for infrastructure, such as being able to connect to power, water, and other critical utilities. For example, many like the charm and functionality of a large Victorian home but have no regard for the infrastructure — a large Victorian home is not likely the best choice for downtown Tokyo. In addition, we need to understand the relationship between the house and its environment, such as what roads are available, what type of services (garbage, cable, etc.) are available, and who are the likely occupants of the house.

Organizations really are closer in analogy to a town than a single building, so it is better to understand the fit of the building (or system) to the infrastructure of the town (other systems and resources). Enterprise architecture is akin to city planning and monitoring the development of buildings to ensure code compliance (developed by the planners). In addition, the enterprise architect (like the city planner) is responsible for ensuring the growth of the town, so that the town functions effectively as the population grows and remains capable of handling the introduction of new services.

Historically in some small villages and towns, the inhabitants would band together to develop many of the main buildings for the community. Throughout the progression of time, the construction of buildings became more specialized; and as villages became towns and eventually cities, the growth made this communal approach unreasonable to sustain. This resulted in dedicated resources for planning and governing of the city's development to best ensure that all the infrastructure needs were in place. Similarly, many organizations have evolved past their start-up stage and now face a complex environment with many constraints and functional needs. These organizations need dedicated resources to plan and govern the evolution of the system landscape — that practice is enterprise architecture.

From an enterprise architecture perspective, systems are the collection of resources and procedures to accomplish a set of specific functions. Resources in an enterprise are human capital, assets, and facilities. This leads us to understand that enterprise architecture comprises all the facilities, hardware, software, people, and processes needed to deliver a function to an organization. The success of an organization is the stewardship of the systems as a whole and not that of a single system.

This leads to the notion that enterprise architecture is a very broad discipline that is beyond the expertise of any single individual to master all the details of these pieces. However, to successfully deploy a technical solution is not just the deployment of a single aspect of these resources and procedures, but the combined effort to unify them into a cohesive solution that comprises a system — and hence the need for a discipline that manages the holistic view of technology deployment. In essence, an enterprise architect would be a "Jack of all trades" and a "master of none." Enterprise architecture focuses at a macro level and avoids the details of specific domains (e.g., software, network, etc.). Unfortunately, there is a caveat because sometimes it is necessary to understand the details to see the larger picture and the issues that affect a macro understanding. Enterprise architecture at times will need to sort through deep details with a good understanding of the high-level implications.

Enterprise architecture is not a single project to manage, but the means to identify which systems are serving the needs of the enterprise, systems to extend, systems to modify, and those systems to retire and replace. The development of an architecture plan manages the prioritization and control of key projects through the enterprise architectural framework. Over the course of designing, developing, and maintaining systems, architecture measures how the systems are to evolve successfully. After system implementation, the enterprise architecture identifies the contract (expected functionality) of the system to deliver the required functionality against standard metrics required by business.

THE NEED FOR ENTERPRISE ARCHITECTURE

One can ask, "What is the real case to formalize a process for enterprise architecture?" as many organizations have managed thus far. While this is a valid question, what happens is that either some small group (or even individuals) has informally created internal enterprise architecture(s) or, more often, the deployment of systems in an enterprise is less than optimal from an enterprise perspective versus at the smaller functional level or business unit. Ultimately, it comes to the issue of who is in control.

Organizations need to balance implementing the vision of the enterprise's leadership and allow the various domain specialists to execute according to their expertise. As stated, no individual can master all the domains of the life cycle of systems, but there must be a mechanism to control the complexities while maintaining the vision and direction of the organization. However, leadership is not the right resource to determine how to resolve deep domain issues that influence the overall implementation. Often, this results in a gap between the vision of leadership and the actual implementation and the main case for enterprise architecture.

An approach often taken by many organizations is to develop a strategic plan and then have the various domains within the organization plan their budgets and respective strategies to align with the corporate goal. However, technology is becoming integral to organizations and the current system landscape can inhibit the realization of a corporate strategy. In addition, this approach creates a gap between leadership and the realities of the systems within an organization. Planning needs to incorporate the realities of the systems in place and build a strategy that not only realizes the vision of leadership, but also is obtainable and provides an accountable mechanism by acknowledging the current environment and requirements of the organization to succeed in the future.

Enterprise architecture best serves as the mediator between leadership and various domains as no single domain should dictate the direction of system deployment. Specific domain experts or architects of a single domain focus on how to best optimize the domain and be predisposed to a narrow perspective of a system view. In addition, there tends to be a bias toward implementation nuances that can affect how a domain expert would deploy a solution. Hence, enterprise architecture fills the need for an arbitrated view to balance all the domains' nuances with the vision and direction of the organization.

To further complicate the environment, systems are becoming increasingly more complex. This only compounds the need for control within an organization that enterprise architecture provides, leaving the increased skill to master the domain for others, but retaining a high-level understanding to make the best judgment for an organization and translate it to leadership in business terms. This is a difficult but critical need for an organization to successfully deploy technology.

In addition, the deployment of a system needs all the elements properly implemented as a whole or the system will be highly vulnerable to failure. The E-commerce failures of the 1999 Christmas season provide a good example of how good technical solutions are not the only requirement for the success of a system. The technical designs of the sites were effective and that attracted and captured larger than expected orders, but the processes supporting order fulfillment were unable to match the demand. This resulted in Christmas gifts arriving after New Year's Day, birthday presents reaching customers after their birthday parties, and other similar failures. This destroyed customer loyalty and harmed future sales for these retailers — not to mention the various lawsuits filed by upset customers. Enterprise architecture helps systems to succeed by overseeing all aspects of the system from a high-level perspective to ensure that everything is carefully considered.

Another phenomenon seen in organizations is that separate domains do not communicate well due to their differences in skills and needs. This results in the "over-the-wall" syndrome, which reduces accountability and often inhibits the success of systems. The enterprise architect needs to bridge these divides and facilitate the coordination between these domains. The overall success of an organization depends significantly on the cohesiveness of resources and the shared vision. Unfortunately, this rarely happens without some type of mechanism in place. One of the charters of enterprise architecture is to ensure that, in new and future efforts, all the domains are addressed and all the right resources informed, thus increasing the successful stewardship of systems.

THE HISTORY OF ARCHITECTURE

In the heyday of the mainframe era, it was clear that the system resources required a more centralized locality for the organizations that could afford them. The need for architecture at an enterprise level was limited because managing resources was minimal, thus entailing little rigor from an enterprise architectural point of view. Early architecture focused on a few domains because the complexities of systems were limited to fewer domains and the emphasis was on the optimization of these resources. For example, a limited pool of resources often developed solutions and these resources closely interacted with the operations staff. The true champions of architecture were the specific domain experts because they were able to readily affect the bottom line for business.

However, IT departments began to closely guard their system resources and the evolution of these systems was slow to meet the demands of the business users. As technology evolved, it also became more accessible, and business units unhappy with the service of the centralized IT departments began deployment of their own systems. This decentralization of systems became a heavily contested issue for these organizations and often divided departments and business units. Around this time, a popular business strategy was to organize a company around smaller business units that responded to market demands more quickly and streamlined their operations to effectively deliver a product or service. Accountability for system deployment and operations became the responsibility of the business units.

The goal of early enterprise architectures was to limit the expansion of systems outside the control of the various data centers within the organization. Through budgeting controls and limiting resources, this was the typical approach and was short-lived as technology became cheaper and departments demanded better control of their functional needs. Thus, the control and influence of systems decentralized even further. Through the struggles of centralized versus decentralized debates throughout organizations, enterprise architecture took a back seat to the political waves of the deployment of systems.

Finally, with organization budget strains and the loss of functionality between departments, enterprise architecture began to develop once again. However, the main technique of enterprise architecture was to reduce costs and regain control of functionality to the enterprise from the business units. This technique was realized through scale of economies by standardizing assets and minimizing the diversity of resource needs for the systems within the enterprise. This was the prominent development of enterprise architecture and often is the practice taken by many organizations even today.

Coupled with the Year 2000 problem and loss of control, organizations began to see enterprise resource planning (ERP) systems as a solution for their current system complexities of multiple legacy systems, fragmented department systems, and limited interoperability. The solution for the enterprise architecture of many organizations was the rationalization of the system landscape by reducing the number of critical systems. The goal of this solution was to realize cost savings through fewer critical systems and gain synergy of like processes throughout the organization. However, many of these projects failed to meet the cost savings and in some cases caused additional operating expense for the organization — thus not realizing a return on their investment.

In one large Fortune 500 company, the effort to standardize onto a single ERP platform resulted in the deployment of more than 60 different instances in various business units that cost many millions of dollars per installation and demanded high ongoing support and maintenance costs. The ERP design of each business unit met the business unit's unique operating model as separate project teams handled each installation. Unfortunately, standardizing onto a single platform did not yield a cost savings and the organization was further hampered by each unique installation's inability to interoperate with each other throughout the enterprise because their configurations varied. This company then acquired another Fortune 500 company that had 16 different instances of the same ERP solution, which would further complicate the system landscape.

Unfortunately, this will cost this company and will continue to cost the enterprise dearly. This all resulted from the lack of a common shared vision of an enterprise architecture, except to standardize on a single platform. Successfully deploying an enterprise architecture requires sharing a vision and communicating through a common framework to achieve results. Limiting budgets and striking high-level strategies often fall short and reveal a need for a better practice.

Another benefit promised by the deployment of ERP systems was to reduce the dependence on in-house development. As systems proliferated throughout an organization, the development of these systems often used different technologies and tools that required large staffing models. In addition, as systems began aging, the original authors of the systems often no longer resided within the organization and maintenance became a liability to the organization. Vendor ERP updates that periodically increased functionality seemed to offer organizations a way to reduce the large numbers of in-house developers.

Unfortunately, many of the ERP installations were highly customized for the organization and required highly specialized resources to deploy the new updates. These ERP systems required the major systems modifications to beneficially function within many organizations, or an organization had to radically change its business processes, which would require unwarranted capital investments. Hence, in-house specialists were still required, along with the addition of ERP specialists that cost these organizations.

With the system landscape further complicated, the common approach for enterprise architecture was and still is the rationalization of system assets to a minimal set. Unfortunately, this approach often has limited success, as the cost to replace systems often does not warrant the investment and the control of systems is usually by different fiefdoms of power within an organization. Thus, systems became highly federated by operating as silos within the organization.

THE CURRENT ENVIRONMENT

Not only are enterprise solutions becoming more complex, but also the functional needs of organizations are increasing. While this is adding to the internal complexity, it is also straining the existing system landscape within enterprises as they struggle to keep pace. Users are demanding more information from companies and often want direct access to their systems to access more timely information. This was unheard of in the early 1990s; but as technologies such as the Internet and wireless connect the planet, this phenomenon has only increased.

In the past, external user interactions with systems were limited, but now are increasing and affecting the need for organizations to evolve their systems at a faster pace. The landscape of federated systems is causing abrasion for the organization's user community, both internally and externally. For example, a customer representative handling a client call needs to understand the history of the caller and all the activity related to the transaction in question to best help that client. Unfortunately, that information can reside on many different systems and can take an enormous amount of effort to reconcile. First, this is a costly scenario for the organization and, more importantly, a serious customer satisfaction issue if not resolved promptly and effectively. Customers are less sympathetic to organizations they feel cannot service their requests.

In addition, more complex systems require tighter integration, shorter transaction cycles, and even interoperability with trading communities. Hence, the days of large mainframe or ERP solutions providing the majority of an enterprise's needs have been changed by diverse systems accumulated through M&A activities, functionally divergent departments, geographic separation, and other factors. The bottom line is that the system landscape in enterprises will become more complex and there is a need to control and manage the evolution of these complex environments.

Not only are user demands increasing the requirement for more functionality, but also companies are forming alliances, merging, and creating cooperative markets that increase the need for interoperability. The success of these activities is not realized by forcing system standardization in each of the companies as time-to-market is a critical component. The reality is that system solutions are different, and to get market advantage requires a means to manage a federated environment effectively.

Organizations today require enterprise architecture to govern and evolve a federated system landscape in a manner that is optimal for the organizations to realize their business visions and strategies. No longer can enterprise architecture dictate that organizations' systems conform to an ideal platform, but need to blend commercial-off-the-shelf (COTS) products, vertical vendor solutions, outsourcing, and even custom in-house development.

New Modeling Techniques

At the same time, technical skills are increasing and the gaps between resources are increasing. For systems to deliver more functionality requires more complex tools and the skills to develop, operate, and maintain these solutions. Either communication between these divergent resources needs to increase in complexity or there exists a need for a better approach to unify the communication between these resources. Today's environment challenges the enterprise architectural approaches and requires a new paradigm shift to meet current realities. First, enterprise architecture must accommodate a heterogeneous system landscape and then provide a framework to communicate to a diverse resource community.

As technology has evolved, so have the tools; and this has provided a more robust design and development environment. As tools progress, there are better means of capturing system logic for the evolution of an organization's systems. These new mechanisms for designing and developing systems can streamline the deployment of a system, but usually require the full adoption of the new tools' nuances to be effective.

In particular, software development has seen the evolution to an object-oriented model. Object-oriented does present a better mechanism to model the physical world more closely, but it is far from acceptance as the sole programming mode. Many systems designed in the past still function quite well, and it would make little to no economic sense for organizations to rewrite code for the adoption of a better programming language. Often, the tool of choice for the development of object-oriented systems is the Unified Modeling Language (UML).

A trend today in enterprise architecture is the use of UML as the primary vehicle to deliver enterprise architecture. The original intent of the UML designers was to create a common notation system for software development. There are many cases of UML being deployed successfully as a tool for development staff, but UML begins to fall short when used outside the original scope intended by its authors in today's environment. As UML became more popular in the industry, it started to become a de facto standard and was extended to accommodate its shortcomings to model the enterprise.

The success of using UML requires the rigorous adoption of the modeling techniques used throughout the organization. However, UML requires a very detailed design that runs contrary to the logic of enterprise architecture having a holistic high-level view of the organization. In essence, UML is forcing all the domains to conform to the standard detail level required by the programming staff. Unfortunately, detailing at this level is often not practical and usually not warranted for standard vendor-packaged solutions.

One could argue that as an enterprise's system landscape becomes more complex, the notation or specifications for these systems also need to be more complex and require a tool like UML. However, the complexities of the systems do not suggest that Enterprise Architecture should begin to expose more detail about the systems through a common modeling language. The success of enterprise architecture is to mediate the various stakeholders with a communication style easily understood by diverse resources and that modeling languages such as UML stay within their respective domains (software development).

Another rationale (no pun intended) for using UML at an enterprise level is to better develop components that promote reusability and increase maintainability. However, time-to-market and minimizing technology costs are often drivers for organizations, as developing software is not a core competence for many organizations. Even a software development company would not likely develop its own accounting solution, so the decision for the enterprise becomes "to what level should in-house development occur?"

In a brief tenure at a dot.com (one that survived the Internet bust), my task was the development of an enterprise program for architecture because many of the systems built were grassroots efforts and were difficult to extend. The company was rapidly growing, and increasing the scope of services was fueling its growth. One mandate from the CTO was to migrate the existing Cold Fusion code to the more popular Java platform and take advantage of object-oriented tools and approaches using UML. The general belief was that this approach would solve the growth problems and create a better code base to make the code more extensible. This would result in code that is easily modified to offer new services.

To test the object-oriented technique was a pilot project that had a low impact on the business and an expected short time for development. Unfortunately, what typically took four to six weeks for development using the old practice took the new technique more than four months. In addition, there were over three times as many resources typically involved, as the team needed to model the system interaction of other systems in UML to properly diagram how the component would be deployed into the enterprise.

The argument initially was that it took time to retrain resources to understand the new technique to design and development. The staff was already versed in Java development, so the main learning curve was around UML and object-oriented development. Soon, other projects identified for code migration were under development and the staff began using the UML notation to capture requirements and get business owners to sign off for new functionality with this new technique. Finally, the analyst group leading the new technique began to model the entire enterprise to better deploy future development efforts.

After six months and slipping project deadlines, the business community began to become frustrated with engineering, as they no longer understood what development was underway and why functionality was taking longer to deploy. It was at this time that our new architecture group stepped in to resolve the matter. After determining that the notation technique using UML was creating another layer of abstraction and the enterprise architecture rarely reflected the current system release, it became readily apparent that the organization needed to fully adapt to the new technique and this would take one to two years, would continue to slow development, and would require the company to hire more analysts to communicate design between the business owners and development.

Our recommendation was to drop UML as the modeling technique and get back to the original practice of developing functional requirements that business analysts could develop and hand to the engineers to develop accordingly (with or without UML). We quickly reduced our overhead and returned to the fast implementation cycles required by business. A key lesson was that this culture was unable to adapt to this new technique universally, so the organization aligned back to their core competence and used a simpler practice for development. This allowed the company to reduce costs and was a factor in the company's survival of the Internet bust.

For the record, let me state that I believe that UML is a viable technique for the development of software code. However, UML is not an optimal choice for creating an organization's enterprise architecture. UML is a very detailed and rigorous notation system that hard-core analysts or Ph.D. types would appreciate. As stated previously, one of the goals of enterprise architecture is to cover a very broad topic, and it is essential to maintain a high-level perspective and avoid detailed descriptions. This is one facet of the lightweight approach of LEA: making enterprise architecture accessible to all the diverse stakeholders in an organization.

STANDARDIZATION BARRIERS

A common practice in many organizations is the use of standardization to shape the enterprise architecture. This standardization is not limited to technology platforms, but includes terms and processes within the organization. While creating common practices and limiting the proliferation of technology are desirable, it becomes impractical at some point. In addition, standardizing terms and processes is not probable in many organizations due to factors such as:

- Language
- Culture
- Laws and regulations
- Business constraints
- Functional departments

Different languages provide an obvious challenge to standardization, and even derivations or dialects of the same languages can create barriers to success. For example, if we could get everyone in England to spell "colour" as "color," then I would concede my point (highly doubtful); thus, this is a serious issue often overlooked by enterprises today, as well as a barrier to standardization.

Culture is another obvious barrier, with different cultures having different expectations from technology. In several global projects, I have witnessed extreme sensitivity to systems designed with a specific geographic bias which resulted in the failure of past solutions. In addition, in systems deployment, culture needs to address the following:

■ Date/time format
■ Monetary format
■ Writing direction
■ Word wrapping and breaking (hyphenation and other)
■ Character classifications (white space, controls, directional indicators, alphanumerics, printable, etc.)
■ Numeric expressions
■ Messages and dialogs
■ Document formatting
■ Page size
■ Line breaks
■ Icons, symbols, colors, fonts

Laws and regulations also cause barriers to standardization, as the definition of terms can vary. A good example of this would be the accounting practices of different countries. In the United States, accounting practices are based on Generally Accepted Accounting Principles (GAAP) and conform to regulations for publicly traded companies complying with SEC rules of disclosure. Even different industries in the United States have constraints on accounting principles; for example, the energy industry must report financial statements according to Federal Energy Regulatory Commission (FERC) regulations. Finally, many countries outside the United States would violate their country's laws if they used the accounting standards of the United States.

Business constraints represent another factor that complicates standardization through the dynamics of the business environment and the constraints placed by business events such as M&A activities, multiple company cooperative agreements, and trading communities that extend the supply chain. These environments have very separate domains of control and hence little leverage to impose a standard model of operation. Economics also deters standardization for the enterprises involved.

Finally, even within many organizations, there exist separate departments and business units that make standardization highly improbable. For example, the term "acquisition" has different connotations at headquarters, in the Marketing department, and in the Purchasing department. A solution could redefine the definition for each department and, hence, headquarters now uses "purchased" (may conflict with another department), Marketing could keep "acquisition" as they have a harder time adapting, and Purchasing now refers to acquisition as "bought-and-received." Unfortunately, Marketing has a conflict with Sales definitions and reporting, so we need more detail. For example, a customer acquired through the Sales department is "Customer Acquired by Sales" (CABS) and a Marketing acquisition is a "Marketing Acquired Customer" (MAC). Now staff can refer to the relation of MAC to CABS that resources outside the department would have trouble understanding.

A simpler practice should allow the various entities to maintain some of their own terms, versus forcing all terms to a standard format. Thus, organizations should only standardize when warranted and only when such action results in a common-sense practice for communicating between departments and not forcing a new language on employees. While a company benefits from standardization, the effort may not always be economical or even practical. Hence, enterprise architecture needs to balance when standardization should occur.

THE NEED FOR LIGHTWEIGHT

The past goal of enterprise architectures moving to a standard platform was to simplify the organization's system footprint to minimize complexity and reduce costs. However, as seen, this is unrealistic and impractical because today's landscape of federated solutions requires a style that is adaptable to this environment. Enterprise architecture must address how to conceptually depict this heterogeneous environment and create a model to help shape and evolve the complex system assets of an enterprise to deliver the needed functionality.

A complex environment does not require a complex enterprise architecture. The goal of enterprise architecture is the successful stewardship of technology, and the primary means is through effective communication between all the diverse stakeholders in the organization. Enterprise architecture is a complex environment that needs to cover a broad field, but yet be adaptable to and approachable by all affected resources.

Enterprise architecture today needs a "lightweight" framework that is easily executable and uses a streamlined means to successfully govern and evolve systems for the enterprise. This book proposes a lightweight framework that uses a simple set of architectural artifacts to address the needs of enterprise architecture (i.e., LEA). In addition, LEA has a greater chance of reaching a more diverse audience and allows for critical communication by all the stakeholders in an organization.

Most architectural disciplines create far too many artifacts that far exceed the law of diminishing returns. In addition, some of the industry architectures (e.g., ISO Reference Model, OMG's Model Driven Architecture, etc.) create a set of artifacts that are too abstract for most users to understand in today's corporate environment. In effect, the artifacts create an additional layer of abstraction for the deployment of technology and typically create issues in versioning or become shelved as developers create what they believe users need, thus ignoring the specification created by the architect.

Finally, unless an organization is willing to invest in and mandate the use of expensive round-trip tools (UML that generates code and code modification that changes the UML diagrams) that also includes training, the effort to manually synchronize the enterprise model to the current environment will be substantial. LEA's premise is to keep the framework simple so that it is usable and adds value while working with the existing tools in the enterprise.

NOTES

1. Compiled search on "Enterprise Architecture" from various online bookstores.
2. From Merriam-Webster's Online Dictionary ©2003 by Merriam-Webster, Incorporated (www.Merriam-Webster.com). With permission.

Chapter 2

ARCHITECTURE IN THE ENTERPRISE

THE COST OF TECHNOLOGY

The amount spent on technology by organizations today is amazing; IDC, the Framingham, Massachusetts-based research firm, predicted that the total worldwide IT industry revenue for 2002 would amount to $875 billion, a figure lower than what was initially forecast, when total IT revenues for that year were expected to remain above $900 billion. However, IDC expects growth rates to improve for several years, followed by slower growth later in the decade that will likely pass the trillion-dollar mark.

To fully appreciate the amount of money spent by some organizations on technology, J.P. Morgan's expenditure on technology in 2002 was $2.6 billion.[1] This figure represents an amount that could fund the estimated cost of rebuilding the World Trade Center in New York City after the September 11 attacks. While J.P. Morgan spent an enormous amount on technology, like many other financial institutions, they are not the highest spender for their industry nor are they outside the average for their industry as a percentage of technology spending to gross revenues.

Considering the cost of technology and the increasing complexity of administering systems in today's environment requires a focus on an enterprise view that enterprise architecture offers. One consequence of not having a mechanism to control the deployment of technology from a holistic perspective is that cost can easily get out of control as separate stakeholders deploy solutions to meet their demand, versus developing solutions from which the entire enterprise could benefit.

Enterprise architecture is a critical component for any organization that depends on technology solutions in its business. While many organizations do not spend an amount close to a Global 500 firm like J.P. Morgan, the amount is significant in most organizations and requires a very diverse set of resources. Not having a means to control these activities can severely influence the line between the success and failure of an organization.

THE BENEFITS OF ENTERPRISE ARCHITECTURE

The cost of technology alone may not provide a strong enough case for deploying enterprise architecture in some organizations, but does provide a good rationale for further consideration. An enhanced understanding of why all organization should have some form of enterprise architecture can be broken down into the two following tangible benefits:

1. Optimize current systems
2. Improve future capabilities

Optimize Current Systems

The optimization of the current system landscape is paramount in controlling the costs and efficiencies of technology resources. An organization can improve the efforts of its technology resources because a system plan created through enterprise architecture identifies projects for deployment in an optimal manner. The identification of system deficiencies through enterprise architecture provides a plan of action for systems to be enhanced, replaced, or retired more readily. Resources are then dispatched more efficiently because a system retired will receive less effort for increased functionality versus focusing resources on developing new system solutions, which has a greater impact to the organization.

Another benefit of enterprise architecture is the identification of similar projects planned or in development. Often, organizations have multiple efforts that accomplish nearly the same functionality because different stakeholders have championed their own projects to meet the goals of their area. Through the adoption of enterprise architecture, the focus is at the high level of systems in the organization, and it then becomes more likely that identification of these efforts are exposed and the organization can then move toward a synergistic solution to better design, develop, and manage the resources for these solutions.

In addition, a good practice (as identified through LEA) views systems as functional components and tries to avoid jumping into the details of implementation. This helps create solutions that are more interface driven and tend to better interoperate with other solutions. For example, developers building a solution to handle customer orders on a Web site will typically initiate their effort by collecting requirements from a focused user group and build it accordingly. LEA proposes that the development community understand the enterprise's need for a shopping cart that must interact with the enterprise's catalog, distributor's inventory, merchant's payment authorization, and other related systems to complete an order transaction.

However obvious this might appear, many organizations as they grow in size develop their own solutions in a vacuum relative to the enterprise. In a start-up organization that grew from 100 to 500 employees in less than a year, I found five separate projects to unify the catalog of the consumer Web site, which was the primary function of the company. The various program managers invited vendors to demo their solutions and separate development resources were actively evaluating products and creating functional specifications for the development of a core function of this start-up. Ironically, these separate groups were the primary source of this problem.

To further illustrate how damaging this approach is for an organization, the management of a large computer manufacturer invited me to help architect a solution offering a new service to its customer base. After a few weeks, I had identified several existing projects that accomplished a similar function to the proposed new service. However, the project could not use these systems because the solutions developed did not interoperate with other systems in the enterprise. These systems were described as "rip and read" solutions because one system's information was either printed or faxed and ripped from the peripheral that printed the information and then manually typed into the other system (the read portion). Hence, an enterprise view of system deployment is essential to avoid this waste of system resources and help to better develop solutions that interoperate effectively within the enterprise.

Another benefit of an enterprise tactic toward architecture is that systems are deployed through a common framework and therefore deployed in a common manner. This implies that systems will behave in a similar fashion and result in better manageability. Technical resources can better deploy common tools to monitor systems deployed in the enterprise and measure them from a common measure that a unified framework provides.

This is an implied benefit of enterprise architecture; handling the difficult enterprise issues such as system management in operations. Without an enterprise framework, various groups' solutions deployed will have limited accountability to meet enterprise standards as these systems are handed off to the operations folks to manage. Many operations folks will refer to this situation as "system babysitting." This and other aspects (e.g., security) have higher success rates if implemented through an enterprise framework that considers how systems influence the overall design of the organization.

Finally, the combined benefit is the improved evolution of the systems in the enterprise. Because the enterprise architecture identifies systems for enhancement, replacement, or retirement, the resources of the organization are better controlled to evolve the landscape of the system solution that comprises the enterprise.

Improve Future Capabilities

As previously stated, improving the bottom line and controlling costs for technology make a good case for enterprise architecture, yet there are additional benefits that all organizations should realize — most importantly enterprise architecture should help answer the question, "Where is the company heading?"

The most obvious benefit from an enterprise framework to architecture is that it leads to a system landscape that is easily extensible to meet the demands of the organization. The framework of enterprise architecture delivers systems with clear functional boundaries and interface points that increase the flexibility of an organization. As leadership identifies new demands for the systems, the option to make, buy, or outsource solutions is easier to deploy and makes an organization more responsive to change.

In addition, as the enterprise architecture identifies future systems to deploy, the tangible benefits of the solution are better realized because the system landscape is more manageable and optimized for the addition of the new solutions. This helps the organization to better gauge the effectiveness of new solutions and ultimately estimate future benefits of proposed systems before they are implemented into the enterprise and before the resources are committed.

Finally, an optimized system landscape promotes interoperability not only internally, but has a higher degree of integration to external systems. This can be a significant market advantage as merged companies can integrate faster and meet shareholder expectations sooner. In addition, as markets become more complex and companies begin to cooperate to improve their position, it will become key to quickly align the technology assets of the organization to leverage economies of scale offered through a strategic alliance.

While leadership generally provides the future direction of an organization, a poorly implemented technical landscape will limit the organization's ability to adapt to new market opportunities or threats and implement the direction from leadership. Enterprise architecture is not the panacea to fulfill all the organization's needs, but it provides a better mechanism to evolve the system landscape to a better position for meeting anticipated opportunities or threats.

Hard Benefits

Through the benefits of optimizing the current systems in the enterprise that lead to the improved future capabilities, enterprise architecture produces tangible benefits to an organization. Specifically, enterprise architecture provides the following advantages:

- Control costs
- Optimize spending
- Identify metrics and benchmarks to better govern technology
- Ensure systems achieve business objectives
- Balance all aspects of technology

The bottom line is that good enterprise architecture reduces costs, as systems are more efficiently deployed. Customer satisfaction increases as systems deliver the organization's intended functionality; and finally, if the strategy of the organization is accurate, then revenue increases as systems match the vision from leadership.

However, the real benefits of an enterprise framework that realizes these tangible benefits leads to potential larger payback for an organization. The enterprise that is able to respond quickly to market opportunities will have significant advantage over the competition and could be the differentiator between a successful organization and a market loser.

THE DOMAINS OF ARCHITECTURE

The success of any enterprise architectural framework is that it properly reflects the direction of the organization as identified by leadership. Enterprise architecture needs to gain input from the leadership team through the development of the business charter, which consists of the vision, principles, and objectives of the organization. In addition, the strategic multi-year plan provides the gauge for current and future projects. The essence of these devices supplies the development of measures and controls for the framework of the enterprise architecture.

As discussed in the previous chapter, enterprise architecture is the macro view of the organization over the more detailed architecture disciplines. Rather than have all the architecture domains interact with the enterprise architecture directly, LEA streamlines the various architectures to like domains that easily represent the full breath of disciplines to deploy systems. This reduces the design effort and communication involved in the evolution of the system landscape. This is one "lightweight" aspect to reduce the number of potential architectural domains to a manageable set of three. These three domains include Information Architecture, Application Architecture, and Technical Architecture.

Figure 2.1 illustrates the relationship of LEA to the domains in the enterprise. LEA is the layer between the business strategy and the three architectural domains. This is both a top-down and a bottom-up model, as the business strategy translates into the architectural requirements to govern the design and evolution of the other domains. However, as key issues that affect the implementation of the strategy or identification of opportunities within the architectural domains, LEA provides the vehicle to translate them back to leadership. This ensures that leadership spends minimal time in the details of execution and receives only the relevant facts in the evolution of the organization's systems.

Also shown in Figure 2.1 is the asset view of each of the three architectural domains. The process, software, and physical views of the assets correspond to Information, Application, and Technical Architectures, respectively. LEA translates the strategy of the organization for how to govern and evolve the assets within these domains. The strategy of the

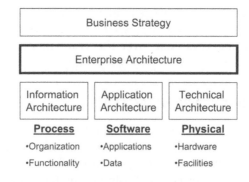

Figure 2.1   Relationship of the Domains of Architecture

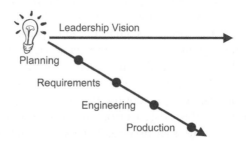

Figure 2.2   The Product/Service Gap

organization provides the criteria for the successful deployment of these assets.

Information Architecture

The domain of Information Architecture primarily focuses on the human interactions with the systems throughout the enterprise. This is not limited to the employees of the organization, but includes customers, business partners, and external systems. The key view of the information architect is the processes and flows of these assets' interactions with the enterprise. A good analogy of how an information architect thinks is the following instruction given on most shampoo bottles:

1. Wet hair thoroughly.
2. Massage liberal amounts of shampoo into the scalp.
3. Leave lather on scalp for several minutes
4. Rinse and repeat.

Given these instructions, it is amazing that anyone ever gets out of the shower, as the last step will have the consumer endlessly repeating the process. This is an infinite loop and one that is typical of how the Information Architect scrutinizes the processes and procedures within systems.

The Information Architect is a key contributor to the functional architecture view discussed in more detail in Chapter 5, "Conceptual Architect." In addition, the Information Architect is a key resource to identify ways to optimize the organization of the enterprise, which is then filtered back up to leadership through LEA and provides input into the development of future strategic plans. Hence, the main role of the Information Architect is to optimize an organization's current assets by involving people through their strengths and weakness, but also to identify potential opportunities and threats to better organize the enterprise for the future.

Application Architecture

Application Architecture is the domain of the electronic bits of an organization's assets that primarily focuses on the software supporting the systems. However, this does not include all software, such as operating systems that are integral to the domain of Technical Architecture, but rather the applications with which users are more likely to interact and that provide the functionality to support key processes as identified by the Information Architects. The Application Architects receive input from the Information Architects on the required functionality and collaborate on the usability of the applications.

Another area of responsibility for Application Architecture is data that most other methodologies have identified as a separate and distinct discipline from applications. However, LEA's success for a heterogeneous environment is the encapsulation of functionality in the enterprise and data plays a subordinate role to persist data in support of the applications. This is an initial paradigm shift proposed by LEA, as traditional practices have historically modeled the data of the enterprise in a pristine form to create an enterprise data model.

The main failures of organizations is grappling with complex systems by creating enterprise data models that do not work for typical systems today. A data architecture method mandates rules such as the non-replication of data elements in different data stores to maintain data integrity. In addition, the goal of a data method is the standardization of all the terms and processes to simplify the data model. This philosophy attributes to early system design, where resources such as storage and computing power were scarce and required the optimization of the data model to deploy a system. Today, systems are lower in cost and the needs of today's environment are challenging the practices of the past.

First, many organizations cannot store data once and in only one location due to system resiliency, network loads, and closed systems. For truly resilient system solutions, data needs geographic replication to contend with system failures and disasters. Next, system load demands from users often require the disbursement of data to load balance peak demands such as reporting solutions with separate data stores that limit the impact on transactional systems supporting key operations. Another factor separating data is the geographic demands as organizations span multiple locations and network capacity is too costly to support a central data store. Finally, many solutions deployed in organizations today do not allow the modification of their data stores (e.g., many ERP solutions), thus complicating the principle of store only once for data-driven architectures.

Another barrier to a data-centric method to enterprise architecture is that standardization is problematic, as identified in the previous chapter. Even if a data model were to accommodate all the restrictions of the organization (i.e., culture, regulations, etc.), it practically would limit its usefulness, as the model would be extremely large and unwieldy. The effort to implement the model is an additional constraint, as many systems would require extensive development resources. This is both a cost and hindrance for time-to-market and lost opportunities.

Technical Architecture

Technical Architecture provides the physical assets to support the applications deployed in the enterprise. In addition, Technical Architecture governs and evolves the facilities of the enterprise to support the resources identified by Information Architecture. These are the assets such as servers, storage devices, and network equipment. In addition, they include the data center facilities and all the peripheral equipment, such as generators, power conditioners, and back-up units.

As stated previously, some software assets belong to the domain of Technical Architecture, such as operating systems, monitoring solutions, and support tools (i.e., backup utilities, asset tracking, etc.), and are integral to the technical infrastructure and usually consist of COTS products with minimal custom software developed primarily through scripting languages.

Unfortunately, Technical Architecture is typically an underestimated and poorly planned aspect of systems and results in significant cost in resources and lost revenue by enterprises. Many projects begin with the development of functional needs that directly relate to application design and often the technical deployment details (i.e., capacity planning, monitoring needs, escalation procedures, etc.) remain unknown until well into the development phase of projects, or later. Further, after system deployment, rarely do organizations measure how the systems operate within the enterprise unless there are failures.

Finally, there are architectures that do not fall into these categories, such as security. Security is a domain that has a process view, an application aspect, and even a physical or technical component. However, to successfully deploy security in the enterprise requires that the implementation of all these pieces are properly and consistently deployed. Organizations will often leave the security aspects to the various domains, but this is an ineffective model, as varying levels will expose the company's assets. The best practice and one that is easily accomplished with LEA is to consider security as a thread within the enterprise architecture layer that is implemented by the domains according to measures and controls set by the enterprise architecture.

THE GAP BETWEEN BUSINESS AND IT

One of the great failings of organizations is the rift between business resources and technology staff. The major factor for this rift is the skill and typical cultural environment of the technology staff. The skill set of a successful technical resource should include a deep technical knowledge that is outside the understanding of most people and should tend to alienate these resources to their own view and understanding of their technical environment. Most of the issues and techniques for this group are difficult to translate into business terms and often can overwhelm most business resources. This has and will always present a challenge for communications between these two types of resources.

The fact is that technology resources are business resources and communication is essential for the success of an organization. Often a trend in IT today is for technology departments to develop a program of internal customer satisfaction wherein the internal customers are the business resources. Unfortunately, this practice also creates a rift between these groups, as the measure of their success is still separate from the objectives of the business.

Technology resources need to understand the issues business faces and actively participate in the processes of the organizations so as to be an integral part of the organization and not a separate fiefdom. LEA begins by bridging business and technology into a common goal, strives to align technology to the needs of business, and serves as a translator for business to understand the actions and decisions IT needs to make.

Another trend observed in organizations is that of technology groups that are tightly coupled to business through fiscal constraints and are accountable for their decisions through ROI models and other cost-based models. These technologists trend to only promote projects with clear and obvious business problems that can easily tie into an ROI model, and often thwart new needs from business by demanding time-consuming business cases. Unfortunately, not all projects have direct, tangible results and often need to happen to support of needed functionality and to support the direction of the organization. Again, this forms a rift between these groups.

All the resources of an organization must cooperate and collectively strive to meet the demands and challenges of a business strategy. Not every action or decision in an organization is justifiable to the penny, as this stifles progress and creates an artificial overhead that often costs far more than is saved through this mechanism. A great example of this is the chargeback used in many shared service models.

A shared service for technology tries to centralize common systems into a centralized model to realize economies of scale. In a recently merged oil company, its shared service model for simple Web services was an amazingly complex model of chargebacks for business units to post Web pages for internal use only. The cost of these Web services to internal units amounted to about $100 per month for intranet (internal only) static pages. This is a factor of three to four times that of an outside vendor providing a more complex solution of public Web access.

The fact in the above example is that Web publishing is a required commodity for an enterprise and is ineffective when subjected to a cost model distributed to the various business units. There was no accountability for the shared service group to lower its operating model as the costs passed on to other units and ultimately the organization paid with the overhead of the chargeback mechanism added.

Another common problem faced in organizations, seen even within the technology group, is the "over-the-wall" syndrome. Again, accountability lies within the respective domains, and groups have no incentive to execute any effort that is not of benefit to the immediate group. Organizations with this type of functional environment, or even through project development, have a difficult time evolving their systems to meet new strategy plans. Often, this environment's philosophy is: "If it isn't broken — don't fix it!"

Hence, the picture painted thus far for today's environment is that it is divided, chaotic, and often unresponsive to change. The question often faced by corporations is how to change this environment to a well-managed and consistent environment across the departments. Often, the solution is to form cross-teams of representatives from different departments and steering groups to achieve collaboration in the organization. While those are good techniques, they are only temporary fixes that are costly, as they require additional time from resources for these cross-pollinations of effort.

Here is the rub: divisions between departments will always occur, chaos is expected, and resources will resist change! That is, diversity is important for new perspectives, evolution often occurs through chaos, and finally, resources want success and fear failing. These are the elements for how organizations need to evolve their systems to beat their competitors. The way to manage this environment is through a shared vision translated from leadership to executable forms for the various domains to execute according to their area, and as challenges occur, relate those that are relevant back to the leadership to adjust the strategy if required. This is what the model identified at the beginning of this chapter depicted and how LEA proposes to bridge this gap.

WHERE DOES LEA FIT?

One of best concepts of technology is the idea of encapsulation, as often described in object-oriented programming. The idea is to remove the details of the object's design from the users, so that the convention of the object is in terms of use and not how the object is developed. Ironically, this is not a new idea, as examples of encapsulation surround our everyday lives. For example, operating a car does not require the driver to understand the details of how the engine works. Our lives improve by removal of the details (or clutter), to allow us to proceed to tasks that are more important. This is what we call progress and the evolution of our society.

Hence, why do we impede our internal processes by not using this model for the organization? Do the customer service representatives handling phone calls really care what design patterns the programming staff used in the application to look up a customer? We need a framework that encapsulates the processes of each department, but allows for an interaction that focuses on the goals of the enterprise.

Figure 2.2 illustrates how LEA interacts throughout the organization, facilitating the design or evolution of a product or service. As shown, the initial idea is a vision from leadership for a particular product or service. However, as the realization of the idea passes from strategic planning to production, the factors of each stage in the life cycle of the product or service influence and reshape the idea. The resulting product or service delivered is not the original idea envisioned by leadership.

This results in a failed attempt by the enterprise to deliver the needs of the business. The enterprise can accept that original ideas will change dramatically yet maintain some essence of the original intent. This results in companies not controlling their destiny and often missing opportunities and threats, which can result in market share loss to competitors. These companies have weak centralized leadership that relies on past successes to survive. Often, these companies grew rapidly from initial market success and the founders (usually gone) have delegated control to manage this growth.

However, it is more likely in organizations that the leadership forces each stage of development to conform to the original idea, with little or no tolerance for deviations. These are tightly controlled companies with very strong central leadership and this creates a tense environment. Usually, the cost to deliver the product or service is higher than average, as efficiencies of design are not likely realized. In addition, this can result in the delivery of either an ineffective product or service. Often, this scenario is in slow-growth companies.

Even companies divided into smaller business units can observe one of the above scenarios for each unit, or a combination of two. The interesting note from the above scenarios is that companies manage to survive even with this dysfunctional behavior. However, a better practice manages these two extremes. This is the primary goal of LEA.

The sphere of influence for LEA is between the expectations of leadership and the realities of producing a product or service, as shown in Figure 2.3. First, LEA provides the stewardship of the vision from the original idea through all the phases of developing the product or service. As the various stages representing different departments or groups identify challenges to the original idea, LEA provides the framework for design adjustments to conform to or meet the original idea. In addition, as barriers identified in each stage challenge the success of the product or service,

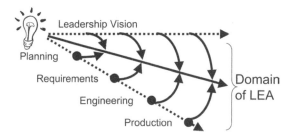

Figure 2.3 Bridging the Gap with LEA

then these issues are raised to leadership and either result in the change of the strategic plan or the original vision of the product or service. The result is that the expectations of leadership change accordingly. Again, we are back to the earlier notion that a successful framework of LEA is that it is both a top-down and bottom-up model.

NOTE

1. Source: J.P. Morgan Chase & Co., Annual Report on Form 10-K, For the Fiscal Year Ended December 31, 2002.

Chapter 3

LEA FRAMEWORK

FRAMEWORKS, METHODOLOGIES, AND APPROACHES

The terms "framework," "methodology," and "approach" tend to confuse many people because books, journals, and articles mix their usage. Even in the previous chapters, I have used these terms frequently and perhaps confused some readers as to whether LEA is a framework, a methodology, or an approach. LEA is a framework with the understanding that true environments use multiple methodologies and approaches. Using a lightweight framework, LEA provides the flexibility of multiple methodologies and approaches selected as appropriate for each project.

To better understand what these terms mean, Figure 3.1 shows the relationship between them. What this diagram illustrates is that the framework provides the boundary or frame for the methodology that comprises multiple approaches. Unfortunately, while that is a concise description, it still is difficult to fully understand the relationship. Hence, an analogy will help clarify the relationship among these terms.

A good analogy is the construction of a family home. The goal of this enterprise is for the family to find the best house to suit its needs. This effort is a substantial investment for the family and one that should not be taken lightly as homes tend to be a long-term investment and an integral part of the family's life. Without a good understanding of the needs, constraints, and values of the family, this effort will likely fail — not unlike many system implementations.

To begin, we need to understand the basic boundaries of what constitutes a house. The *framework* describes the basic elements of a house, such as the number of bedrooms and bathrooms, the size of the lot, the size of the house, and other elements. The criteria of these elements are critical in understanding what the family needs in a house. The combination of these elements can vary between a single-family home, a condominium, a townhome, or a loft.

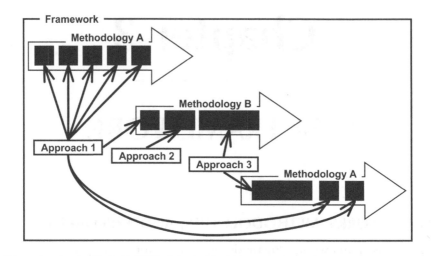

Figure 3.1   Relationship of Framework, Methodology, and Approach

The family usage of the home is another factor that will help develop the framework. If this is a large family, then the choice of home is likely either a single-family home or a townhome. In addition, it becomes important to understand the values of the family to better select the type of single-family home or townhome through more detailed elements such as large windows for more natural lighting, a backyard for the kids, and other factors to weight the decision of which house to choose.

Another consideration of the framework determines whether the family should build a new home, buy an existing home, or continue to rent. If the family decides to build a home, then there is a choice of whether to use a builder, find a new development project, or manage through subcontractors. Together, these considerations provide the framework that creates the boundaries of what type of house the family needs.

Next, we need a plan for the family to get into the house. This is akin to the methodology that is the *life cycle*, from the identification of the need for a house to moving in. The family must identify factors such as financing, time constraints, budget, and then manage the effort to design, build, and move into the house. However, without the framework, it is difficult to proceed with this effort if it is unclear what type of house we are building or buying.

Another factor in the methodology is the approach of how to build the house (if in fact the family is building) — factors such as what materials and techniques will be used to build the house. The family may prefer a durable home and want a metal roof that requires a different skilled resource than a shingle roof. This influences the mechanics of the methodology (different cost and timeframe), but the methodology does not need to change dramatically to accommodate different approaches. Also, this does not affect the type of house or the framework, because either a single-family home or a townhome can have a metal roof, but a single-family home has a higher chance of accommodating this need. Hence, the framework needs to anticipate potential future requirements so that the solution will accommodate the needs of the family.

All these views are critical in matching the right house to the family. As in the evolution of systems in an organization, the organization needs a framework that provides the criteria for the successful evolution of its systems. Methodologies provide the governance model for the life cycle of projects identified through the framework and, finally, the approach of how the organization will build or modify the system. Table 3.1 summarizes these terms.

An important note is that the ideas of framework, methodology, and approach are often highly sensitive topics. There is significant work and thought around various practices that have garnered good followers that believe in one doctrine and will fervently defend its use. The purpose of this book — and ultimately the framework of LEA — is to provide a viewpoint to assess these various methodologies and approaches (even frameworks) from a common perspective, thus helping to find the right balance for an organization. It is my firm belief (proven multiple times) that no single methodology or approach is the best, nor can it accommodate all situations. In addition, methodologies and approaches that seem to have the right fit in an organization have failed miserably; and likewise, poor fits of methodologies and approaches have had tremendous success in other organizations.

Success and failure are contingent upon one simple factor: the fit with the resources of an organization. First, the people of the organization must buy in to the idea that a given methodology or approach is the appropriate match for the task. Next, the culture of the organization needs to match

Table 3.1 Comparing the Terms

Term	View	Typical Question
Framework	Structural elements	What kind of house?
		How will the family use the house?
Methodology	Life cycle of the effort	What is the budget?
		When does the family need the house?
Approach	Action	How do we build drainage?
		Do we use a panelized home, or is the frame built on-site?

the methodology or approach for it to be effective. And finally, the right match of skills must be present or accessible to make the methodology and approach succeed.

For the enterprise architect, it is important to understand all the potential methodologies and approaches and their potential impacts in realizing the evolution of the system landscape. Thus, an enterprise architect can more effectively invoke change when dealing with a complex environment and know how to collaborate with different methodologies and approaches.

THE FRAMEWORK OF LEA

As stated in the previous chapter, the goal of LEA is to provide a framework for a diverse environment. The framework needs to align the strategy of the business, identify projects to realize the strategy, and provide the criteria for success. At the same time, it should be sufficiently flexible to accommodate multiple methodologies and approaches. The framework of LEA necessitates the need for tangible metrics that are developed and accepted by the key stakeholders.

LEA as a macro view of the system landscape provides a structural view that is not a detailed design. For example, LEA is not primarily concerned with the details of resource needs (resource loading/leveling, skill matching, etc.) or of the work plan details except at high-level setting of goals and criteria for success. For example, the details of the work plan are best developed through the domain of the methodologies deployed by the project managers, of which architecture is supportive. In addition, LEA is not primarily concerned with the "how" of the system design, as this is the domain of the approach. LEA places the initial "stake-in-the-ground" for where the system landscape needs to evolve, but then is a partner in the development of the details. It is the methodology and the approach that own the details of execution. Similarly, an architect does not tell a carpenter how to pound a nail, but is on-site to see the work and comment on the general direction of progress and offer any guidance if needed.

As a framework, LEA provides a lightweight model that is not rigorous in practice, thus allowing methodologies to do what they do best and govern the implementation of change. Not integrating a methodology or approach keeps LEA light in implementation, as there are no rigorous controls to capture at all the levels (macro and micro view) of system evolution that require tight integration. LEA provides the needed output for methodologies and ultimately the approaches for them to succeed, and watches for key milestones to help govern the progress.

Focusing on delivering a clear macro view of the enterprise and a roadmap for its evolution requires this framework to be concise and approachable to a divergent audience. This demands that LEA provide a toolset that is a balance of delivering the right amount of detail but not overwhelming the audience. This means that deliverable artifacts are at a minimum and this calls for a light framework.

LEA provides flexibility by allowing multiple methodologies and approaches as long as the criteria of the evolution of the systems are satisfied. Selection of the right methodology and approach is the match between the culture of the resources and the ability to meet the goals set out by the framework. In addition, LEA as a framework interacts with all the domains of architecture (technical, application, and information) and is not centric to one or two domains (as some of the other architectural models propose), thus making it flexible to all the needs in the enterprise and not tied to a specific domain.

Finally, LEA gains flexibility through a macro view that encapsulates systems and components, and facilitates an adaptable mindset for design. Not burdening the design with the details of the system implementation issue allows for freedom in evolving the system landscape to better meet the needs of the enterprise. For example, it would be difficult to design an off-road vehicle if the designers had to reinvent details such as a tire and how it would mount to the vehicle, rather than supply performance requirements and have the experts choose from the selection of available off-road tires from the various manufacturers to best match the specifications.

TYPES OF METHODOLOGIES

Organizations adopt methodologies with a fanatical doctrine that does not allow the organization to realize the need for a framework. These organizations believe their methodology is applicable to all projects and, if properly followed, will develop the right system landscape. Unfortunately, these methodologies primarily focus on how to deploy a given project best, but do not ask the questions of whether the project is viable or, worse, what priority of projects should be undertaken.

Again, a methodology is generally a project-centric view and not an enterprise-centric view. The framework is essential to identify the right projects that a methodology governs.

The past few decades have seen the development of several types of lifecycle models that resulted in the creation of the following major methodologies:

- Standard Development Life Cycle (SDLC)
- Waterfall
- Spiral
- Rapid Application Development (RAD)
- Rational Unified Process (RUP)

There are more methodologies than those cited in the above list, but these are the more popular and are in existence in organizations today.

Standard Development Life Cycle (SDLC)

Most methodologies follow a variation of the SDLC that consists of concurrent phases in the life cycle of a system. At the most basic level, the phases can condense into three phases, as shown in Figure 3.2.

In the definition phase, the main events are the analysis of the current environment, system feasibility, and project scope. This then leads to the construction phase, which involves design, development, and testing. Finally, in the implementation phase, the major goals are to install and operate the system.

Many organizations define their SDLCs in various formats that consist of a varying number of phases, with four or five phases being the optimal number. In my experience, I have witnessed many variations in different organizations, including one large consulting firm with several dozen phases within its own practice. The irony is that these methodologies are usually far from unique as one can simply map the phases between different SDLC methodologies.

The advantages of the SDLC methodology is that a project following a proven SDLC method generally produces high-quality systems that are well designed and contrasted. Without a proven SDLC methodology, a system may lack some desirable characteristics and not meet the requirements of the organization. Another advantage of the SDLC is the well-defined processes, and life-cycle intelligence from past efforts generally translates into predictable results and the efficient use of resources.

The disadvantage of SDLC is the rigor of the phase approach as defined by this methodology. For example, system requirements need to occur early in the project. Often this can be difficult as there may be many unknowns in a project. Improper requirements can negatively affect the success of a project through delays and increased costs, or worse — delivering the wrong system.

Another disadvantage is that this methodology tends to create long projects and this influences the cost of the system. First, any additional cost to an organization is undesirable, but needed functionality in an

Figure 3.2   Basic SDLC Methodology

organization may not occur because the cost and coordination of resources can obstruct the justification of the project as a whole. Hence, some functionality may not occur, as it would take another large project cycle to implement the new feature set.

The best fit for the SDLC method is for large system implementations that are likely very predictable. Small projects and unfamiliar technologies can be a poor fit for SDLC.

Waterfall

A variant of the SDLC is the waterfall methodology, which many credit to Winston Royce. Even in Royce's original article, "Managing the Development of Large Software Systems," published by the IEEE in 1970, there is no mention of the term "waterfall" as this was a label added later by others. As Figure 3.3 shows, the image resembles that of a waterfall and has led to much misconception about this methodology. As water flows over a waterfall, the concept is that there is no return to the former stage. This has led to the belief that at the end of each phase, the activities of that stage are frozen and passed on to the next stage. Unfortunately, this is the common approach used by some organizations.

However, Royce improved the nine phases of the Stage-Wise model from Benington by adding explicit feedback loops and introducing the concept of prototyping. Royce stated the following in his article:

> *If the computer program in question is being developed for the first time, arrange matter so that the version finally delivered to the customer for operational deployment is actually the second version insofar as critical design/operation areas are concerned.*[1]

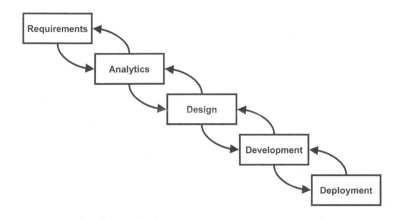

Figure 3.3   Waterfall Methodology

In addition, Royce described the concept of "Feedback Loops"

> *At any point in the design process after the requirement analysis is completed there exists a form and closeup baseline to which to return in the event of unforeseen design difficulties. What we have is an effective fallback position that tends to maximize the extent of early work that is salvageable and preserved.*

The benefit of the methodology proposed by Royce is that system design is improved. In addition, the idea of prototyping a system helps clear up any unknowns in the system development. Unfortunately, this methodology is usually very resource intensive, as it requires an exchange at each phase for resources to provide the feedback loops, and this methodology tends to extend the length of the life cycle because there is a long gap between project initiation and delivery.

Like the SDLC methodology, the original method proposed by Royce provides a good fit for large technology projects, but gains the added benefit of allowing for some unknowns.

As for the common waterfall approach (not Royce's method), its benefits include well-defined requirements and documentation. However, the negatives of this variation are that the methodology is too rigid and unable to accommodate change or wrong specifications (unlike Royce's original model). In addition, this variation trends toward a federated approach to the system life cycle as separate groups are accountable for different stages and an "over-the-wall" syndrome is present as one group tosses their work to another.

Although this methodology sounds undesirable, it is very effective in systems development of large systems that iterate slowly in design over long periods. Groups can become very specialized in adding functionality to large complex systems that are unlikely candidates for retirement and core to business functionality. Business would suffer if these systems, including the associated processes (often very complex), abruptly stop and are modified to accommodate a new system. Imagine making sweeping changes to the air traffic control system because the need to add some functionality is initiated.

An interesting note on some recent offshore project developments: the methodology was surprisingly similar to the variation of the waterfall. The life cycle of the projects are highly departmentalized as requirements are developed on-site with the client and then shipped to a design group from the offshore team for development and then back on-site to the operations staff for implementation. This methodology seems a good fit as each stage presents a decision point to move forward or send the work back to the previous stage and group for improvements.

This is a case-in-point of what appears to be a bad methodology that works quite well if applied to the right application and, more importantly, the right people having the right skills buy in to the methodology.

Spiral

The spiral model as developed by Barry Boehm in his initial article entitled "A Spiral Model of Software Development and Enhancement"[2] was an approach to provide a more iterative methodology to system development.

As shown in Figure 3.4, the model represents iterative development cycles as an expanding spiral, starting with system analysis and prototyping, and expanding rings denoting iterations with a risk analysis, and then eventually spiraling to the typical phases of the SDLC. The radial dimension denotes cumulative development costs, and the angular dashed lines denote progress made in accomplishing each development spiral.

The benefit of the spiral methodology obviously lies in its ability to iterate over initial design because the model allows for the refinement and clarification of the requirements. The spiral method can promote faster

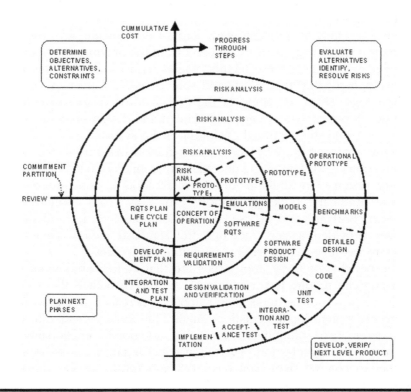

Figure 3.4 Spiral Methodology

system life cycles as overcoming development challenges and arriving at requirement consensus occur early in this methodology and actual development starts even earlier. However, an iterative methodology may develop solutions that are not robust if they have not had sufficient design work, as a traditional SDLC would allow.

Spiral is a good fit for system development on established platforms that really require customization of the system to meet the demands of the organization. Vertical packages and COTS are usually good candidates for the spiral methodology. Users agree early on about system needs and then development can proceed quickly over iteration of design as the solution evolves for the environment.

Rapid Application Development (RAD)

There are many rapid development methodologies but Rapid Application Development (RAD) is the most popular. The variations of these models lie in their approach versus how they manage the life cycle of system implementation. As defined previously, a methodology in the context of enterprise architecture is the governance of the life cycle of a system (not just the software).

It is interesting to note that many Rapid Development advocates claim that their methodology is vastly different from the previous methodologies identified but, in fact, these methodologies tend to have distinct phases of development similar to SDLC and some iterative aspects of the spiral methodology. However, some of the central ideas of these models are short development cycles, joint requirement and design sessions between developers, and the continual evolution of the system.

These practices grew out of the recognition that businesses need to respond quickly to change and uncertain environments in the development of their systems. In addition, development tools became more robust, offering automatic code generation, especially from companies like Microsoft, Borland, and Sybase. In addition, the Internet and the Web browser provided a new medium; the standard methodologies were ineffective as time-to-market was paramount to success.

The benefits of these approaches are that system implementation is faster and can require fewer resources. Another benefit is that users can slowly adapt to new systems as functionality increases over time and not in one big system implementation. Finally, the environment can test the new incremental solution, ensuring that additional functionality is of benefit to the organization. This allows the organization to determine whether to commit significant resources and further evolve the system accordingly.

The negative aspect of this approach occurs when this methodology happens on poorly developed systems. Hence, the iterations will only exacerbate the fundamental flaws of the core system as maintenance costs will be high and, at some point, the system may become unstable. Finally, these practices tend to believe that systems are never complete and, while partially true, care is paramount to balance system refactoring with the needs of business from an economic view. Resources for system development are limited within organizations and best served to exploit systems to leverage market opportunities and reduce internal costs versus creating a great system.

These methodologies are best suited for small to medium-sized applications and where fast implementation is critical for success. However, these methodologies best fit when systems are deployable in a phased approach and likely are not a fundamental process to the business, but provide more of an ancillary functionality for the organization.

Rational Unified Process® (RUP)[3]

The Rational Unified Process® (RUP) is a methodology developed by Rational Software, which was subsequently acquired by IBM. The founders of Rational Software were pioneers in the advancement of the object-oriented (O-O) approach for design and development. The efforts of these founders were in the standardization of key software models to aid in the design and development of software solutions. RUP is a methodology that closely resembles SDLC, with the approach heavily influenced by O-O nuances and iterative processes similar to previous methodologies.

This methodology has four distinct phases — inception, elaboration, construction, and transition — which is similar to a SDLC model. The difference between RUP and SDLC lies in the acknowledgment that these phases repeat over the traditional model over time. Hence, unlike a traditional SDLC, the design (or other activities) do not occur only once, but cycle over several iterations, thus providing a phased methodology for software solutions. Essentially, RUP is an iterative process of software releases that is a well-defined and well-documented software development process.

A benefit of this approach is that it takes advantage of some of the newer modeling tools and the modeling language of UML, which is closer to the business environment. Organizations with good analysts can benefit from a methodology that mandates various models and ultimately creates a good documentation base.

However, the commitment for most organizations is too steep, as this model requires training and the learning curve can impede progress initially. In addition, documentation of the systems using this methodology creates very detailed specifications that are not readily accessible to nontechnical resources and can contribute to a gap between end users and the technical staff. The commitment to maintaining the models for this approach is significant, or systems get out-of-sync from their documentation easily.

It is also worth noting that RUP has a framework for the view of Software Architecture called the 4+1 View. This consists of a logical, process, physical, and development views plus the use case view. The logical view captures the functional requirements of a system and the process view concerns the nonfunctional requirements such as performance and availability. The physical view is how the software maps to the hardware, with the development view packaging how the software is developed. Finally, the use case view provides scenarios to test the other four views.

The best fit for this methodology and framework is for custom-developed systems where there is minimal use of packaged solutions. Many packages will not reveal the internal design, and it becomes a significant effort to model software that in fact is already in place and not easily accessible. In addition, it is important that the resources within the organization buy in to the benefits because this methodology requires different skills and a greater influence of analysts and the programming community. In organizations where programming is a strong competence, these are viable techniques because RUP is a highly software-centric style of architecture. However, RUP does not serve well as an enterprise model because it is very solution oriented and is not a framework that supports the stewardship of all the technology (other than customized software).

Why SDLC Is Popular

Of all the methodologies presented, the most commonly used in today's environment is some variation of the SDLC methodology. Many organizations need to understand when will they get specific functionality and how to budget and manage accordingly. In addition, the bottom line is that leadership will always ask when will they get "x" and how much will it cost. SDLC is the easiest methodology to answer this for the enterprise.

First, SDLC provides a good subdivision of the project in a linear fashion that easily breaks the project into discrete chunks of time, which makes the project more manageable and thereby promotes better project control. Management can commit the right resources at the beginning of the project and their time is budgeted accordingly.

SDLC also promotes time-boxing of activities; although different parts of a project may develop independently during a stage, the parts of the project are forced to reach the same point of development at the end of each stage. This promotes coordination between the various components of large projects and provides clear milestones to report to leadership.

Finally, projects usually get commitment from leadership once and rarely will extending an evolving development cycle be acceptable to leadership. Leadership will require results for any investment of resources and even non-SDLC methodologies will ultimately get flattened to mimic a SDLC model to gain corporate buy-in.

CMM[4]

The Capability Maturity Model® (CMM) is not a methodology, but rather a technique that determines the effectiveness (or maturity) of the development life cycle within an organization. This model is under development by the Software Engineering Institute (SEI) and was originally developed to measure the software life cycle, but has since expanded into other domains.

At the core of CMM are five levels of expertise, to include initial, repeatable, defined, managed, and optimizing. Figure 3.5 shows the relationship of these levels. For an organization to move up this model, CMM offers key practices that need to be in place before an organization can rise to the next level.

In *initial*, the lowest level (level 1), the process can be chaotic and often requires the strength of individual effort and heroics. This is often the domain of a start-up company and not sustainable for any company. The next level, *repeatable*, is often observed in companies that have survived the initial level and have learned from their mistakes, but usually have minimal processes defined. In the *defined* level, at level 3, there is a standardized process in place with supporting documentation. When an organization begins to collect metrics and evaluate their life cycle, they have reached *managed*. Finally, the highest level (level 5) of *optimizing* occurs when there are programs in place for continuous process improvement with emphasis on innovation.

Figure 3.5   CMM Methodology

While this model was originally centric to software development, it does provide an important tool for organizations to measure how well resources evolve software, and these principles are useful to gauge the overall system life cycle. The basic ideas for CMM provide useful tools to measure an organization's effectiveness (or maturity) of life-cycle management, but the CMM literature is a bit overwhelming. Not all organizations should reach level 5 or even pass the defined level, as system life-cycle development may not be the core competence of an organization.

The investment of time and resources to reach higher levels can be significant and really be a case of diminishing returns for organizations—except for either consulting firms or outsourcing vendors. However, the tool is still a good metric in evaluating project management expertise and potential steps to improve if needed.

TYPES OF APPROACHES

Unlike methodologies that concentrate on the process of the life cycle, *approach* focuses on the "how" of system evolution. Unfortunately, many approaches have loosely wrapped methodology around these techniques and have thus helped convolute the industry. This trend is not a detriment to organizations as these techniques have proven successful, but successful system evolution should not be the bane of strict guidance to methodology or approach. However, the mixing of approach and methodology has led to confusion over accountability within organizations over which methodology or approach should dictate the direction for resources. In addition, new approaches have improved system development and often spurred practices that have proven successful for many organizations and, when formalized, present a compelling process for organizations to replicate.

The main approaches seen in organizations today include the following:

- Standard
- Prototyping
- Object-oriented (O-O)
- Agile
- Process

While these are a few of the approaches, with many more existing in the industry, these provide the best spectrum and popular approaches with which the practitioner of enterprise architecture should become familiar.

Standard Approach

The standard approach is the typical practice of organizations that take a formal, staged approach to system evolution that follows an SDLC methodology. It is usually a formalized approach with some form of a hierarchical structure with typical resources such as a Program/Project Manager, Technical Manager, Technical Lead, and engineering staff. The standard approach is a project-centric style for system evolution and effort is fragmented between different skilled resources.

This approach begins with a need identified that forms a group that builds a charter by specifying the scope, estimating the timeline, and estimating the resource demands. Once the charter has sufficient support from business owners, the Program/Project Manager leads the building of the work plan and the functional specification. The functional specification typically includes system criteria for success, user requirements, and a conceptual design of the system.

After developing the functional specification, collaboration usually occurs between engineering and the business community, clarifying system needs and then identifying the best means to move forward. The paths along which to proceed include:

■ Write a change specification for an existing system.
■ Develop a technical specification for a new system.
■ Create a Request for Proposal (RFP) sent to outside vendors.
■ Use a combination of the above.

Next, resources are allocated for design, development, and implementation of the solution to the organization, with the effort divided between separate resources specialized for the various tasks. Items such as documentation and training are often the domain of specialists removed from the development process and in many instances not of high priority for the completion of the project.

The standard approach is an easy-to-understand process for most resources and can result in good overall system design if the organization has good resources or a mature process (CMM level 3 or higher). However, this approach can be resource intensive and result in long system life cycles.

The optimal fit for the standard approach occurs for organizations with fairly predictable needs and a good mix of junior and senior skilled staff.

Prototyping Approach

As discussed in the methodology section, some of the methodologies have been highly influenced by the approach of prototyping and the methodologies have adopted their life cycle by taking advantage of prototyping. It is important to note that prototyping in itself is not a methodology, but rather an approach because it is useful within any of the methodologies. Even SDLC can successfully incorporate some prototyping activities in the design phase of its life cycle to better refine resource needs in the development and implementation phases.

The difference in prototyping activities is how the approach integrates into the methodology. In the SDLC methodology, prototypes are usually only proofs-of-concept that typically are thrown out when system development occurs. Other methodologies use the prototype as the core of system evolution and build upon the prototype through successive iterations. Hence, prototyping from an approach perspective is a technique validating design, and prototyping from a methodology standpoint is an iterative process that many have labeled as prototyping.

Prototype is defined in the *Merriam-Webster Online Dictionary* as follows:

An original model on which something is patterned

or

A standard or typical example

or

A first full-scale and usually functional form of a new type or design of a construction (as an airplane)[5]

It is important to note that none of the above definitions suggest that a prototype serve as permanent solution or system. Unfortunately, the use of the term in the industry has caused confusion and its use is widespread. For the enterprise architect it is better to understand from the perspective of approach that prototype is typically a proof-of-concept and prototype from a methodology standpoint is an iterative process within the life cycle.

Prototype as an approach is a very useful technique to deliver results when there are unknowns and is very adaptable to most environments. However, prototyping should not replace good system design and planning. Thus, only through careful consideration, testing, and analysis should actual prototyping be part of the final system design.

Object-Oriented (O-O) Approach

The object-oriented (O-O) approach takes a new paradigm in system design and development by modeling systems closely to their business form. As tools evolved from products like Smalltalk, the basis of the new programming model was on objects versus structured techniques using procedural and modular coding. A light understanding of the O-O approach is that programmers initially model objects and then develop methods that other objects call, providing a system of interaction between objects and ultimately form needed system behaviors. A variety of other techniques and terms fill the O-O domain, helping to create a robust toolset, but are beyond the scope of this book.

Essentially, the O-O approach involves identifying key objects the system needs to model and the needed interactions between these objects. An interesting note is that good coding techniques in traditional systems can closely resemble object techniques, but developed (with great effort) without the foundation of a toolset, that supports this technique.

A common and often associated notation system for O-O is the Unified Model Language (UML), which provides standard models for designing and developing solutions using the O-O approach. While, the O-O approach does not mandate the use of UML, many of the models of UML provide a good means to capture and document system characteristics. However, the O-O approach and tools have been around longer than UML, and many successful systems designs exist without the use of UML.

A fundamental difference in the approach of O-O is the need to understand a holistic view of the business domain in which the system operates. While this would be good practice for traditional approaches, it is not necessary. As traditional approaches focus on algorithm design versus the object interaction of the O-O approach, traditional techniques can develop and optimize code based solely on the needed inputs and outputs of the system.

The benefits of the O-O approach are that systems tend to have more of an adaptable design for later system extension. In addition, software can become reusable as design and development techniques are easily transferable for new solutions through the modular design of the O-O approach, thus resulting in faster system life cycles.

The negative aspect of the O-O approach is that it requires more analytical expertise, thus necessitating a larger resource need, and is a software-centric approach. Hence, if not managed properly, O-O can promote the oversight of the other areas of system, especially within the domain of the technical architecture. Finally, documentation produced by the O-O approach often provides excellent documentation; but unless there is rigor to updating this documentation, the O-O models (or UML, if used) quickly become obsolete and ineffective. It is important to note that this is a common problem with any approach, but O-O requires a strong skill set to maintain and understand the documentation.

The O-O approach is best suited for organizations that require extensive user interfaces and differentiate their products or services through custom system solutions. The O-O approach is not a good candidate for packaged solutions unless these packages support the O-O approach with O-O-friendly tools. In addition, O-O is problematic in highly complex environments that have a mix of systems because the O-O approach models the business environment and in some mixed environments many of the solutions are unavailable to analytic design or even modeling due to their closed application architecture.

Agile Approaches

Based on the success of the O-O approaches, an agile approach advocates the notion of collaborative design and changing requirements. The O-O approaches do not advocate strong collaboration and, in fact, many organizations have seen analysts and programmers work independently, which has led to inefficient solutions. The agile approach mandates group efforts through frequent collaboration between all the stakeholders in the organization and that software is an evolving process. Hence, taking some of the principles of iterative design, agile approaches tend to quickly promote production updates for software and iteratively add new features as needed and expect unforeseen needs and changing requirements.

There are several agile approaches, the most popular of which include the following:

■ Extreme Programming (XP)
■ Feature-driven development
■ Adaptive Software Development

The nuances of these approaches differ and again are outside the scope of this book, but are important because these approaches arose from the need to have a more flexible technique than the typical process-heavy approaches of the past. These approaches are appealing to the development community as they empower these resources to control the design and evolution of systems and have greater feedback with smaller and shorter development cycles.

The benefits of the agile approach include the ability for risk assessment occurring early in the system life cycle and the close collaboration of resources, thus generating stronger buy-in to the solutions from all the stakeholders in the organization. In addition, this approach expects that requirements will change and can accommodate this reality of environments that greatly impede other approaches. However, this does require that engineering staff get involved with business and accept a moving target of system development that culturally can be a tough fit.

Agile is an approach that, despite it weighing heavily on O-O principles, is applicable to traditional design and development. Agile is a good fit for small teams and projects that can evolve over time in an environment that is conducive to learning. Projects that have tight deadlines and require the coordination of a large number of diverse resources can be difficult for an agile approach.

Process Approaches

Unlike the previous approaches, a process approach first emphasizes the redesign of processes and then identifies technology to best fit the redesign. This approach is compatible with any of the previous technical approaches (to a degree) if the domain of effort between the approaches separates and balances their benefits and, in some instances, compromises are mandatory for the approach's doctrine.

There are a variety of process approaches, to include the following:

■ Total Quality Management (TQM)
■ Business Process Reengineering (BPR)
■ Lean Management

I have categorized these into a single section because they all offer similar efforts when related to technology, but initially have different drivers for the redesign of the system processes.

Total Quality Management (TQM) and similar approaches (e.g., Six Sigma and others) focus on the best optimization of a current system to achieve better products and services for consumers. TQM emphasizes continuous, incremental improvement of processes to achieve the best system. This is primarily a bottom-up approach of system redesign.

The scientific study of work began with Frederick Winslow Taylor,[6] who many regard as the father of scientific management. Taylor's work mainly defined the unit of work as a task that an individual performs. Taylor referred to this view as a system of task management and later it evolved into the label of "scientific management." This view of system understanding was prevalent in management theory, beginning during the Industrial Revolution until even today. However, the tasks were changing, as processes shifted from materials-based to information-based activities, from the production of tangible products to the production of information and knowledge.

Hence, just refining tasks was no longer having a significant impact on the business. The approach of Business Process Reengineering (BPR) had become popular through the works of Hammer, Davenport, and Short in 1990.[7,8] BPR emphasizes a top-down, radical (nonparticipative of resources like TQM) redesign of business activities. Essentially, the knowledge worker now changed the idea of management of tasks, so the focus shifted from task optimization to process redesign.

Many have associated BPR activities with enterprise downsizing, but downsizing is often a separate event not required by BPR that management has used to justify the BPR approach. More appropriately, companies need to rightsize their resources by redistributing them throughout the organization to better match the needs of the enterprise with the skills of the resources. This, however, is more difficult and ultimately more effective because acquiring new resources usually has a higher cost than retraining or reallocating resources.

However, the popularity of the task optimization has resurfaced, as the time and motion studies of Taylor are the driver for *lean management*. Lean management is the focus on value and the reduction of waste. Lean management concentrates on providing value for the customer by relentlessly striving for waste reduction and the identification of the value stream for each product and/or service. This results in the customer finding value when needed from the organization. Lean thinking has been predominant in the manufacturing industry for the past decade and is now gaining acceptance by other industries as well.

The important notion for the architect is the understanding that there exist multiple approaches to achieve the best solution for the enterprise and these impact how technology should evolve. Not all approaches are embedded in technology-focused approaches.

ACTUAL SYSTEM ENVIRONMENTS

If only real environments would clearly fit the scenarios these methodologies and approaches paint; however, environments are highly volatile, highly charged environments. Systems are a mix of packages, legacy systems, and custom code. Even organizations that begin with a fresh start will evolve into a mixed collection of systems as they grow. More importantly, the landscape of personalities is usually a diverse crowd that will believe in various methodologies and approaches. The important tactic in using any methodology and approach is that there are the right resources responsible for the task and that they believe in the chosen path (or at least they are persuadable).

Evolution is a chaotic process, and highly charged and successful organizations display this phenomenon. Diversity of resources and practice is healthy and often results in high-quality systems. Some of the worst meetings I have witnessed that had in-fighting and strong disagreement ultimately ended in some of the best solutions. Many participants would agree to disagree and move on, but their strong beliefs in a particular approach or even methodology were only due to a strong sense of wanting to succeed. No methodology or approach provides instant success if the resources are not willing. In addition, poorly matched methodologies and approaches have resulted in effective solutions when the resources believed they were doing the "right thing."

Not all efforts require a full methodology or even an approach. Some projects are simple modifications to systems that, when matched with the right resources for execution with a clear expected completion date, it is often best left to the resources to manage their effort accordingly. Unfortunately, as is common in large organizations today, management will implant too many processes and controls that inhibit resources from performing their job effectively. In effect, every effort becomes micromanaged and the cost to the enterprise influences the profitability of the organization.

Another side effect of micro-management and rigid methodologies and approaches is the increased tension and rift that can result from enforcing all efforts to conform. This can effectively destroy innovation and often creates a tense environment that can result in high turnover rates. A changing environment that can adapt in its methodology and approach has a higher chance of success than the environment that dogmatically applies the same practice to all efforts. Conforming to uniform processes is the result of not having a solid framework in place that places confidence in management where controls and expectations exist.

Organizations that become entangled in a particular doctrine(s) often lose sight of the goal of system evolution. Systems provide the functionality for the organization to realize revenue growth while balancing costs — it is all about keeping the business profitable. The final analysis of any endeavor is whether the organization benefited from the effort, and not that a particular methodology or approach is the recommendation of an industry guru or trade journal. With a framework such as provided by LEA, changes in methodologies and approaches are less dramatic as the framework provides the chart for success with the resources to match the best technique.

With an understanding of common practices in the industry, the enterprise architect can understand what may and may not work in a given environment. More important is that a framework exists that can guide the efforts of the organization to better optimize its resources and shape the technical landscape over time. This is the domain of LEA and the subject of the next section.

NOTES

1. Royce, Winston W., Managing the Development of Large Software Systems, IEEE, 1970. With permission

2. Boehm, B., A Spiral Model of Software Development and Enhancement, IEEE-CS Computer 21, 5 (May 1988), 61–72. With permission

3. IBM Corporation, Rational Unified Process®.

4. Carnegie Mellon University, Capability Maturity Model®.

5. From *Merriam-Webster's Online Dictionary* ©2003 by Merriam-Webster, Incorporated (www.Merriam-Webster.com). With permission.

6. Taylor, Frederick Winslow. *The Principles of Scientific Management*. New York: Harper and Brothers Publishing, 1911.

7. Davenport, T.H. and Short, J.E., The New Industrial Engineering: Information Technology and Business Process Re-Design. *Sloan Management Review*. Summer 1990, Vol. 31, No. 4.

8. Hammer, M., Reengineering Work: Don't Automate, Obliterate. *Harvard Business Review*, 1990.

SECTION 2

FRAMEWORK FOR LEA

Everything should be made as simple as possible, but not one bit simpler.

— Albert Einstein

Chapter 4

LEA OVERVIEW

OVERVIEW

LEA bridges the gap of business vision and the technical community through a simple framework of architectural responsibilities. These responsibilities require a minimal set of deliverables other resources use (or consume) that progressively transforms the visions of the enterprise into structured, executable artifacts for technology. The simplicity of LEA is that in progressive stages of enterprise architecture, the artifacts support and build into the next set of artifacts. By keeping to a minimal set and building the artifacts onto each other, LEA is a simple framework to understand. This ultimately increases the chance of success as this design is more usable by diverse resources, simplifies communications, and reduces drifts of interpretation from vision to implementation.

As stated in previous chapters, architecture at the enterprise level is a broad discipline. The involvement of enterprise architecture requires varying degrees of interaction in organizations to be successful. However, it is important to maintain the correct context for the architect's participation to have a successful impact in evolving the system landscape within an organization. There are varying degrees of responsibility for an architect that range from hands-on involvement and design to observation and mentoring.

To better help the architect with these various levels of responsibility, LEA frames these into three separate and interrelated perspectives. LEA consists of three realms (or perspectives) of architecture that include Strategic Architecture, Conceptual Architecture, and Execution Architecture. These realms are progressive areas of focus that are interrelated, as shown in Figure 4.1. The realms of LEA focus on different views of the enterprise, including enterprise, system, and project.

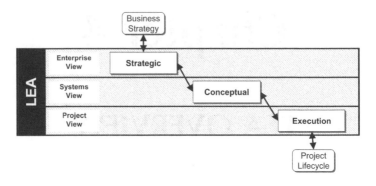

Figure 4.1   Overview of LEA

REALMS OF LEA

The Strategic Architecture focuses on building strategic principles and developing guidelines by working closely with the leadership of an organization. Taking input from the business vision and goals, the Strategic Architecture frames the measures and practices for the enterprise's technology. Essentially, the Strategic Architecture sets the direction for LEA to ensure effort on technology is consistent with the needs and visions of the enterprise.

Often in organizations, some of these activities are in the IT strategic plan. However, IT strategic plans often are vehicles promoting the budget requirements of a department versus an enterprise view. In LEA, the Strategic Architecture is a continuous, ongoing process to translate business strategy and provide the framework guiding technology stewardship as best interpreted from leadership. IT strategic plans still serve as an excellent communication tool for leadership to understand the general direction of technology throughout the organization and, with a Strategic Architecture in place, providing a context (framework) for these plans.

The outputs of the Strategic Architecture provide the means to develop the next realm of the Conceptual Architecture. Taking the efforts from the Strategic Architecture, the Conceptual Architecture begins to map at a high level the view of an organization's system landscape. It is these observations of the conceptual view that shape future system evolution and they are used to best understand resource needs and the functional needs of an organization.

It is important to note that the Conceptual Architecture is at a high level to prevent too much detail entering into the designs which averts these artifacts from becoming obsolete. By not capturing too much detail, the models can survive the realities of most environments that have dynamics that limit any potential detailed model. New demands from the enterprise will necessitate changes of details, so this effort is wasteful and rarely productive. The fact is that many solutions are not pristine, and the architecture best serves to keep a sensible and organized vision of the technology landscape versus creating pristine systems. Hence, LEA is a framework serving as a simple model versus a rigorous architecture defining system blueprints through detailed analysis and design.

Finally, the last realm, that of the Execution Architecture, provides the macro view of the implementation details and helps in the realization of system evolution. Using inputs from the Conceptual Architecture, the Execution Architecture assists in overcoming implementation hurdles by providing techniques and practices that facilitate the progress of evolving the system landscape and meeting the needs of the business. The outputs of the activities in the Execution Architecture produce artifacts that help guide project implementation.

The Execution Architecture builds on all the previous efforts of both the Strategic Architecture and the Conceptual Architecture. By leveraging these previous efforts, the project details are consistent with the vision of the business and the intended direction of the evolution of the technical landscape. Thus, projects are aware of these needs and their scope boundary reflects the initial efforts of the Strategic and Conceptual Architectures and does not recreate the needs that influence scope.

Feedback

Not only are these realms interrelated from a top-down perspective, but LEA also provides feedback and thus a bottom-up approach into the Enterprise Architecture. The conceptual design has the ability to feed back into the Strategic Architecture if there are significant barriers for the given Strategic Architecture to succeed as identified in the Conceptual Architecture. The architecture group, with leadership appraises the significance of these barriers and either changes the Strategic Architecture or removes the barrier at the conceptual level through a redesign.

The Execution Architecture also has a feedback mechanism to the conceptual design when implementation issues can affect the success of realizing the conceptual design. The architecture group then evaluates these issues and determines whether to modify the conceptual design or work through the issues in the Execution Architecture.

It is important to note that the Execution Architecture does not have a direct feedback mechanism to the Strategic Architecture, but issues identified in implementation can influence the Strategic Architecture via the Conceptual Architecture. This can occur when significant changes to the Conceptual Architecture created by issues identified in the Execution Architecture now provide barriers for the Strategic Architecture. If the

Conceptual Architecture is unable to adjust and still realize the direction of the Strategic Architecture, then the feedback mechanism between the Conceptual and Strategic Architectures is used.

It would make little sense to involve business leadership with implementation issues, especially when it is technical in detail, as this undermines the competence in the technical resource by the leadership. Only when technology truly becomes a barrier to success and this has been worked through the conceptual designs and thus affects strategic ideas should business leadership be consulted. The leadership then more readily recognizes the barriers as issues that affect strategic design rather than technical aptitude. This also reduces the noise or technical babble that is a common complaint in the business community.

To bridge the gap between business and technology, the LEA framework connects both the business strategy and actual project implementations through these realms and their relationships. As stated previously, the Strategic Architecture receives input from the business strategy driving the activities of the Strategic Architecture. However, the activities of the Strategic Architecture can influence some of the decisions created in the business strategy as issues arise and require clarification or refinement from the business strategy. In addition, the Execution Architecture acts as an oversight to project implementations and as issues arise from these projects, they can reflect back to the Execution Architecture to address the issues and better refine future efforts.

Framework Significance

The significance of this framework is that each realm requires a different level of involvement from the architect. In the Strategic Architecture, the architecture mainly serves as a translator from the business leadership to provide the direction and sets the boundaries needed to evolve the system landscape. The architect group is the owner and creator of the activities in the Conceptual Architecture and is the fundamental communication vehicle for the architect between all the stakeholders. Finally, in the Execution Architecture, the architecture group acts as a mentor for the resources implementing the changes to the enterprise.

Figure 4.2 shows an expanded overview of LEA. Each realm has a specific view that is reflected in the core activities and deliverables needed in these realms. The core activities divide into three distinct activities: Measures, Fit, and Means. In the Measures activities, each realm will answer questions according to their viewpoint, such as the following:

- What should it do?
- What is success?

	LEA		
	Strategic	**Conceptual**	**Execution**
	Core Responsibilities		
Measures	Enterprise Principles	System Contracts	Project Requirements
Fit	Enterprise Patterns	System Models	Project Diagrams
Means	Enterprise Guidelines	System Objectives	Project Vision
	Deliverables		
	Technology Charter	**Technology Roadmap**	**Project Scope**

Figure 4.2 Expanded View of LEA

- When will it be complete?

In the Fit activities, each realm concerns the suitable location and answers the "where" for technology. These activities answer questions such as follows:

- What will it look like?
- Where will it fit?

Finally, the Means activities describe the way to accomplish the goals set out in the Measures. These are the "how" as it pertains to technology. The following are questions that these activities address:

- How will we build it?
- How will we maintain it?

In each realm, these questions easily translate into the proper context by placing the viewpoint into the word "it." For the Strategic Architecture, "it" becomes "technology of the enterprise." Hence, the first example question becomes, "What should the technologies of the enterprise do?" In the Conceptual Architecture, the word "it" turns into "The Systems" or "The System Landscape;" and for the Execution Architecture, the noun "The Project" or "The System" is the replacement.

The results of these activities turn into deliverables that resources consume in the next realm within the related set of activities, but with a deeper focus addressed in that realm. Deliverables that serve multiple uses over time become artifacts within the enterprise and reflect an organization that is using its resources in an optimal manner that a framework like LEA helps promote.

A successful enterprise architecture compels the reuse of artifacts throughout the enterprise as artifacts appear in various proposals, presentations, and even specifications. In contrast, many organizations will re-invent prior decisions and hence contribute to the common phenomenon of the communication gap as changes to original ideas transform into different meaning and even goals.

In essence, to bridge the technology gap using LEA begins by ensuring that these core activities happen and, in each successive realm, the activities expand into more detail but support the previous realm's results. The question of how complete and detailed each activity is will vary, depending on the culture and the resources within the organization. However, any of these activities are replaceable with artifacts from prior activities or, if strongly understood by all within the organization, then portions of the activities are not as critical to complete in detail. LEA outlines these activities or artifacts as the minimal needs for a successful enterprise architecture, which increases the success of system stewardship in the enterprise.

Through the three realms, the architect is able to focus his efforts on value-added activities and create tangible deliverables for the enterprise. Keeping with a simple framework relies upon using the activities identified within the realm to compile into a final, single deliverable that the enterprise could use, thus reducing wasted effort.

The activities of the Strategic Architecture lead to the development of the Technology Charter (described in Chapter 5), which guides the use of technology in the enterprise. The Conceptual Architecture activities result in the delivery of the Technology Roadmap, which provides the implementation plan for the evolution of the systems of the enterprise discussed in Chapter 6. Finally, in Chapter 7 on Execution Architecture, the deliverable in this realm is the continual creation of the Scope Documents, which drive the actual project implementations as identified in the Technology Roadmap and using technology solutions as identified in the Technology Charter.

THE GOALS OF LEA

The basic philosophy of LEA is that simpler is better for the enterprise architecture. As stated previously, technology is increasingly becoming more complex and the needs of enterprises are also increasing in complexity. Developing a complex enterprise architecture only compounds the management of technology within the enterprise.

Enterprise architecture as seen by the framework of LEA must provide a simpler view of how technology currently affects the organization and how best to influence technology that realizes the visions of the enterprise. When all the resources of an organization can rally around enterprise architecture achieved through clear and concise representation of technology, then LEA has succeeded.

WHY NOT LEA?

LEA succeeds when senior management identifies significant principles critical to the enterprise and completely captures the needs of key stakeholders in the Strategic Architecture. From a sound Strategic Architecture, the development of the Conceptual Architecture provides the Technology Roadmap for system evolution. Finally, when the Technology Roadmap is clear and acceptable to the organization, then the Execution Architecture provides the means for implementation of the Technology Roadmap. While this appears obvious, it is important to understand these activities as separate and interrelated distinct processes, and not allow any single realm of activity to overshadow other realms.

Not Following a Framework

Many of the failures of enterprise architecture are the result of the failure to proceed in a progressive fashion from strategic to conceptual to execution. Weighted by system nuances, many talented architects in organizations are architecting from a poor foundation and are in a reaction mode to the needs of the organizations. Hence, there is no structured approach in the stewardship of the enterprise's technology.

Without formulating a framework for success and working with all the major stakeholders, it becomes a staggering task to achieve success. An architect will fail to prepare the system landscape, without looking at the macro-view of the systems and understanding the general future direction of the enterprise both expressed and anticipated. Then, without a clear conceptual design to communicate to all the stakeholders, there is a limited chance that the stakeholders will understand how the systems are to evolve and, worse, the stakeholders are less likely to buy in to any future effort.

Leadership to Direct Implementation

In some organizations, the architecture proceeds directly from the business strategy to the Execution Architecture when leadership communicates an IT Strategy Plan directly to the specialty resources. Then these specialists immediately implement changes to systems they believe the plan implies. While this approach is fast and can have limited success, it will eventually fail because no system landscape endures for long periods of time without major shifts in design. Hence, the specialists can best tweak their systems, but any major change creates the potential for systems evolving into solutions that eventually break or become too costly to operate. In addition, these organizations can miss opportunities to innovate new technologies and processes by not constraining their solutions with the current environment.

Companies that show this behavior usually have leadership resources who have a strong technical understanding. In addition, these leaders often believe that their current environment will endure over time and have great level of comfort for their environment. While this operating mode can be successful, time will change this phenomenon; and unless there is some framework reviewing the position of the environment to the future needs of the organization, the chance of a significant failure that impacts the viability of the enterprise increases over time.

Designing in a Vacuum

In other organizations, architects will immediately proceed to conceptual modeling with limited interaction from the business domain. Then the conceptual designs closely control the implementation of the system evolution. This can result in better quality systems, but often the ultimate result is systems that do not meet the future needs of the enterprise. In addition, the stewardship of the systems becomes technically centric and this results in a gap of expectations between the business owners and the technical resources.

This often happens when architecture is narrowly defined to limited domains like software architecture and modeling becomes a process of evolution in itself. Without establishing a solid Strategic Architecture and a process to continually control this realm, the conceptual design will have limited success as expectations from leadership change over time and well-intentioned directions from past strategies can become ineffective.

Why a Light Framework

Understanding that the scope of successful enterprise architecture is a broad discipline that requires the interaction of diverse resources requires some means that will provide a guide. The basic premise for LEA is that there exist many successful techniques for evolving systems to meet the demands of the enterprise, but without a framework to view these techniques one creates a directionless enterprise of resources over time. Placing tight controls and demanding specific approaches do not guarantee success and results in eventual failure. A simple perspective on the stewardship of the system enterprises and facilitating the growth of these systems requires a good understanding of the realms presented by LEA and not the adoption of a highly specialized series of tools and techniques.

As the following chapters reveal, LEA is not a rigorous style of enterprise architecture that interweaves notions of methodology and/or approach within. Methodology and approach are best left for the domain experts and specialists within the enterprise. Enterprise architecture is not purely an engineering discipline, as there are no clear, distinct paths for any specific industry because they all have unique influences through environmental factors such as people, culture, and technology. Even within a single organization, projects can change over time as new influences appear, because the enterprise cannot always anticipate these future influences.

However, enterprise architecture is not solely an art that is the domain of creative talents and left to the "winds of change." Enterprise architecture needs the development of a map that an organization can follow. The organization must have confidence that the systems will evolve as the business needs change. This map needs to balance between the discipline of science and art to be successful.

LEA is lightweight in that its focus is on a minimal set of activities and the creation of artifacts for the enterprise to ensure consistent effort and direction. Essentially, a philosophic way of practicing the art and science of architecture, realizing no single individual or group is charged to deliver a specific task or even that all tasks must occur every time change, is identified.

LEA is better understood as a viewpoint for enterprise architecture that works to bridge the vision of leadership and the physical realities of the system landscape. LEA provides no vigorous modeling techniques and processes, as the realities of most environments is one of constant change and complexity. LEA provides a simpler understanding of the environment, fostering an environment that can rally around a vision and implement systems to meet the needs of the enterprise and realize profit. Thus, a simpler style results in a lightweight framework that has an increased chance of being understood and is actionable for the organization.

Chapter 5

STRATEGIC ARCHITECTURE

GOALS OF THE STRATEGIC ARCHITECTURE

Strategy is core to the success of any enterprise. Without a sense of purpose, any endeavor becomes meaningless after awhile. As well, without predicting future trends and understanding the current marketplace and making the appropriate adjustments, an enterprise will lose its market share to competitors. Strategy shapes the vision and helps steer the course for an enterprise. It requires not only strong leadership, but also a means for the organization to embrace the strategy.

The Strategic Architecture goal is to capture the vision of leadership that translates readily for adoption in system design. Many strategy plans are well designed but are written by and mainly for the adoption of the business owners. Very few strategies offer the perspective of how to change systems, but rather focus on the intended outcome — either functional or budgetary needs. Some strategies provide some indication of how systems should change, but these are again mainly to reflect the business needs with minimal account for the technological impacts.

However, this does not mean the reformulation of the strategic plan to benefit technology, but rather the need for the translation of the strategic plan into tangible guides for technology to be successful. This is a clarification of the strategic plan and consensus on what the translation of the plan implies and the focus of the Strategic Architecture. The final deliverable of the Strategic Architecture is the Technology Charter that structures the success for the other realms.

Business Strategy and LEA

In the Strategic Architecture, the architect needs good interaction with leadership and the business owners to best understand their stake in the future of the enterprise. This often entails participation in strategy meetings and identifying impacts on technology and the potential effect on various strategic scenarios. However, the key to a successful Strategic Architecture is the development of a core Strategic Architecture that remains consistent over time.

At first glance, this may seem impractical and a bit contrary to previous statements on LEA. However, fundamental organization values should not change radically within an organization or that organization will never realize its full potential. A great example of a successful strategy that remained unchanged is that of the beginnings of NASA through the Apollo missions, sparked by the speech from John F. Kennedy on May 25, 1961, addressing the U.S. Congress.

> First, I believe that this nation should commit itself to achieving the goal, before this decade is out, of landing a man on the moon and returning him safely to the earth. No single space project in this period will be more impressive to mankind, or more important for the long-range exploration of space; and none will be so difficult or expensive to accomplish. We propose to accelerate the development of the appropriate lunar space craft. We propose to develop alternate liquid and solid fuel boosters, much larger than any now being developed, until certain which is superior. We propose additional funds for other engine development and for unmanned explorations — explorations which are particularly important for one purpose which this nation will never overlook: the survival of the man who first makes this daring flight. But in a very real sense, it will not be one man going to the moon — if we make this judgment affirmatively, it will be an entire nation. For all of us must work to put him there.

> Secondly, an additional 23 million dollars, together with 7 million dollars already available, will accelerate development of the Rover nuclear rocket. This gives promise of some day providing a means for even more exciting and ambitious exploration of space, perhaps beyond the moon, perhaps to the very end of the solar system itself.

> Third, an additional 50 million dollars will make the most of our present leadership, by accelerating the use of space satellites for worldwide communications.

> Fourth, an additional 75 million dollars — of which 53 million dollars is for the Weather Bureau — will help give us at the earliest possible time a satellite system for worldwide weather observation.

Let it be clear — and this is a judgment which the Members of the Congress must finally make — let it be clear that I am asking the Congress and the country to accept a firm commitment to a new course of action, a course which will last for many years and carry very heavy costs: 531 million dollars in fiscal '62 — an estimated seven to nine billion dollars additional over the next five years. If we are to go only half way, or reduce our sights in the face of difficulty, in my judgment it would be better not to go at all.[1]

The main goal Kennedy presented to Congress and ultimately became the goal of NASA was the successful and safe landing of an American on the moon by the end of the decade. The goal breaks down into the following:

1. Get an American to the moon.
2. Provide a safe mechanism.
3. Accomplish this by the end of the decade.

In addition, Kennedy outlined several objectives that he felt provided the means to accomplish the following goals:

1. Accelerate the development of the lunar spacecraft.
2. Develop alternate liquid and solid fuel boosters.
3. Research of other engine development.
4. Develop worldwide communication via satellite technology.
5. Extend the capabilities of the Weather Bureau for launch windows.

Now go back to the original statement that the core of the Strategic Architecture remains relatively unchanged. The core strategy outlined for NASA remained the three goals as outlined by Kennedy and they did not change. Neil Armstrong landed safely on the moon on July 20, 1969, just five months before the end of the decade!

Some of the objectives outlined by Kennedy changed slightly as unforeseen technical challenges presented themselves, but the goals remained. For example, research efforts into other engine developments, especially nuclear-powered engines, were successful. However, they were not a factor in reaching the goals initially set, as the danger of a nuclear-powered vehicle was contrary to goal 2.

At no point in the NASA mission did the goals change to include a lunar craft that would provide comfort and ergonomic design for the astronauts. While an astronaut's comfort is a good intention, it is not key to the initial goal. However, the development of a safer lunar spacecraft remained a fundamental goal, despite many design changes and initial objectives.

Many feel that after landing on the moon, NASA began a gradual decline as it lost its main purpose after achieving its lofty goals. However, NASA remains a viable innovator with successes with the space probes (e.g., Voyager, Galileo, Mars Pathfinder, etc.), Skylab, the Hubbell telescope, the Space Shuttle, and the International Space Station, despite many setbacks.

Over time, NASA has had to revise its goals to meet new opportunities, and this required a transition of the system landscape at NASA to support these changes. Primarily, the objectives of NASA evolved to meet new challenges. LEA outlines the development of the objectives in the Conceptual Design, but the goals are within the realm of the Strategic Architecture.

A successful enterprise identifies key goals that the organization can rally around; these are often identified as the principles in Strategic Architecture. Next, the objectives of how an organization accomplishes the goals need to embrace standard tools and techniques to optimize the resources of an organization.

A good Strategic Architecture contains the following three fundamental components:

1. Enterprise Principles
2. Enterprise Patterns
3. Enterprise Guidelines

Enterprise Principles refer to the translation of the goals for the adoption of technology that remain consistent within an organization, forming a set of values or goals. Enterprise Patterns are the identification of where functionality resides in the organization, and Enterprise Guidelines are the general techniques governing the application of technology to the patterns while achieving the principles of the enterprise.

ENTERPRISE PRINCIPLES

In various fields (e.g., engineering, marketing, human resources, etc.), the terms of goals and principles have different contexts and, hence, meanings implied. In LEA, goals are specific to the business strategy that provides the input to the principles, which is a translation for the measure of technology across the enterprise. The key to the successful practice of applying principles to the enterprise is that they are tangible metrics.

Historic Examples of Goals

For example, the goal outline for NASA was to reach the moon by the end of the decade. However, that meant the technology for the support of this endeavor needed to be in place well before that date and specific systems had various deadlines to meet as the systems evolved through advancement in research and system design. The command center and infrastructure needed upgrades to support the future projects with the advancements in weather and communication, as outlined in Kennedy's speech.

Finally, the various projects that led to the eventual landing on the moon had progressive dates associated starting with Project Mercury (1961 to 1963) to determine whether humans could survive in space. The next endeavor, Project Gemini (1962 to 1967), used the success of Project Mercury to place astronauts in orbit around the Earth. Then, Project Apollo (1961 to 1972) finally reached the goal of landing on the moon, but depended on the earlier successes of the previous projects. Apollo, along with the other projects, achieved the true principle for the enterprise of landing a man on the moon before the end of the decade.

The failure of many companies lies in not realizing that principles need permanence through business planning and visioning. Companies cannot continually change their principles every year, as evidenced by many of the failed Internet start-ups. Companies that survive are identified by their principles, which distinguish them from their competitors, and only change these principles slightly over time if markets necessitate the need.

A historic business basis often cited for the need to be flexible is the case of the Empire Buggy Whip Manufacturing Company. At the turn of the century, this company was the most efficient manufacturer of the buggy whip and focused on internal quality. However, as the market changed from the horse and carriage to the automobile, the market declined and eventually the buggy whip company closed. While it is imperative that enterprise architecture watches for changes in the market to not become obsolete, it is important to note that the demise of the buggy whip company took ten years!

A company's principles need to ground the values of what that company stands for and the company must design technology to best serve those values. The buggy whip company could have still held to the internal quality value but continue to search for new markets with many of its core values intact. Hence, principles are a foundation for an organization, but the objectives can gradually change over time.

Defining Tangible Principles

Enterprise Principles need to provide a tangible set of measures that technology can readily adopt. Often, companies make principles that are vague, using "-able" terms. These include the following principles:

1. Systems need to be scalable to meet future demand.

2. The architecture needs to be flexible to add future functionality.
3. The designs need high adaptability to minimize effort.

While these are worthy attributes, they are useless because they have different meanings for various resources. Scalability for an operations manager means handling current capacity demands with the given infrastructure and adding hardware as demand increases. A marketing manager sees scalability as the ability to handle current and future numbers of customers.

For an organization's success, scalability needs to have tangible boundaries to design the system environment optimally. An organization cannot continually just add more customers and then have operations increase hardware, because this approach will eventually fail as the processes and resources become strained handling the increased need for productivity. For example, filling hundreds of orders becomes logistically more challenging as this number rises to thousands and even millions.

Systems require a design that clearly anticipates tangible measures. Hence, a better statement on scalability would be:

> Initial systems needs for the next three years require the enterprise to handle 750 orders per day the first year and a 33 percent increase each year after. Peak hourly orders can reach 25 percent of a daily total. Planning for additional years will happen after analyzing the first year's data of growth through better forecasting models. The goal of the enterprise is to achieve 2500 orders per day within five years to reach profitability.

How an enterprise develops a system that needs future growth to handle 2500 orders per day is very different from building a solution that can scale to millions of orders per day. It does not limit the organization to never realize a million orders a day, but rather the organization must realize that this new goal may require replacement of this initial system. Building a system that can scale to a million orders a day is likely prohibitive in cost and influences the profitability or even the rationale of the organization.

Limiting the Scope of Principles

Another important aspect of developing measures is that they be reasonable within the context of the realm. In one Fortune 500 computer manufacturer, I approached a vice president of the Architecture Group and asked what the organization perceived as acceptable transaction cycles for a consumer Web site. The VP responded that all Web site interactions with any customer required sub-second performance, as was the principle of the technology outlined in their architecture.

While this is a tangible measure, it is unreasonable to believe that system performance should obtain such metrics, as they would become cost prohibitive. This is especially the case when response depends on outside influences, such as network response time at the customer location, transactions that span multiple companies (e.g., credit card purchases are handled through financial clearing houses), and other factors. Additionally, the customer may not expect all transactions to be sub-second responses (although that would be nice). For example, the ordering of a new computer does not complete in a sub-second timeframe, but rather consists of the following chain of events:

- Selecting the computer
- Selecting the payment method and obtaining approval
- Building/configuring the computer
- Testing the computer
- Shipping the computer
- Receiving the computer

Even if each of these sub-transactions could achieve sub-second performance, it is unlikely the company would lose a customer if, for example, the payment approval process took 30 seconds to complete online.

Hence, principles should not become hard, fast measures for technology's sake, but rather measures for the success of an organization. A better response from the vice president would have been that the enterprise needs to support a maximum of a 48-hour turn-around time from when an order is placed to when the product ships. All the system responses need to support the customer's confidence by providing status updates in a timely manner.

Even going into more detail on transactions (not the realm of Strategic Architecture, but Execution Architecture as we will see in Chapter 7), the measures that become system requirements could be:

- Computer selections: sub-seconds
- Payment approval: less than 45 seconds
- Payment problems: have a customer representative call within two hours if order does not complete (sub-seconds on this transaction could actually scare customers!)

How Many Principles

In some organizations, I have encountered several documents that have outlined the principles for technology. A common mistake that I have noticed is the inclusion of dozens of principles for technology to follow.

Unfortunately, as the number of principles increases, the "law of diminishing returns" comes into effect and eventually principles begin to contradict each other. A good analogy is the engineering picklist.

> For new system development, the system designed needs the selection of the following attributes chosen before development occurs:
>
> ◼ Fast
> ◼ Cheap
> ◼ Good
>
> Unfortunately, only two of the above three items can be selected for any new projects.

The point of the engineering picklist is that selecting all three attributes is contradictory and would be impossible to achieve. This is an important notion for the development of principles in LEA; these principles are first measurable from an enterprise perspective and optimally contain between five and seven principle statements. Too few principles do not provide enough criteria to define a product or service, and too many principles widen the scope, which again prohibits the execution of technology to support a product or service.

Another failure of too many principles is that enterprises cannot readily adopt all these principles in their efforts. As they become esoteric, more principles are lost to resources due to saturation of too many ideas. In addition, an increase in the number of principles is usually the result of too much detail and is really system-specific measures or requirements.

The number (i.e., 5 to 7) of principle statements is not an exact number to achieve, but it does seem optimal for most organizations. Even in the previous example of NASA, there were only three principles. However, upon reflection, it is easy to see that there were several additional principles. One principle outlined by Kennedy was budgetary constraints, as the American people would only tolerate a certain level of expenditure. In addition, another principle was security, inherited from a previous charter by the government agency — NASA.

Hence, the principles included, whether implied or not, were as follows:

1. Get an American to the moon.
2. Provide a safe mechanism to minimize the loss of life.
3. Accomplish this by the end of the decade.

4. All research and development of this program is classified and subject to the guidelines of the Department of Defense (DoD) and NASA.
5. Budget: $531 million for 1962 and $7- to 9 billion additional over the next five years.

Notice that principle 2 is not a measurable item, but has caused much grief for NASA in the past and even today. While no one wants to put a limit on how many lost lives are acceptable (a morbid concept), the assessment of this principle occurs each time there is a disaster and life is lost. This is not a bad choice, and pause in advancement is an acceptable event. Hence, the principle could contain additional detail to become measurable:

> Provide a safe mechanism to minimize the loss of life; in the event of a loss of life, review the safety precautions and assess whether to continue the program if loss of life is avoidable and new precautions are plausible.

In addition, note that principle 4 refers to further documentation for more detail. This is expected because national security is the principal concern and implementation is again a matter of detail not within the realm of the Strategic Architecture. However, it is important that security is addressed in system design other principles such as lowering operating costs through open public bids on key technologies that affect security.

The bottom line for LEA is that there exists a core set of Enterprise Principles (around five to seven) that are measurable and indicate the priorities of the enterprise identified to the organization. At a minimum, basic measures of the principles should include the following:

- Product or service demands at various phases (including hourly, daily, annually, etc.)
- Time constraints
- Resource constraints (resources are not infinite in any organization, so what are the limits)

However, the notion of profitability or any generic money related statement is not a principle. Every organization needs to be profitable and not spend all of its capital. Even nonprofit organizations cannot deploy technology that costs more than the monies raised in funding. Profitability or maintaining capital assets is a given; principles need to identify how the organization expects technology to achieve this basic idea.

Why Principles Are Critical

A start-up that I stepped in to help was developing an amazing product that would automate the dispensing of prescription medication in large medical facilities such as hospitals. After three years and spending over $10 million in venture capital, the company still did not have a product to sell and was in need of additional funding. There was significant conflict and distrust between the various stakeholders in the start-up.

When I arrived, the immediate task was to settle architectural disputes and get the project back on track. After listening to the staff for a few weeks, it became apparent that the hundreds of issues raised were primarily focused on coding techniques and approaches. The underlying rationale was the development of code for ease of maintainability. The fear of the group was that the leadership was pressing hard to meet timelines and continually adding functionality for market opportunities, thus compromising the quality of the product.

The leadership feared that not meeting certain market expectations for the product would be disastrous; meanwhile, engineering was responding with esoteric issues. Unfortunately, upon realizing that the product was still several years off and required another significant investment, the leadership was dramatically changed and most of the engineering staff was let go.

Although the engineering staff used solid techniques such as design patterns and UML for development, they missed an essential principle: that the delivery of a product in a short time was even more critical than getting it perfect. In addition, leadership did not have a uniform view of what the principles of the organization should have been and hence created a conflicted environment in which the engineering staff had difficulty delivering technology.

In several days, we were able to gather the expectations from leadership and sit through just two meetings before we arrived at a list of seven principles for the organization. Unfortunately, it was clear to leadership and engineering that the organization was not adhering to these principles and it was no surprise when the company almost shut down.

The CEO later confided that had this process occurred at the beginning, the company likely would have succeeded and had a product in the market already. It was the uncertainty of what the achievement for the company was, and many of the leaders were giving conflicting guidelines to the resources and causing unnecessary effort by lacking a unified sense of purpose and direction.

ENTERPRISE PATTERNS

Another important activity for the Strategic Architecture is the determination of the fit of technology within the organization or, more specifically, how the technology looks within the organization. Immediately, many enterprise architectures lead to the development of a list of standard hardware and software identified by vendor, product, and version. The notion of the standardization of assets is important within an organization to realize economies of scale through uniform purchasing and to optimize resource skills.

However, this is more of an ongoing operations activity versus a strategic activity, as most companies will always have more than one in-house technology. While negotiations of contracts with vendors and limiting the proliferation of different products appear as strategic activities, they are really best managed by the engineering community working with the products because the engineering community understands the impact of the specific technology and this requires a focus at the system level versus the enterprise level.

From an enterprise perspective, it is often a better strategy not to limit vendors. First, limiting the selection of the best product for the enterprise is not advantageous and, more importantly, this gives better advantage in negotiating deals with vendors, even preferred vendors. The notion of a "preferred vendor" is an activity within the Conceptual Architecture and covered in the next chapter.

Identifying Patterns

More importantly, from the viewpoint of the enterprise, is how the technology will look in the enterprise. Once an organization understands its principles, then the next question becomes that of what the appearance of the major technical components will be and how they fit together. From the principles, there should be some indication of some best styles of technology that match the needs of the enterprise.

The identification of patterns in LEA should not be confused with the concept of software design patterns, a concept that has gained recent popularity in software architecture. Software architecture design patterns were initially discovered through the efforts of Ward Cunningham and Kent Beck working with the O-O language Smalltalk. Design patterns in the software community are solutions using sound programming techniques to solve common problems. Hence, many programming efforts can build from these design patterns without reinventing the solution each time, thus becoming more productive and producing better applications.

The software architects borrowed this notion from the architect (construction, not technology), Christopher Alexander in The Timeless Way of Building. His belief was that architecting is a timeless art, that building is really the reflection of the people and the society.

> Those of us who are concerned with buildings tend to forget too
> easily that all life and soul of a place, all of our experiences
> there, depend not simply on the physical environment, but on
> the patterns of events which we experience there.[2]

Enterprise patterns for Strategic Architecture in LEA also need the discovery of where the events of the organization lie and through this discovery determine where technology can find its fit. Patterns in LEA are closer to the ideas of Christopher Alexander because LEA focuses on an enterprise approach and, as stated in an earlier chapter, enterprise architecture is like city planning. Essentially, the Strategic Architecture for enterprise patterns answers the question of where, as it relates to technology in the enterprise. The enterprise patterns are broken down into four areas:

1. Functionality boundaries
2. Internal users
3. Customer access
4. Management

Functionality Boundaries

An important concept to best understand the preceding sections is the idea of segmentation of functionality. First, understanding what and where an enterprise does things is a driver in the design of technology and not the reverse, as technology should not dictate the course of the enterprise. Hence, we need to understand how the enterprise functions.

LEA identifies the highest level of functionality or the aggregation of like business events as the function. The next level consists of the sub-functions that comprise many activities or processes. Both the function and the sub-functions are the primary focus in architecting patterns, but it is important for the architect to understand the further breakdown of these components for several reasons. Figure 5.1 captures the relationship of these terms.

First, for the Strategic Architecture, it is important to not involve too much detail or the task to reconcile patterns becomes onerous. At the levels of function and sub-function, it is important to note that this is primarily an enterprise view as major functions impact the business more readily than the processes/activities that comprise them. Because the processes/activities that support the sub-function can vary, the result of the processes/activities needs consistency for the sub-functions to succeed.

In some instances, the functions of an organization may require the identification of more levels at the Strategic Architecture level to capture

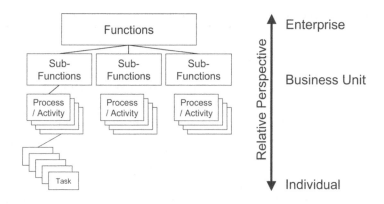

Figure 5.1   The Relationship of Terms through functional Decomposition

patterns, but this does not mean going into more detail and bringing processes/activities that are the focus of business unit optimization to influence strategic design. Many organizations will use different terms and different levels of hierarchy of these terms. However, for LEA, segmentation needs to remain light with fewer levels.

The first question to ask in identifying patterns within the Strategic Architecture is where to segment the functionality of the enterprise. The architect needs to determine which are of like functionality and then assess the impact of the functionality on the organization. Hence, the Architect must look at the major functional components of the enterprise, which usually include departments such as Finance, Customer Service, Marketing, Sales, etc.

In addition, for each functional component of the enterprise, the architect also needs to identify the main sub-functions. For example, for finance, these could include billing, payment authorization, financial reporting, etc. As shown Table 5.1, the best mechanism to capture these lies in a spreadsheet (as we will see later) that includes the relationship of sub-functions to the functions and their impact on the enterprise from a technology perspective. For example, "pricing" can be a low priority from a technology standpoint but critical for the business to control various price lists and product pricing. The Marketing department may have an appropriate manual process that handles pricing well for the business and not require a technical solution, but future growth may change and be revisited later.

Many organizations will have identified their internal processes, and this information can be readily available for the architect without having to recreate it. In particular, many organizations will have identified their process view by business analysts using modeling techniques such as

Table 5.1 Enterprise Function Decomposition

Major Function	Sub-Function	Description	Technology Impact
Finance	Billing	The calculation, generation, and collection of billing for customers.	Critical
Finance	Payment Settlement	Handle money transfers and related transactions (e.g., clearing house approval [credit cards], transfer funds, fraud check, etc.).	High
Finance	Financial Statements	Generate required financial reporting, including Balance Sheet, Income Statement, etc.	Critical
Marketing	Market Analysis	Profile customer base and product development using demographic and other statistical tools.	High
Marketing	Advertising and Promo	Design, develop, and monitor advertising and promotional campaigns.	Moderate
Marketing	Pricing	Develop product pricing and maintain multiple pricing lists for different customer segments.	Low
Customer Service	Order Tracking	Locate the status and details of any order placed in the organization.	High
Customer Service	Order Modification	Change order details before product has shipped e.g., billing information, product selection, etc.)	High
Customer Service	Customer History	Look up all past and present customer orders and personal data, including shipping address, payment detail, etc.	Moderate

value chain, workflow models, functional decomposition diagram (FDD), etc., which are great resources upon which to draw.

The architect needs to understand what functionality exists in the enterprise, the relative importance of each, and how the functionality interrelates. Once the functional boundaries are defined, the architect then plans where the functionality resides in the following activities of internal users, customer access, and ultimately management.

Internal Users

Next, the architect needs to address where these functions and sub-functions reside within the organization. An important first step is the determination of how best to divide the organization, as this must align with the business strategy. For example, if planning is at the regional level, then break the organization into the same regional segments. Other factors that influence segmentation include business units, functional departments, product divisions, etc. Typically, most organizations have a combination of these factors, so it becomes important to identify the hierarchy and capture it in the spreadsheet.

A great mechanism to determine the segmentation of an enterprise is through organizational charts and abstracting the segments of control. However, many organizations periodically change the organization and this captures an important issue and cause for many system challenges. Control is ultimately the factor addressed when dealing with the system challenges and how best to evolve the systems and meet the needs of the enterprise. How the architect should deal with such circumstances is a topic found in Chapter 9. However, for developing the architectural patterns, the architect only notes the similarities and the variations.

A common misconception that I have witnessed many times is the belief that organizations not only do things differently than other organizations, but that different divisions, regions, or departments do things differently within the same organization. Often, this is only the result of different resources approaching the same function or sub-function with different tools and techniques. It is important for the architect to not fall into this trap. The best technique is to note any variations and only separate sub-functions if the results with in the sub-functions are different.

Ultimately, the goal of building this worksheet lies in the discovery of patterns of common use. Hence, even if processes are different today, they can conform later and help optimize the system landscape. A good means to determine whether a different segment of the organization truly has a different sub-function is through abstraction of use by resources. Very simply, this means determining whether the resources are highly specialized for a given business domain to perform the tasks supporting the sub-function and these resources are highly integrated into that segment.

For example, logistics may seem very similar in process, as shipping a product is simply handing package delivery to a freight company. However, different countries have varying customs requirements, and freight companies are often outside the control of many organizations.

Hence, resources in different geographic locations need to understand the nuances of their respective business rules involving the logistics of their region. In this instance, the sub-functions may reflect different practices and hence we have Logistics-North America, Logistics-France, Logistics-China, etc.

Table 5.2 shows capturing the internal segmentation into the spreadsheet initiated in the previous section for the various functional boundaries.

Customer Access

After understanding where functionality and technology serve the organization, the architect should address what channels in the organization will interact with the customer base. In the previous activity (functional boundaries), the functions identified may have lead to some indication of potential channels that already exist. Channels include:

- Telephone
- E-mail
- Web site
- Store front (brick-and-mortar)
- Etc.

While almost every organization has all the above items, what is of particular importance to the architecture is the technology needed to support these channels. For example, the telephone can require call centers, interactive voice response (IVR) equipment, voice recognition, and other related technology. E-mail support can include mailing lists, bulk mailers, Web site support, reporting, and other applications running on multiple systems.

Rather than just cataloging the channels of an organization and planning future capabilities (an important endeavor in itself), the architect must not see these as separate customers in different channels, but the customer base accessing the organization in a variety of modes. This is an important concept that many organizations struggle to get right. Customers do not want different answers from different modes; rather, they want consistent and timely answers to their questions.

Unfortunately, many companies have developed different systems of channel communication that do not readily integrate to other channels. In fact, some systems may never integrate fully, but the planning and designing of these channels must have functionality implemented in a consistent manner. For example, when accessing order status, the customer must receive the same details whether access by a customer service agent via the telephone or on a company's Web site.

Table 5.2 Adding Geography Detail

Major Function	Sub-Function	Description	...	Geographic					
				HQ-San Francisco	SF-Design	Dallas Manuf.	Dallas	Toronto	Tokyo
Finance	Billing	The calculation, generation, and collection of billing for customers.	...	Yes	No	No	No	No	Yes
Finance	Payment Settlement	Handle monies transfer and related transactions (e.g., clearing house approval [credit cards], transfer funds, fraud check, etc.).	...	Yes	No	No	No	No	Yes
Finance	Financial Statements	Generate required financial reporting, including Balance Sheet, Income Statement, etc.	...	Yes	No	No	No	No	Yes
Marketing	Market Analysis	Profile customer base and product development using demographic and other statistical tools.	...	Yes	No	No	No	Yes	Yes
Marketing	Advertising and Promo	Design, develop, and monitor advertising and promotional campaigns.	...	Yes	No	No	No	Yes	Yes
Marketing	Pricing	Develop product pricing and maintain multiple pricing lists for different customer segments.	...	Yes	No	No	No	Yes	Yes
Customer Service	Order Tracking	Locate the status and details of any order placed in the organization.	...	No	Yes	Yes	Yes	Yes	Yes
Customer Service	Order Modification	Change order details before product has shipped (e.g., billing information, product selection, etc.).	...	No	Yes	Yes	Yes	Yes	Yes
Customer Service	Customer History	Look up all past and present customer orders and personal data, including shipping address, payment detail, etc.	...	No	Yes	Yes	Yes	Yes	Yes

Adding to the table created in the previous activities, the channels accessed by the customer are matched by each sub-function. The architect can easily add this information by creating new columns for each new channel and identifying whether the channel supports the sub-function (Yes or No) or is intended for future development, as shown in Table 5.3.

It is important to not fall into the notion that activities are different in the channels, due to varying business logic and processes. These are the syndromes of a system evolving separately and likely by different resources, which is similar to the scenario identified in the previous section by the various internal groups within an organization. This is the benefit of getting the macro view of the enterprise and not encumbering strategic design by system nuances, which the Conceptual and Execution Architectures address. However, if these are real issues, then the feedback mechanism will capture these variations.

Management

Now the functionality of the enterprise resides within a single source that details where functionality resides for internal and external use as identified by the spreadsheet. The architect can now sort the spreadsheet using various filters and sort levels, and discover the patterns of functional and mainly sub-functional usage in the enterprise. This then leads us to the best interpretation of where technology can serve the enterprise optimally to support these patterns.

Typical questions to ask concerning the management of technology from the design perspective in the Strategic Architecture include:

- Does the enterprise require a large data center(s)?
- Where (geographically) should the enterprise locate the data center(s)?
- Where should the enterprise centralize versus decentralize functionality?
- What functions are global, local, departmental, etc.?

The best technique to map where technology is the best fit is to start with a blank sheet and not use the current state as a model. Using the current state could bias the result of where to best optimize the technology landscape from the enterprise perspective. From the patterns, identify where technology should exist to best serve the enterprise, and use simple modeling techniques devoid of implementation issues.

For example, despite the cost of technology in Tokyo, let the initial data center exist in the area to serve a segment if the pattern indicates it, and let the Conceptual Architecture determine that Singapore could

Table 5.3 Adding Customer Channels

Major Function	Sub-Function	Description		Customer Channels				
				Tokyo	Cust. Srvc	IVR	Web	E-mail
Finance	Billing	The calculation, generation, and collection of billing for customers.	...	Yes	Yes	No	Future	Yes
Finance	Payment Settlement	Handle money transfers and related transactions (e.g., clearing house approval [credit cards], transfer funds, fraud check, etc.).	...	Yes	N/A	N/A	N/A	N/A
Finance	Financial Statements	Generate required financial reporting, including Balance Sheet, Income Statement, etc.	...	Yes	No	No	Yes	No
Marketing	Market Analysis	Profile customer base and product development using demographic and other statistical tools.	...	Yes	N/A	N/A	N/A	N/A
Marketing	Advertising and Promo	Design, develop, and monitor advertising and promotional campaigns.	...	Yes	N/A	N/A	N/A	N/A
Marketing	Pricing	Develop product pricing and maintain multiple pricing lists for different customer segments.	...	Yes	Yes	No	Future	Yes
Customer Service	Order Tracking	Locate the status and details of any order placed in the organization.	...	Yes	Yes	Yes	Yes	Yes
Customer Service	Order Modification	Change order details before product has shipped (e.g., billing information, product selection, etc.)	...	Yes	Yes	Future	Yes	No
Customer Service	Customer History	Look up all past and present customer orders and personal data, including shipping address, payment detail, etc.	...	Yes	Yes	No	Yes	No

serve that segment at a better cost. However, in the Strategic Architecture, the architect should identify that a dedicated data center needs to serve the Tokyo segment. This can either be captured in a narrative form, through a list of key fits, or even a simple diagram.

Centralize versus Decentralize

A common stumbling block in identifying where to place technology is the notion of centralization versus decentralization. Many organizations have smaller business units that fear losing control when technology identifies cases for centralization. However, centralization has many forms, and control is only a product of how centralization is accomplished — not a restraint.

Again, remember that in the Strategic Architecture we identify where functionality resides and where to apply technology best. Centralization is first a consideration of centralizing functionality and then conforming the functionality to minimize resource efforts in the enterprise.

As shown in Table 5.4, centralization has two main attributes: physical location and distribution. An instance refers to how functionality implements into technology and how it is released for the organization. A single instance of technology is a common version of a system that all users interact with without any variations to the system. Multiple instances are separate technology products with varying functionalities. Boxes are a purposeful term used to enforce the idea of technology without the implementation detail. Boxes centralize into one location for better optimization of resources directly to manage and support the boundaries of the box. Multiple boxes minimize technology infrastructure demands over wider geographic or large system demands by spreading box resources closer to the demand, which reduces network resources.

Table 5.4 Centralization Approaches

Versions of Functionality	Technology Location	Centralization Attribute	Functionality Profile
Single instances	Single box	Central physical location	United functionality
Multiple instances	Single box	Central physical location	Federated functionality
Single instances	Multiple boxes	Central distribution point	United functionality
Multiple instances	Multiple boxes	Central distribution point	Federated functionality

A variation of the idea of centralized versus decentralized is the concept of federation. Federation is the balance between the centralization and the decentralization of resources. As in most organizations, it is not optimal to be completely centralized or decentralized, but rather to have federated areas of centralization and decentralization within the enterprise. In other words, federation is segmenting the enterprise, taking advantage of either a centralized or a decentralized model for the deployment of technology in support of a specific functionality. Hence, the concept of centralization is not simply moving all resources to one location, but rather optimizing the disbursement of resources throughout the organization.

While many of the examples given for the responsibilities around the enterprise patterns were on global segmentation (more to illustrate a point), LEA can scale to a more localized organization. Instead of countries, the strategic segmentation could reside in buildings, floors, or even server rooms. The point of the examples was to illustrate the idea that in the Strategic Architecture, identification of enterprise patterns should begin at a high level devoid of implementation detail.

ENTERPRISE GUIDELINES

The third piece of the Strategic Architecture, which follows the enterprise principles and enterprise patterns, comprises the enterprise guidelines that determine the "how" for implementation of technology. Enterprise guidelines are not details on implementing technology, but rather a strategy for helping in the Conceptual and Execution Architectures. Enterprise guidelines are based on three factors:

1. Construction
2. Resource
3. Control

Construction

The first activity in LEA for enterprise guidelines is the identification of how best to construct technology within the enterprise. This is a hot topic in many organizations and is often contested by the engineering staff as they feel that any worthy effort is best created from internal staff. While this is not a false statement (in and of itself), the objective of a strategic view is to think "enterprise," so not every effort in an organization requires all efforts built from scratch in engineering. For example, it would make little sense for an organization to create its own operating system when there are viable solutions available. For this reason, it is more important to focus the resources on higher-value efforts for the organization.

The opposite view is that using packaged technology is a better model for optimization of resources. However, packages tend to be too rigid in their functionality, and customizing packages can lead to extra effort in many cases. Hence, the goal of developing the guidelines for construction is to create the outline of what factors will identify how to build solutions.

There are no forms or formulas for this portion of the Strategic Architecture. The following solutions are the various options that the guideline needs to identify as to when best to use for the enterprise.

- Internal customization
- Package implementation
- Vertical vendor solution
- Contract/offshore development
- Canned solution

Internal customization best matches when existing solutions are not available and the efforts of the resources required are available and capable. In addition, the organization needs to accept the cost to the enterprise as this usually has the highest associated cost, both short and long term (especially if key resources leave).

Next, packaged implementation and vertical vendor solution offer similar products but are differentiated by packages having a broader industry focus versus a vertical vendor niche. The package implementations also tend to have more customization capabilities and can require more resource effort from the enterprise. Vertical vendor solutions can provide better matches if the product design was to meet the technological gap currently identified by the organization.

Contract or offshore development can offer organizations better solutions but often require higher capital costs to develop up-front and ongoing. Contract or offshore is comparable to internal customization and appropriate if the right resources are not available within the organization. Finally, canned solutions provide a low-cost alternative but this is at a cost to the organization having to adapt to the solution.

The other factors influencing how to write the enterprise guidelines for construction depend on the culture of the resources and their productivity level as well as the core competence of the organization. It would make little sense for a sales-centric organization to build a contact management system as these are well defined and many solutions exist, from packaged to even canned. A better use of internal resources could require the custom building of a unique Web site to entice potential customers.

However, the most important factor for developing an enterprise guideline for construction is that limits and constraints are identified and understood by the enterprise so this issue is not reinvented for every project and the system design is consistent with the enterprise principles. It is common in organizations to waste effort during projects by trying to determine what the organization's policy stance is on using alternative means of development versus custom internal efforts. An enterprise guideline provides a consistent use of resources, both internal and external, that is optimal for the organization.

Resource

Resource identification in the enterprise guideline is the determination of when to deploy technology in-house or when to outsource technology. For example, a company that has limited resources and tight timelines may consider strategies of outsourcing of commodity functionality.

The business owners often consider outsourcing a loss of control and a threat to internal security. While these are valid concerns, industry has historically intertwined the sourcing of other companies to better focus on core competencies. Some of the first merchants relied on shipping companies to bring products to sell, relied on bankers to manage the money, and relied on government to enforce laws. This dates back to the Babylonian Empire over 4000 years ago; hence, the idea of outsourcing is not a new idea.

The main consideration is that internal resources are finite and that consideration must be given to identifying when using external solutions can provide the needed level of service for an enterprise, without sacrificing the security or integrity of the organization. This requires great care in developing the right measures and identifying competent outsourcing solutions.

Another consideration to understand in the development of the resource guidelines is that engineering staff can fear job instability when the notion of outsourcing exists. The right attitude for a company is that outsourcing best serves in situations of commodity functionality that other vendors have refined over time (with other companies). Reinventing this by staff is really a waste of their time as there should be more exciting challenges for the staff to address.

Outsourcing is more common than many people realize, as the following list attests:

■ Payment authorization is outsourced to companies that immediately verify the availability of funds and will transfer monies for a fee. This is in contrast to the old method of swiping a card in the hand imprinter and depositing the credit receipts into the bank, a process that took several days to post.

- Shipping has been outsourced for a long time with government developed postal systems, but recently the trend for express delivery has offered additional services such as online tracking. Hence, customers rarely call the company from which they purchased the product, but rather check online directly with the shipping company via the tracking number.
- Many companies have their Web site systems at hosting companies rather than building the necessary infrastructure in-house for a Web server and related gear.

Hence, it is not a matter of whether to outsource but when does it make sense for the enterprise and when does it not. The enterprise guideline should offer the enterprise basic strategies, so that this is not a political struggle each time, but rather an accepted enterprise guideline.

Control

Finally, control is concerned with who will govern specific technologies and this is likely the most difficult in a politically charged environment. The objective of the Strategic Architecture is to best advise on the optimal source of control for the enterprise patterns identified, but foremost to support the mandates set forth by leadership. It has been my experience that this is best a gradual process. Many times, the architecture has identified an optimal placement of technology that is not consistent with the current environment, but has required the culture and leadership time to accept the change or, in some cases, the changes were not implemented and thus a contingent strategy was required.

The most important activity in control is managing the expectations of leadership. It is rare that a well-informed business group in a leadership role will make an obvious bad choice for an enterprise. However, the architect must understand the stake the business owners have in the enterprise to best manage their expectations (this topic is discussed in more detail in Chapter 8) and to sincerely respect the directions of the business community and provide insightful business-related feedback and not technical babble.

Mapping control is often a design of where the resources reside, who owns the budget, and ultimately who approves the budget. Little else influences control other than changing these and that typically is the leader who approves the budget. Chapter 8 touches on this topic and the role of the architect in these matters.

TECHNOLOGY CHARTER

Often, the objective of the enterprise architecture in companies is to rationalize the technology portfolio from the perspective of what exists within the organization. From this rationalization comes a roadmap of system evolution that many organizations implement with minimal success. Rationalization in this style is based on what works well from internal best practices or external influences that govern industry best practices (a common approach used by consulting firms).

However, many factors influence the ability to replicate the success observed in other endeavors. While much is learnable from the success (and failure) of other efforts, jumping into the implementation of best practices without understanding the functionality of an organization first will lead to a high probability of failure. The best chance for an organization's success requires that first the direction of the business is understood through the vision and goals stated by the leaders.

LEA takes these goals and then translates them into tangible measures for technology as enterprise principles to adopt and determine what constitutes success. Next, how the business currently functions and the impact on the technology allows for the identification of enterprise patterns and determines where technology best fits to align with the business.

Finally, enterprise guidelines address the major technical issues that are strategic to the enterprise and developing these guidelines ensures that technology evolves in a uniform fashion. All these pieces of the enterprise principles, enterprise patterns, and enterprise guidelines compile into the final deliverable of the Strategic Architecture, the Technology Charter. For the success of an enterprise, the Technology Charter should remain consistent and not easily change over time. The initial Technology Charter will take time to realize in the enterprise and should be consistent with multi-year planning efforts of the business.

With this initial framework from LEA, the identification of a strategy focused on the success of the enterprise will better influence the efforts of the Conceptual Architecture that will optimize the systems within the organization to realize the Technology Charter.

NOTES

1. President John F. Kennedy, Special Message to the Congress on Urgent National Needs, May 25, 1961.
2. Christopher Alexander, The Timeless Way of Building, Oxford University Press, 1979, 62.

Chapter 6

CONCEPTUAL ARCHITECTURE

GOALS OF THE CONCEPTUAL ARCHITECTURE

Once the needs of the enterprise are made clear through a well-defined Technology Charter, the architect can begin the development of the Conceptual Architecture, which focuses on the system landscape in an enterprise. It is often tempting for architects to immediately model conceptual designs of the enterprise with the working knowledge of the current environment. However, without gaining buy-in at the strategic level from the leadership and understanding what the enterprise requires, there are high risks that the current environment may bias the correct evolution of the systems.

It takes skill to modify systems to meet specific functional channels but it takes expertise to understand the direction of an organization and plan system evolution accordingly. Conceptual Architecture is not merely the models to implement projects to satisfy short-term planning, but a gradual roadmap of how the system landscape of the enterprise needs to change.

A clear Conceptual Architecture helps organizations as it is the true communication medium between the various stakeholders in the enterprise. Many of the conceptual models that I have developed in the past have transformed into tools used in ways that I had not imaged or envisioned. The reason the models became widely used mainly occurred from resources understanding the technology landscape and being able to use the models to express new ideas or communicate key concepts.

My favorite instance was when I created several conceptual models that outlined functions and sub-functions in a relational model (discussed in a later section in this chapter). This was the first time anyone had modeled the current state and the model included some future enhancements. My intent for the model was several-fold. First, I wanted key engineering resources to buy in to a new technology that would evolve the systems more effectively. Next, I could show the needed technology and how it would affect the future requirements in a more cost-effective manner over time to leadership, thus obtaining initial funding for the effort. Both of these activities had proven successful, and the models even helped in the evaluation of potential vendor solutions to launch the development.

However, what surprised me was that the engineering leadership from the various domains grabbed onto the model. First, their initial reaction was that this was not the correct interpretation of the systems within the enterprise; and after a short one-hour session, they agreed that even as simple as the model was, it effectively communicated the essence of the system landscape, both present and future.

The following day, one ambitious director of the programming department color-coded the model to reflect systems of influence and control by the various departments. Apparently, there had been much confusion over which department controls which technology; and when the business community identified needed system functionality, there were instances of uncertainty regarding which department needed to own the development of the new functionality. The CTO then prompted me to validate the color-coding and adapt the model to a RACI (Responsible, Accountable, Collaborator, Influencer) matrix. My next task was to meet with the vice presidents and directors of each department and confer their roles and responsibilities through the model I had created for an entirely different purpose.

Despite some politics, the task completed successfully and many of the departments welcomed the clear boundaries. Hence, the fundamental philosophy of LEA proven many times is that simple and concise artifacts that are consumable by many different resources become vastly more influential than complex detailed designs that only specialized resources can adopt. Hence, the key to Conceptual Architecture as discussed in the following sections adheres to this basic philosophy.

A successful Conceptual Architecture focuses on the system landscape of the enterprise by optimizing the systems currently in existence and potential solutions. LEA identifies three areas within the Conceptual Architecture:

1. System contracts
2. System models
3. System objectives

System contracts are the measures of what the systems need to perform for the success of the enterprise. System models provide the fit for the systems within the enterprise, and the system objectives identify how the systems are to evolve. Ultimately, the Conceptual Architecture creates the deliverable: the Technology Roadmap for the systems of the enterprise.

SYSTEM CONTRACTS

In beginning to envision the system landscape, the first activity identified through LEA is the understanding of what the systems of the enterprise are doing. Each system in the organization is tasked to perform specific functionality to the enterprise and the first notion is to inventory those systems key to the enterprise. The key notion is the classification of critical systems and identification of systems that are complementary, conflicting, or even overlapping in functionality.

What is important in developing the system contracts initially is not to evaluate the systems against each other as that is a later activity in the objectives, but rather to gather as much detail of each key system as possible. There have been companies that I have dealt with that had thousands of systems and any Enterprise Architecture that would consider all of these systems would fail. Hence, the architect must concentrate on the major systems that support multiple sub-functions for large groups of users. For example, the Microsoft Access database that an analyst wrote to handle internal department reporting is not likely a key system to include.

In addition, companies that have fewer systems still benefit from this activity and can complete this quickly and easily. Small start-ups with less than 200 employees have benefited from this exercise as most resources are not familiar with all the systems and their exact functional support for the enterprise. The example of the company that had trouble identifying which IT group was responsible for functionality and developed the roles and responsibility map from my conceptual models was a company with fewer than 500 employees in the entire organization.

The areas of focus for the responsibility of the system contracts include:

- Categorization of systems
- Map systems to functionality
- Supporting principles

First, the architect needs a way of grouping systems by determining a categorization scheme. Then the architect can map those systems key to the organization to the functions within the enterprise using the same functional boundaries identified in the Strategic Architecture. Finally, the systems are measured against the supporting principles to determine their effectiveness in this Conceptual Architecture.

Categorization Systems

The most important aspect of categorizing systems is to identify their impact on the organization. This process is best captured through a variety of ways, but mainly a scale of criticality to the enterprise is needed that help assess systems. Some critical systems are not directly related to business functionality and are infrastructure systems, but key for the enterprise and the architect should identify these systems as well. A crude categorization that I often use is the following:

■ Key functional system
■ Minor functional system
■ Specialized system
■ Support system
■ Non-critical system

Truly, most systems are often a combination of the above but through LEA, they must reflect the primary category. While a system can be both a key functional system and a specialized system, it is better identified as a key functional system. We are assessing the impact of the system on the enterprise, so the higher categorization prevails.

Key functional systems are solutions that span multiple sub-functions and even multiple functions, and serve a large user base relative to the size of the organization. Many ERP solutions fit this categorization in companies.

Minor functional systems span multiple sub-systems, but rarely across functions unless they serve a very specific niche within the organization. Unlike specialized systems, minor functional systems serve a larger community and can support the adoption of different procedures.

Support systems are often very critical to the organization but do not directly contribute to any business functionality. These systems can include trouble ticketing (internal), configuration management, enterprise integration tools, and others. Often, these infrastructure systems provide valuable services for the internal systems that are key for the daily operation of the organization and those required by the architects to identify to best evolve the system landscape.

Finally, there exist systems classified as non-critical, as the process of identifying systems will later evaluate these systems as non-critical; but again, this process should first identify major systems and later evaluate their impact on the organization.

This classification can change to different categories that are more appropriate for the classifications of systems in an organization. The best practice is begin with a classification system and make changes later if the classification does not stratify the systems in a manner that builds the best conceptual view.

Map Systems to Functionality

Next in the determination of the system contracts is to map directly the functionality of the systems against the functions and sub-functions identified in the Strategic Architecture. Through LEA, the systems should not only identify their significance to the enterprise, but also identify what business events they support. Accomplishing this goal is possible through a variety of techniques, including:

- Modify the spreadsheet from the Strategic Architecture.
- Create a new spreadsheet and reconcile later.
- Develop a database that can map the relationships of the systems, regions, channels, etc.
- Write down system attributes on index cards.

No single technique to map system functionality is best, as all these techniques work. The important factor is to capture the information as clearly as possible and begin to see patterns of systems versus functional support in the enterprise, so that the modeling techniques of the following activity can develop.

The most successful technique I have deployed for this activity was to send e-mails to all the key IT resources from the various departments to identify their systems and provide quick detail on each system on a simple one-page survey form for each system. It is important to not leave the fields of these forms open, as they will become impossible to compile. For this reason, attaching the proposed functions and sub-functions definitions created in the previous Strategic Architecture for patterns helps to level-set the responses and keeps them consistent.

Supporting Principles

An important question to ask at this phase is whether the systems identified in this activity support all the principles outlined in the Strategic Architecture. While a system like the financial system does not support an enterprise goal of obtaining a specific percentage of a market, it will support the operations of the organization. Not every system maps to all or any of the principles but the collective set of systems need to support all the principles outlined in the Strategic Architecture or the enterprise is likely missing key systems or their exists a significant gap between business vision and the current system landscape.

In addition, systems have varying degrees of measures and do not directly map to principle measures. For example, a company that anticipates the transactions of thousands of orders per day will not require the CRM solution to process thousands of requests per day because not all customers will enlist the support of customer service for their orders. Hence, many systems will have a fraction of the goals identified by principles set by the Strategic Architecture.

In addition, systems will have different timelines and requirements because not all business functional needs are met immediately. However, they as a whole need to support the principles as set forth by the Strategic Architecture.

Together, the categorization of systems, mapping systems functionality, and the identification of supported principles provide the information for the understanding of the system contracts in the enterprise.

SYSTEM MODELS

Modeling is the most frequently recognized responsibility of the architect and often the most difficult to get right. Developing usable models requires an abstraction of the physical environment, which is more art than science. The architect must balance the need for informative designs, but at the same time not capture so much detail as to overwhelm the models and make them difficult to interpret. The designs of models in organizations frequently lean toward more detail rather than less detail as an attempt to validate the designs from architecture.

Complex and detailed models cause the designs to be consumable primarily to the engineering staff and begin to direct the approach for development. Detailed models become exact replications of the actual environment and are not a conceptual design. While this is perceivable as a viable use of modeling, it really becomes another artifact of system documentation that easily turns into outdated models as system design changes more readily affect a detailed model than a simpler, more abstracted model that is more conceptual. In addition, detailed models must make implementation assumptions to progress the systems for future needs and this can bias possible future alternatives.

In a large healthcare insurance company, my task was to help redesign the submittal process of electronic and paper transactions from the providers (i.e., doctors, hospitals, labs), to better streamline how the insurer processes these transactions. A main principle of the enterprise was to reduce customer distress, including to the providers. The submittal process was a major offender.

One hurdle was to get the many resources in the enterprise to recognize that all modes of submittal, paper, fax, EDI, etc., needed to filter through a single portal to process the business rules to handle these transactions consistently.

There were many arguments on the fact that paper had different rules for processing than an EDI transaction. Discussion got very detailed as to why the processing of a paper claim was more involved than an EDI transaction as staff mapped in detail the steps of how paper claims were processed in the organization; from getting scanned, keyed, and checked for accuracy. Through the keying of transactions, for example, the typist would check for valid codes and information in the system, then make changes as appropriate, and then submit the transaction to the processing system. However, the EDI transactions just passed through to the processing system and were either rejected or accepted based on the contents of the transactions.

The arguments went from checking EDI transactions for accuracy to letting paper transactions go directly to the processing systems as submitted. The arguments ranged from how resource costs increased to how abrasion is realized through changing various processing techniques. However, all this discussion, even though valid, was unproductive from the perspective of designing the system to move forward. A single portal can either provide the same process regardless of mode or provide additional processes depending on the mode.

Essentially, the design of the current environment was not allowing the resources to understand that regardless of the mode, the systems can evolve and handle the processes as appropriate and have them evolve over the various modes to the optimal state. However, resources felt that all the processes needed resolution in detail before system design so as to support the detailed processes faithfully. The flaw with this rationale is that true system design requires an open architecture when processes are not well understood within the organization. Hence, architecture best serves an enterprise when systems can evolve over time and are not built to exact specifications with little regard for future changes.

In addition, systems designed by constraints identified by detailed design can challenge the success of realizing the principles of the organization. In the healthcare provider scenario, the main reason for abrasion was through transactions having different results through the various modes as handled by different resources and systems. As the LEA framework would dictate, first determine the system contracts (what the system should accomplish) and do not focus on the details that often stalls progress, as these details are the implementation issues and the domain of later efforts.

In fact, the solution for the healthcare provider was relatively simple, but difficult to convey to the resouces of the enterprise. First, the enterprise needed to architect a solution that served as a single point for the organization to handle all processing for the claims and initially spend minimal effort to reconcile and reduce the various rules. Then, over time, using a single solution would provide a better means to find the right balance of policies to best reduce abrasion. Trying to intitially solve all the organization's policies before building the system was cresting a major challenge.

System Segmentation

A complex system is usually too difficult to fully understand when viewed as a whole with all the processes and details diagrammed. This increases in complexity when modeling needs to include the relationships of other systems to better understand how systems serve the enterprise. The best mechanism is the capturing of a high-level view that is the encapsulation of key systems and sub–systems, including their relationship to the enterprise and other systems. These views help slice the enterprise into discrete systems and sub-systems that are more readily identifiable, and that helps coordinate efforts between IT and business on technology.

In modeling, we separate a system into its component sub-systems, which in turn can segment into smaller sub-systems (if needed). Each of these levels of abstraction reveals more or less detail about the overall system or a subset of that system, and we can map the functions and sub-functions of the enterprise to these components. More importantly, the implementation detail is not included in modeling as the system contracts and the relationships in the system landscape are of higher value at this stage.

In LEA, there are two types of system models used in the Conceptual Architecture:

1. Functional model
2. Physical model

These two models are common in the industry, but how these models evolve in various organizations varies greatly and each has different connotations in different domains (data modeling, programming, business analysis, etc.). However, for enterprise architecture, the conceptual design is an abstract view of systems and sub-systems in their entirety.

The creation of the functional model and the physical model is not to perfectly represent the enterprise, but rather serves to capture key concepts of systems and their relationship in the enterprise. In LEA, we need a business understanding of the enterprise that the functional model provides and then a physical model that captures where key systems reside. LEA builds upon the activities of the previous system contracts and the efforts from the Strategic Architecture.

Functional Model

The functional model begins to map how the systems interrelate throughout the enterprise. What this model provides is a common system view of the enterprise. Both technical and nontechnical staff can communicate and agree upon how the model supports the business functionality.

There are many techniques to create a functional model, including:

- Functional
- Time progressive
- Domain

The functional technique is perhaps the easiest to develop as much of the groundwork was captured through the previous activities and now requires that the functions and sub-functions be mapped throughout the enterprise. Figure 6.1 provides an example of a functional model using the functional boundaries created earlier.

The time progressive technique takes the vantage point of how products and/or services progress through an enterprise and finally end with reaching and supporting the customer. Figure 6.2 shows an example of this modeling technique.

Finally, Figure 6.3 shows the domain technique of creating a functional model. The main aim of this technique is to highlight functionality as it is supported through the various domains (e.g., geographic, business unit, etc.) in the enterprise.

Any of these models are sufficient to communicate conceptual design to all the key stakeholders in the enterprise. Many of the efforts from the previous activities provide insight into the development of these models as the previous activities have captured far more detail. However, these models provide a simpler view of the enterprise and help better communicate new ideas for the evolution of the systems. In my teaching of undergraduate students in Fundamentals of Business Systems Development, I used the following example to painfully illustrate the power of simpler modeling techniques:

> Read the case carefully as it describes how a typical individual tax return is processed. There are several questions at the end of the case to determine your understanding of the tax systems.

> Tax returns can be received either via postal service or electronically. Electronic filings are captured by the Electronic Services Center that checks the returns for completeness and accuracy, mainly to ensure the integrity of the electronic transfer.

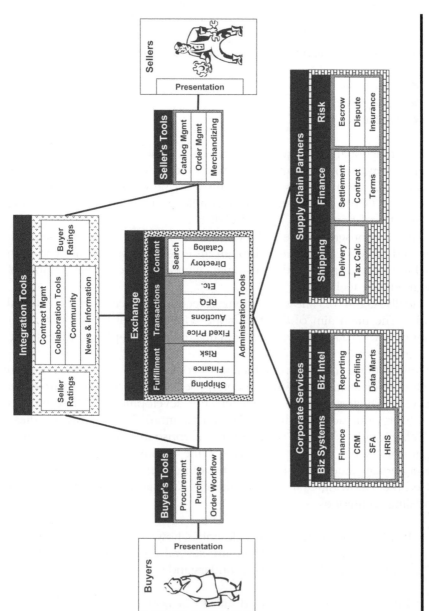

Figure 6.1 Functional Technique for the Functional Model

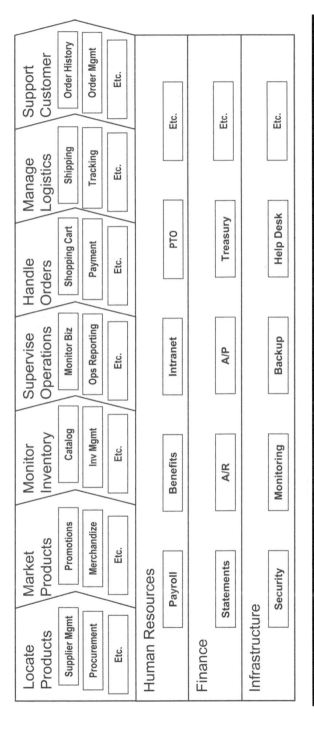

Figure 6.2 Time Progressive Technique for the Functional Model

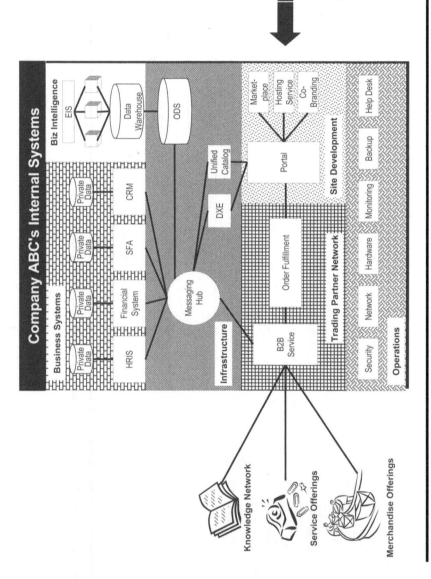

Figure 6.3 Domain Technique for the Functional Model

The verified returns are then forwarded to the Federal Computation Center, which then controls the processing of the returns.

The mailed tax returns are received by the Regional Center for sorting. The Receipt and Control department opens the returns and codes the return types. The number of received returns can hit extreme loads towards the end of the filing period. Hence, the mailroom must sort the returns in several passes to effectively manage the volume. There are several dozen categories of returns received by this department.

The first and primary sort divides the business returns from the individual returns and then forms requesting refunds and returns that contain a payment divide the individual returns. Next, the forms with simple filings requesting a refund are scanned. These validated returns are immediately sent to the Federal Computation Center to initiate a refund request and to the Examination department within the Receiving Center that stores and later further processes the returns.

The Federal Computation Center calculates the correct tax, decides whether a refund should be sent and updates taxpayers' files. Once the returns pass through various filter criteria and validated for a refund, the Federal Computation Center initiates the Treasury to issue the actual refund checks. Letters, notices, and other correspondences are sent to Local Offices for distribution to the taxpayers.

The processing of complex returns varies slightly from the simpler returns due to the number of forms and schedules involved. Complex returns initially sort into batches and are numbered to ensure that no returns are lost or excessively delayed. The batches are then forwarded to the Examination department that checks for accuracy and codes the returns for processing.

The Examination department, via the Local Offices, can request more information from taxpayers with incomplete or uncorrectable data in their returns. Additional documentation from the taxpayer is received through Receipt and Control department (not the Examination department) and then forwarded back to the examiners. Finally, the control of the return passes to the Federal Computation Center.

Now answer the following questions:

1. Which systems can request the Treasury to cut a refund check?
   a. Federal Computation Center
   b. Receiving Center
   c. Electronic Services
   d. A and C
   e. All of the above
2. Where is the taxpayer information stored?
   a. Examiner
   b. Regional Center
   c. National Computer Center
   d. A & C
   e. None of the above

To understand how much better functional modeling works, see Figure 6.4 and answer the previous questions using the functional model. While this functional model is simple, it provides an excellent medium for various resources to understand and discuss how systems exist today and how they should evolve. Often, these models have long documentation life cycles and can be reused in many new ways, such as color-coding for roles and responsibilities.

Physical Model

Physical modeling captures where major system resources reside within the enterprise. Often, physical modeling is used after the conceptual stage in many organizations, but encapsulating where key systems are physically located in the current environment is a valuable endeavor at this point in the LEA framework.

Up to this point, much has been captured around where functionality resides and some detail around the key systems. Now LEA needs to capture the system viewpoint of where these systems physically reside, so that we can understand the impact of the patterns and guidelines developed in the Strategic Architecture and compare this against how the enterprise currently deploys its resources. The physical models provide the foundation (with the functional) for the next set of activities in the objectives of the systems.

Many organizations capture the physical designs of their systems, so the architect need only compile the diagrams from the engineering departments. Often, the operations resources have good physical models of the systems that they support on a daily basis. These models usually offer much more detail than is required because they usually represent a

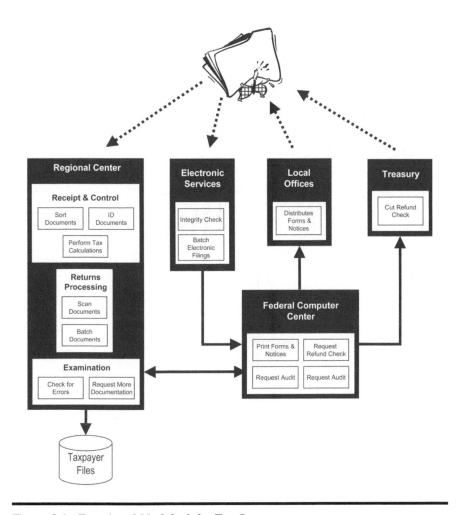

Figure 6.4   Functional Model of the Tax Systems

departmental or business unit view. Hence, there must be an abstraction to a higher level that consists of a more enterprisewide view of the systems. Figure 6.5 shows an example of a physical model.

SYSTEM OBJECTIVES

Through the activities of the system objectives, the architect begins the development of the evolution of the system landscape by balancing how best to streamline the technology and still provide increased functionality for future demands. The previous activities captured through LEA at this point begin to unveil potential areas of opportunity of how to best simplify the system landscape and provide future functionality. In addition, efforts

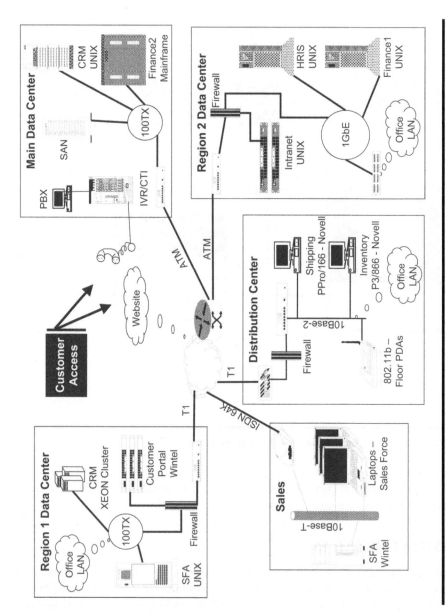

Figure 6.5 Example of a Physical Model

in the Strategic Architecture began the identification of functional patterns and presented guidelines for technology solutions.

System objectives for the enterprise's systems include the accomplishment of the following activities:

- Portfolio rationalization
- Preferred solutions

Portfolio rationalization is the process of minimizing the technology footprint in an organization. To support the portfolio rationalization is the creation of a preferred solution tactic that outlines ideal solutions from vendors. The completion of the system objectives in the Conceptual Architecture will lead to the development of the Technology Roadmap. The Technology Roadmap is the main deliverable for the Conceptual Architecture.

Portfolio Rationalization

As Figure 6.6 shows, there are five main layers for portfolio rationalization of technology within an enterprise. These layers are best restructured in a top-down process as the portfolio rationalization of process (or the patterns identified in Strategic Architecture) influences what applications are needed for the rationalized processes. Next, the applications rationalized dictate the best deployment of operating systems that the enterprise requires for the applications. Then finally, the network services and the infrastructure follow as best rationalized in the support of the applications and operating systems.

Why Progressive Rationalization?

Another problem that I encountered working with a large healthcare insurer (discussed in the previous section) was in recognizing that technologies like EDI, FTP, and other transmittal modes are like systems. Hence, the rationalization of these systems was an obvious choice to benefit the organization. However, the VP of the EDI solutions and the staff argued that EDI systems were different and required the providers to have submittal software and that rationalizing the technology with other transmittal modes was not possible.

The barrier for the staff was in the insight that the process of submitting transactions to the company needed a rationalized model first. Providers (i.e., doctors, hospitals, etc.) needed a simple and single method to send their claims and other related information to the insurer. It was determined

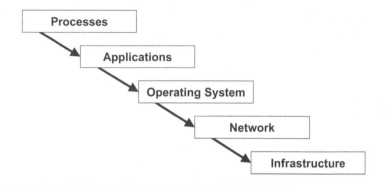

Figure 6.6 The Technological Layers for Rationalization

that almost all providers had access to Internet services and that a portal with secured access would service all provider needs.

Providers could send transactions in whatever format and the portal would then redirect the transactions to the appropriate system internal to the insurer. Hence, there was no requirement for providers to have specialized software to send even EDI transactions as they could use their existing systems and redirect the transactions to the portal. However, the staff obstruction in understanding this was due to the implementation of their current tools and the belief that rationalization of processes occurs after technology is in place.

The main technique is to create a target or optimal architecture against which the layers are progressively rationalized, achieving the mandates set forth by the Strategic Architecture. There are three main techniques to create an optimal architecture:

1. Best of breed
2. Internal optimization
3. Reference architecture

The best-of-breed technique uses either commercial solutions and/or industry-proven practices that closely match the required business functionality as the target. The benefit of this technique is that it is often a faster approach for rationalizing an organization's current technology portfolio. However, it usually requires significant modification of business processes, has a higher initial learning curve (for both IT support and the user community), and it proves difficult for the integration of existing systems.

Internal optimization works to identify the best-of-class solutions internal to the organization as target and provides integration through a robust messaging infrastructure. This technique is the most flexible approach because the organization likely has perfected systems over time and provides the lowest adoption rate for both IT support and the business community. The negative of this technique increases if the current technology is poorly developed, which will then add complexity to the portfolio. In addition, this technique can take longer to rationalize the technology portfolio if technology expertise is not a core competence of an organization.

Reference is through the development of a pristine enterprise model of the business and uses it as target. Then, portfolio rationalization is the process of manipulating the layers to achieve alignment with the reference architecture. The benefit of this technique is that it enables integration of best-of-breed package applications with custom applications. However, this approach can have high cost due to customization and provides a slower approach to a rationalized landscape.

The most likely scenario for most companies is a combination of the above approaches to achieve the most advantageous portfolio. Finally, the main goal of portfolio rationalization is the reduction of duplicated functionality in the enterprise, so that the resulting layers of technology can better rationalize.

A common obstacle is the belief that more than one system needs a particular function and hence the systems are to retain the delivery of the functionality. This goes back to the notion of the system contracts and that portfolio rationalization efforts need the identification of one system to act as the primary provider of a function. However, if other systems require this functionality to operate successfully, then every effort is needed to make those systems subscribers to the primary system. Working toward a provider and subscriber view of system functionality helps avoid systems duplicating functionality and hence convoluting processes over time, as separate development efforts with duplicated functionality in systems will eventually influence the efficiency of the organization.

Initial system contracts in an organization will have multiple occurrences of duplicated functionality. It is the goal of portfolio rationalization in the design of the Technology Roadmap to reduce these duplications. An important architectural consideration is that duplication will always exist, and elimination is likely impossible and very likely unproductive for the enterprise. The goal is to minimize the occurrence of duplication.

Figure 6.7 is an example of a plan for the portfolio rationalization of the application landscape. As shown in the figure, the many applications that are duplicating functionality can reduce to a much more manageable set that still delivers the needed functionality to the enterprise. Adding functionality is easier in a rationalized environment because there are fewer systems to enhance.

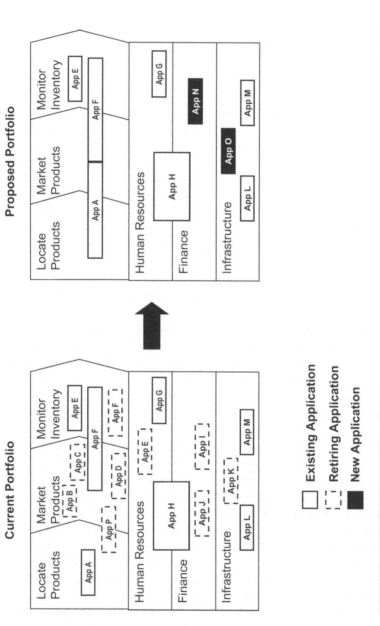

Figure 6.7 Rationalizing an Enterprise's Application Portfolio

Preferred Solutions

The preferred solution is usually a list of key platforms and technologies that have a descriptive usage associated. The list contains the supported vendor solution(s); that is, hardware, software, services, or a combination of these. Combinations are classified as technology profiles that define best uses in the enterprise as a complete solution and not portions of a solution. Multiple vendors are expected but this must be balanced with time-to-market and support of the principles because an environment with too many different solutions breeds complexity and is to be avoided if possible.

In rationalizing the system landscape, there is balancing between minimizing the number of platforms and not limiting an organization's technology solution. In developing the preferred solutions, the first activity is the identification of the current landscape that builds upon the efforts of the physical modeling. Next, boundaries and criteria are defined for the various vendors that help rationalize the specifics of the system landscape.

Many IT departments have claimed that they support only certain technologies, but I have found this to be rare — even in organizations that are fervent UNIX shops and have claimed that all their critical systems were on UNIX servers and not on any Microsoft platform. However, I often find the business community using Microsoft Office and Outlook[1] extensively, so many inter-department applications were built with Microsoft Access and Outlook was supported by a Microsoft Exchange server that the business community felt were critical systems.

Hence, standardization of technology is best understood where specific products are best suited, but not does mandate the use of any single vendor product. Rather than the idea of standards, LEA chooses the term "preferred solution" when rationalizing technology solutions.

The preferred solutions outline the specific tools, platforms, and solutions best suited for the development of the technology solutions in the enterprise. The solutions must reflect the principles outlined previously and provide a clear selection of all the major categories (e.g., OS, database, etc.) versus having multiple standards that create complexity in the design and support of a product.

Often when a company standardizes upon given solutions, they are susceptible to unforeseen failures as this limits the selection of technology solutions. Forcing standardization may appear as a viable means for system rationalization, but true environments are much more dynamic. Thus, companies will eventually make compromises to their standards, so it would stand to argue why not prepare for the exceptions by stating when technologies are optimal — not required.

A consultant working for a freight company that spanned the globe and heavily relied upon technology once related a great example of forcing standards to me. The company had a standard model of the technology needed at each shipping site that provided a means to streamline the company's operations. However, in an Asian facility, the shipments had large backlogs during specific seasons and productivity dropped significantly for that facility.

A team was dispatched to investigate the causes of the errors. Upon arriving at the facility on a particularly cold day, the team observed the employees working in the extreme conditions. Upon acceptance of parcels, the receiving staff had to type the parcel information into the computer terminal. However, due to the cold weather, every worker wore large gloves that prevented them from typing, so they would use chopsticks to enter the parcel data.

Hence, the keyboard was an ineffective tool in the functional layout of this facility for this environment. Even bringing heat into the receiving area was not a complete solution because the receipt of parcels was from trucks and staff was continually moving in and out of the cold environment. A new process of staging parcels was designed, along with a simplified keyboard that could be used with gloves.

TECHNOLOGY ROADMAP

Through the activities of the Conceptual Architecture, the main deliverable for this realm is the creation of the Technology Roadmap. Taking the artifacts of system contracts, the system models, and the system objectives, the Technology Roadmap compiles these into a single document and places a timeline against the system objectives, thus creating major milestones of activities to drive in the next realm of LEA in the Execution Architecture.

Figure 6.8 shows a sample of a summarized roadmap. How the Technology Roadmap identifies and outlines the milestones will vary, depending on the environment and the needs of the enterprise. It is important to realistically plan the timeline for a successful implementation as project realities can influence delivery dates and likely have a great effect on the enterprise achieving its strategic goals. However, as with most endeavors in organizations today, taking too long to deploy technology and not seizing advantage of market opportunities or threats are detrimental to the organization.

Hence, the Technology Roadmap needs to identify the key milestones and gain the buy-in from all the key stakeholders while balancing the desires of leadership to move forward with the limits of resources to

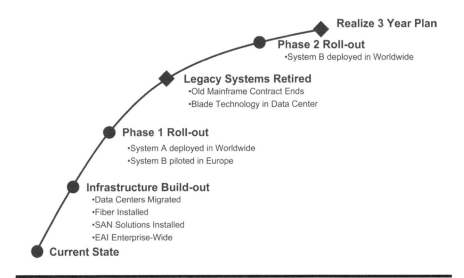

Figure 6.8   Highlighting the Roadmap

evolve the system landscape. The Technology Roadmap is an important tool that bridges the business and technical communities.

FEEDBACK TO STRATEGIC

Upon the development of the Conceptual Architecture, the system contracts should collectively support the enterprise principles identified in the Strategic Architecture. Not every system requires the support of the enterprise principles or even a single enterprise principle, but all the principles must be addressed in the system landscape. If there exist significant challenges to any enterprise principle, then these need reassessment in the Strategic Architecture.

Similarly, any challenges to the enterprise patterns or enterprise guidelines through the development of the modeling designs or portfolio rationalization efforts are best resolved through a reconsideration of the ideas initiated in the Strategic Architecture. However, sufficient effort must occur to reconcile the design in the Conceptual Architecture to ensure that the original strategic visions are obtainable and not subject to change every time design challenges confront the architecture team.

NOTES

1. Microsoft Office, Microsoft Outlook®, and Microsoft Exchange are products of the Microsoft Corporation.

Chapter 7

EXECUTION ARCHITECTURE

GOALS OF THE EXECUTION ARCHITECTURE

Once the Conceptual Architecture has a Technology Roadmap and system models of the enterprise, the architect can more effectively influence the outcome of system implementation and help in the prioritization of the technology projects presented. Execution Architecture focuses on specific systems and helping projects implement the Technology Roadmap developed through the Conceptual Architecture and helps in the realization of functionality needs from the organization.

The Execution Architecture primarily mentors and helps set the guidelines for implementation activities. It is not uncommon for architects to get involved in actual implementation detail, but it is not the best use of resources, as architecture needs to be unencumbered by implementation tasks, which are the domain of the skilled resources. The architect is the owner of the overall vision and should not be involved in detailed activities unless there are barriers to success that cannot be resolved by the technical staff. The roles and responsibilities of the architect are the focus of Chapter 8 and discussed there in more detail.

The activities of the Execution Architecture include the following:

- Project requirements
- Project diagrams
- Project specifications

The Execution Architecture really sets the foundation for projects by outlining what systems need for their success through capturing of *project requirements*. Next, the architect helps craft the *project diagramming* of the key system's design to enable better integration of the system to the system models. Finally, the development of *project specifications* bounds the approach of the system to be implemented.

The efforts around the Execution Architecture are planning and high-level design for systems and the projects to realize the evolution of these systems. The result of the Execution Architecture provides the scope documents for the system implementations that the technical and business resources can develop in more detail for the deployment of the solution.

The Execution Architecture has the most changes over time compared to the other realms of LEA, because the Strategic Architecture is really a refinement of the direction for the enterprise and the Conceptual Architecture is a foundation for the system landscape. The Execution Architecture is the detail work for LEA and provides the deliverables of the project scope documents that project staff and engineering can embrace.

PROJECT REQUIREMENTS

The capturing of project requirements is often an activity that every organization has in place but often creates artifacts that an engineer can rarely fully implement in system development. Hence, in almost every instance of system development, I have witnessed the paring down of system requirements. Unfortunately, many times what was excluded from the final system was not due to lack of need, but that the initial design of the system could not support the requirement without significant effort.

The goal of project requirements in LEA is to understand that resources are limited and project requirements need to reflect true business requirements and not functional wants or unnecessary details. Often, requirements activities lose sight of the goal of creating requirements — every notion is captured to the list of requirements and left for project management and engineering staff to deliver a system to satisfy all needs.

Ultimately, this leads to an excessive list of requirements that becomes nearly impossible to design into a system. Some projects I have been on collected requirements that numbered into the tens of thousands! When requirements are too numerous, they are in fact the collection of detail specifications.

In typical organizations where the efforts of system planning produce an excessive number of requirements, there are three approaches to handle the requirements:

1. Status quo
2. Requirements triage
3. Collaborative requirements

Usually in organizations, requirements gathering is a separate and distinct activity that the business community participates in with little to no involvement from the technical community. Status quo allows the business analysts and program managers to drive the development of excess requirements gathering, because the factor for these stakeholders is to capture all the ideas of the business community. However, this approach tends to place the burden of delivering on the technical community as the business community feels that it has articulated its needs and now the technical resources need to execute them.

In due course, the number of requirements needs to be addressed in either design or development and often the business community views the technical community as unable to deliver functionality to the enterprise. Unless the technical community has great diplomatic resources within or a very sympathetic business community, this results in a rift between these resources and reasoning by each side to disbelieve each other. Even the technical community begins to view the business community as unrealistic with its compilation of numerous requirements.

Another approach takes a more proactive tack by the technical community through triaging the requirements at the very beginning. This approach requires the architect and skilled technical resources who can work with the business community to rank and prioritize the requirements and manage the initial expectations of the business community early.

Typical categorization of requirements fall into the following scale:

- Critical to business
- High impact
- Medium value
- Low value
- Nice to have (usually unknowns, as impact has not been tested or realized in the current environment)

After categorizing the requirements, the next step is to evaluate the effort in implementing the requirements using simple metrics (i.e., High, Medium, and Low). Finally, the requirements are sorted and filtered in a variety of ways to help bundle requirements into phases of delivery for the technical community. This helps provide a timeline of releases that the business community can expect for functionality and the technical community can better budget their resources.

This is a better approach than status quo because the technical community takes a more proactive approach and works more closely with the business community. However, there still can exist friction between the groups as the prioritization process and staging into releases might not be readily agreeable between the business and technical communities.

The last approach is to change the typical requirements gathering process and use a collaborative process in developing the requirements. The previous two approaches are typical of environments that support SDLC as the effort is highly segmented by effort type, delineated by type of resources. In other words, resources are involved only as needed to minimize cost within the enterprise because resources usually have multiple responsibilities. Hence, technical resources are usually busy either building or supporting systems in the enterprise and are not available for planning and early design activities.

Using a collaborative approach is a technique embraced by other approaches, such as prototyping and O-O. Some of the agile approaches even mandate collaborative design for more effective delivery of functionality to the enterprise. This means that technical resources have a wider domain of responsibility that, depending on the culture of the technical community, can be highly successful or disastrous.

The success of this approach depends on the technical resources' willingness to leave the technical domain, work within groups, and participate in planning and design meetings. Many technical resources are reluctant (to put it mildly) to go to a meeting with business resources, so fostering this environment is important in helping the technical resources realize that this is a more empowering environment for technologists and one that ultimately leads to better system design.

In all these approaches, the number of requirements can still reach the law of diminishing returns and invariably result in the capturing of requirements that inhibit the delivery of a successful system to the enterprise. The important notion to instill for the process of capturing project requirements is only to capture business-related functionality that readily translates into tangible measures. Within the LEA framework, project requirements are the boundary of measures in Execution Architecture. Hence, the requirements need to reflect what the system should do and not how (how is the boundary of the means).

However, it is difficult to not get involved in developing the details as there are many pain points within organizations and the user community wants them resolved. An approach I have used successfully in the past is to give the case of the "Soda Pop Initiative," which goes as follows:

> In an office design meeting, resources gather to lay out the offices of a new building for the Finance department. As discussion produces some good arrangements of the staff, the

discussion then turns toward the location of the break area. It is at this point that someone presents their need to solve a problem with the soda machines in the current building. Apparently, when purchasing a carbonated beverage, the vending machine drops the can in a manner that agitates the contents and when opened usually sprays the purchaser.

Everyone agrees that this is problem, but some want to continue the design process. However, a few people who have been sprayed argue that this is indeed a problem and needs to be resolved in the new office. A few argue that this has led to instances where some staff members have left the facility to change their clothes. Finally, to move forward, the group collects the requirement that the new office location will host a vending machine that does not agitate soda cans.

The point of this case illustrates that while requirements may be valid, they need to reflect the effort at hand, as these can grow and potentially offset the original intent of the effort. While the soda can spraying instances are truly a problem, they are not qualified for the inclusion of requirements for a new office layout, but should be forwarded to the appropriate resources. The appropriate resources should replace all the vending machines, and the project team for the layout should focus on the office build-out.

Planning and design meetings capture significant ideas on how to deliver the system and collection of these ideas is a wise endeavor. However, the how is not included in the project requirements. The system must first meet the success criteria of the enterprise through measures. The appropriate time to determine the best approach on how to deliver the system is during design and development.

Use Cases

Use cases are a popular form of capturing requirements in enterprises today. There are many techniques to create use cases, ranging from narrative to UML diagrams. However, often these efforts easily increase the requirements further and force design constraints, as use cases are primarily a design tool. The real benefit of use case design is if the environment needs to map very complex business logic and processes that the technical staff knows little about. However, rarely do complex process models constitute a requirement, but really force a system to mimic preconceived notions of how a system should deliver functionality in the guise of capturing business logic.

A good requirement states a tangible benefit to the enterprise and not just the capture of an idea for functionality. For example:

Good Requirement:
>   Users will vary in expertise for the system, so the solution must ensure that all transactions are valid requests from the user.

Not a Good Requirement:
>   Upon the user clicking the submission button, a pop-up dialog box appears to confirm the user submission.

Actually, both examples above capture the same notion but the latter would be replicated at every user instance in the system and become redundant. By better formulating the need, the technologist may have better means to ensure transaction integrity. Rather than a dialog box that many users click too quickly, a confirmation e-mail or some other control mechanism may be more appropriate.

The specification discussed later in this chapter covers the domain of capturing business logic. Requirements need to minimize as best as possible to a set of criteria that determines success for the system. The ideas of how to develop the system should not influence design, which can limit the success of the system. Not including the "how" in requirements does not equate to these ideas not being embraced in the system, but they are a secondary consideration.

It is often the "how" that creeps into requirements, increases the scope of system design, and negatively affects the outcome for system delivery. A primary goal of a system is the delivery of functionality for the business to operate; next, the "how" of interacting with the functionality is only a matter of preference for the organization.

In keeping with the philosophy of a simpler approach, a system is better captured through the initial understanding of the enterprise needs. How this is accomplished is an implementation detail and not a direct enterprise architecture concern. This is not to say that the enterprise architect is not involved with how the system is implemented, but it is not within the domain of the Execution Architecture as first the system scope needs identification. Project requirements provide an excellent mechanism to capture the enterprise needs, but become a hindrance when they also include low-level design detail.

There is a balance for system evolution and delivering key functionality to the enterprise. We want enough detail to know when a system is successful, but too much detail can prevent the delivery of a practical solution. Working through the framework of LEA helps accomplish balance at the right level of detail at the right time.

Issues

An important consideration for implementations is that not all criteria or success factors are identified in planning. Factors such as system limitations, new technologies, and changing business environments are all large contributors for changing requirements. The management of new or changing requirements is important as they can easily cripple an organization if the system design is continually changing and never finalized long enough for the system deployment to mature.

Systems usually evolve over time and rarely remain unchanged, so future updates for changes are normal. However, introducing change within the system development and delivery stage increases the risk of a poorly implemented system if not managed well. Changes are not allowed at this stage if they are not critical to the success of the system as identified by the system contracts or even the enterprise principles.

However, it is important to capture the changes into an issue log that then can assess whether these changes are critical. For critical issues, they form into new requirements that the system must incorporate in the current implementation phase. Changes that are not critical need to go into a list of requirement considerations for the next release of the system.

PROJECT DIAGRAMS

In the previous Conceptual Architecture, the activities of modeling provided good abstractions of the system landscape; but as the focus shifts to a system or project view, there becomes a need for more detail. Project diagrams provide the next layer of abstraction detail from the modeling done previously. An enterprise can have many variations of diagrams, and LEA does not mandate a specific set but rather provides a minimal set that helps frame actual implementations.

There are primarily three types of project diagrams outlined in LEA:

1. User interactions
2. Interfaces
3. Logic diagrams

User interactions provide the detail of where functionality resides. *Interfaces* are primarily the details of the various information stream locations; and finally, *logic diagrams* provide the details of where business logic and physical logistics are best located and how the solution fits within the enterprise.

User Interaction

User interaction has four areas of concern to frame where functionality needs to reside. These areas:

1. Types of users
2. User mapping
3. Input needs
4. Output needs

The various types of users are important to capture so as to ensure that all stakeholders of the system are a design consideration. In addition, characteristics of these users are useful, including items such as descriptions, population, and frequency of use. This illustrates where, architecturally, the system demands reside for the proposed system.

Next, what functionality each type of user requires is the activity for user mapping. This gives the project team a sense of the needed functionality by user and potentially different design considerations (i.e., GUI design, business logic, etc.) for similar functionality, but for different sets of users.

Input needs is about capturing the information required for a given functionality. Various approaches require different details, as O-O approaches the need to understand the business objects and the messages between the objects versus standard approaches that capture basic data models of input needed. However, LEA simply requires a basic understanding of the information required for specific functions. For example, to complete an order online for an Internet store requires the following:

■ Customer (e.g., name, contact information, shipping address, etc.)
■ Billing (e.g., method, payment detail, billing address, etc.)
■ Order (e.g., item code, quantity, price, etc.)
■ Transaction (e.g., date/time submitted, referring page, etc.)

The project staff will then develop the specific data needs and identify the complete list of information.

Output needs capture the reporting functions of the system. Either samples of the existing reports can be collected or the users polled for their needs, but essentially the output needs with this activity focus on mainly the type of reports, general attributes, and the selected audience. Like the input needs, only a basic understanding of the reporting is required as the details again are developed by the project staff. The goal of LEA for project diagrams is to capture the scope of the proposed system. It is not essential and discouraged at this stage for the architects to develop the details of the system.

Interfaces

Interfaces are external to the proposed solution and are a consideration of the relationship of the systems information stream relative to the other systems in the enterprise. In almost any organization, a new system cannot exist without integrating with current systems, so early planning is required that maps these interfaces.

Context mapping provides the simplest and most effective mechanism to capture the needed interfaces for a system. A context map, as shown in Figure 7.1, is a centered, simple box for a proposed system with directional lines of messages to all systems with which it must interact. The messages are unique names that are then easily referable in a separate spreadsheet that captures the message detail.

Logical

Logical diagramming presents the next-level of detail from the system models previously developed in the Conceptual Architecture. However, the logical diagrams are still not the detailed design that the project will develop. The main purpose of logical diagramming is the identification of key tools and techniques to deploy the solution.

There are mainly two types of logical diagrams: functional logistics and physical logistics. Functional logistics segments where functionality resides in the potential solution as most solutions will span over multiple systems and share functionality. Figure 7.2 shows a functional model and its fit within the enterprise using layers of abstraction to segment types of functionality of the system.

In particular, as mentioned earlier in the portfolio rationalization activities within the Conceptual Architecture, the goal was the minimization of replicated functionality. The portfolio rationalization activities proposed a reduced technology footprint that promotes the idea of a primary system providing the function and secondary systems as subscribers to that primary system. This functionality will need to map across the systems and reflect how the solution will leverage existing functionality or even future functionality in the enterprise.

Finally, the physical logistic diagram identifies where the system best resides. This is particularly important in understanding where the physical equipment and software reside, so that the operation staff can begin planning the fit of the solution within their facilities. Only simple diagramming is required that identifies the solution using physical models from the Conceptual Architecture.

It is important to note that both of these project diagrams are initial ideas for where the solution would best fit. However, later project devel-

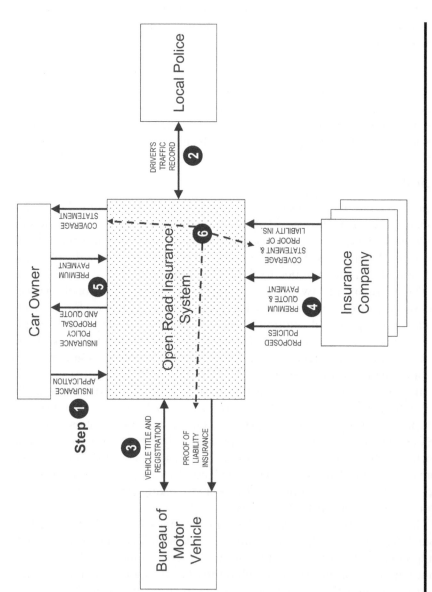

Figure 7.1 Sample Context Map

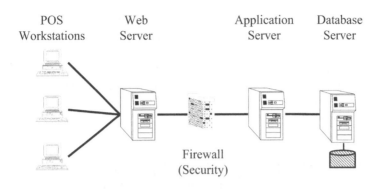

POS Workstations   Web Server   Application Server   Database Server

Firewall (Security)

Figure 7.2   Sample Logistical Diagram

opment can change these initial assumptions, as they are only guide considerations for the project resources to build upon.

PROJECT VISION

The last set of primary responsibilities for the architects in the Execution Architecture is the development of the project vision. This is the beginning of how the project needs to evolve for the Technology Roadmap realization. Ultimately, this is the initial idea for the design of the project. There are three primary areas of focus within the development of the project vision:

1. Impacted systems
2. Potential solutions
3. Key business logic

To best develop the project vision, first the architect must understand the relationship of this project to the current systems in the enterprise, discover what type of solutions are applicable, and then identify the key business logic the solution must provide.

Impacted Systems

The impacted systems have already become familiar to the architects, as the previous diagramming responsibilities should have identified many of the systems impacted. In addition, systems that have been identified also need assessment on how this solution affects these current systems in the organization. This requires the identification of key resources for these systems and discussing the design plans of the project with these resources.

While there is not a specific approach or format to proceed on these tasks, the architect needs to meet and have discussions with as many of these resources as possible. The input of these resources will be invaluable and this is an excellent beginning to gaining buy-in. These key resources can affect the success of the project. In addition, these resources also can provide potential insight into the project vision.

Potential Solutions

An additional area of responsibility within the project vision is the discovery of potential solutions that can offer the needed functionality to the enterprise. Identifying a list of candidates for the project provides a list that can:

- Modify a current system
- Provide internal custom development
- Find an external solution
- A combination of the above

The goal of the architect in this area is not to restrict to a single solution, but rather identify a short list of candidates that the project resources select in their initial activities. Finally, in the potential solutions, there is identification of the possible candidates, which includes some due diligence of why these solutions made the short list for this project.

If the solution is clear and only a single choice is appropriate (this must be definite), then this effort only requires a verification of resources on the selected solution. However, the goal of the potential solution is to clear the path for the project team to quickly come to a selection on the solutions.

Key Business Logic

Finally, the architect must determine what functionality the solution provides and the critical business practices that characterize how the organization operates. These components comprise the key business logic and are important for capturing the initial scope of the solution. In addition, this provides the criteria for selecting the right choice from the previous activities captured in the potential solutions.

Together, the impacted systems, potential solutions, and the key business logic set the initial foundation for the design for the project. This initial idea of the project is captured in the responsibility of project vision that feeds into the deliverable of the Execution Architecture, the scope documents.

PROJECT SCOPE

The project scope is the compilation of all the previous work done through LEA and some additional detail of how to best approach the evolution of a system. This should prove to be one of the easier activities of LEA, but still generate an invaluable deliverable for project implementation.

It is important to note that these activities within the Execution Architecture are identified through the Technology Roadmap deliverable created in the Conceptual Architecture. The project scope is generated for each major milestone on the Technology Roadmap. A portion of the project scope will remain consistent in format and the contents are pasted from the artifacts generated in previous activities in LEA.

The project scope is project focused and provides the boundaries of the system needs. The document should include, at a minimum, the following information:

- Timeline
- Key stakeholders
- Architectural background
- Project requirements
- Project diagramming
- Project vision

The timeline comprises the specific details identified for the project. The timeline should reflect only major phases of the project and the date when leadership expects the solution implemented. The actual timeline can change if the project team identifies significant challenges for the realization of the proposed timeline. However, the changes need to feed back to the architects and be checked against the Technology Roadmap developed in the Conceptual Architecture, because pushes to the timeline influence the success of the overall Technology Roadmap.

Key stakeholders include not only the proposed project team, but also the business community involved. Business users need to be identified to help validate design and key business owners to approve the designs.

Architectural background is the packaging of the artifacts captured in the Strategic and Conceptual Architectures that is relevant to the project. Important aspects are principles that the system is to support, the fit of functionality, and the guidelines for finding the best solution (e.g., build versus buy, etc.) and evaluation criteria. In addition, the system contracts, system models, and the portfolio rationalization are excellent supporting material for the reasoning for the project.

The previous activities, which include the project requirements (preferably a minimal set), the project diagrams, and the project vision, are included. In addition, the issue log is an important tool for the ongoing challenges as the design and development of the system unfolds.

Output to Implementation

Once the project scope is complete, the project team takes this document and pulls together a project charter around the proposed scope of the solution. The project scope increases the chance of project success as many of the main ideas for the project are captured and now the project team can focus on the implementation details to deliver the solution.

Any significant barriers for the project that limit the ability to realize the project scope are then fed back to the Execution Architecture for consideration. As mentioned, impacts on the timeline, resource constraints, and implementation barriers that conflict with the architectural design are all valid issues for the architects to address and determine whether the Execution Architecture is impacted.

FEEDBACK TO CONCEPTUAL

Over time, an organization that has effectively executed enterprise architecture activities will notice that less effort is required in the Strategic and Conceptual Architectures as the systems more closely align with the vision and need of the enterprise. Furthermore, the technology can only rationalize to an extent and the Roadmap will become less dynamic as technology optimizes, so future activities will have less need for portfolio rationalization efforts. Hence, the focus shifts to more Execution Architecture activities that maintain the designs of the systems by the architects.

However, Execution Architecture will identify barriers in new system implementations and uncover new challenges, as the enterprise requires functionality not originally intended for the current environment and these challenges then trigger the reevaluation of the Conceptual Architecture. Then again, no company remains unchanged for long, so the need to recycle through the three realms of LEA will begin as new markets, products, services, or technologies identify new opportunities to the organization.

SECTION 3

IMPLEMENTING LEA

Any intelligent fool can make things bigger, more complex, and more violent. It takes a touch of genius — and a lot of courage — to move in the opposite direction.

— E. F. Schumacker

CHAPTER 8

PHILOSOPHY OF LEA

BELIEFS OF LEA

The fundamental belief for LEA is the observation that most organizations use technology inefficiently and that complexity is the culprit in these organizations. This results in cost overages, long implementation cycles, and failed expectations within these organizations. Often, the resources in these organizations attributed the failures to the diverse technology within the enterprise.

However, diversity is a reality in many organizations, and creating a standardized environment is highly unlikely and very likely impractical. The main failing of many diverse environments is the existence of a complex communication process and a lack of understanding of the values within an organization. Many endeavors involve complex designs that justify effort because many regard simple results as ineffective and unproductive.

The result of adding complexity in an organization is the introduction of additional barriers to success for organizations. Ultimately, this translates into poor technology solutions that only complicate an already complex environment. Simplicity itself is neither easily obtained nor is it ineffective. LEA provides a simple framework to reduce the complexity that causes difficulty in the communication and realizations of ideas.

The standpoint of LEA is that there are too many organizations encumbered with complex lines of communication. This complexity places a strain on the organization's ability to execute upon new visions or, worse, realize old visions. This inhibits the health of any organization and causes mistrust between the business and technical communities.

For LEA to succeed, the participants need to have a goal of simplicity. Obtaining simplicity in the framework requires five basic premises for LEA to thrive:

1. Environment of trust
2. Unbiased vision
3. Minimal clutter
4. Consumable artifacts
5. Simplicity

By developing an environment of trust, providing an unbiased vision, reducing clutter, and creating consumable artifacts, an organization can foster a culture of simplicity. These are the beliefs of LEA that help deliver a simple framework for enterprise architecture.

Trust

Initially, trust is the most difficult task for many resources, as their efforts are often required to be comprehensive and without any ambiguity or their efforts are incomplete. Many demand the "how" for system design to be comprehensive. Trusting is not so much the release of dictating the "how" to skilled resources, but rather providing a direction. This fosters an environment where resources have a higher esteem as they proceed, using the best approach with the knowledge of their craft. If resources are unclear of how to proceed, then this is usually an indication of too many junior resources and the need for more senior leadership in the technology domain.

The architects cannot perform all the activities within technology or even anticipate all the required tasks. This fact indicates that the architects need to trust resources at some point. Hence, the better strategy is to minimize involvement in the details of how, provide the vision for technologists, and provide support only when requested. If requests are frequent, then the technology staffing is inadequate.

Unbiased Vision

Next on the demands for the architect is the desired state of not being a technology zealot. The primary goal of any organization is the success of the enterprise's ability to reach the intended market and not how the technology works. Technology is a great advantage for organizations to better realize success, but it is not a guarantee. Architects need to understand this fact.

The first unbiased view is that technology does not solve all problems and that the latest technology is not always the best. Technology needs accountability against the bottom line for organizations, as resources (mainly financial) are finite, so technology needs to become accountable for this fact. Usually, technology is very expensive to deploy and support, so the benefits must be significant and measurable for the organization.

In addition, unless an organization can risk failure, most new technologies need careful consideration before they become candidates for a proposed solution. All technology needs verification through established use or a clear demonstration of how it can fit in the organization before serious consideration is given. Only under extreme circumstances, when an enterprise is willing to risk failure, is an unproven technology used in order to gain first user advantage in a competitive market.

Finally, relying on a single platform or putting faith in a vendor is risky for any organization. Very few organizations can afford to limit their options for technology, as this usually requires significant resources and is usually the viewpoint of technology shops that internally build all their solutions. These organizations need to analyze whether custom coding is the core competence of the organization and the best use of resources.

Clutter

Clutter is a common result of the various skilled resources in an organization and little cooperative vision to unify effort. Technology is a broad field with resources that rarely understand completely the domain of other technologists. Hence, a usual outgrowth of this fact is the proliferation of technical artifacts that rarely align in design and interpretation. This then leads to additional supplemental material for these artifacts to be self-sufficient.

First, this implies that there is significant duplication of effort and, again, resources are limited in an organization. Second, it implies that there exists a higher probability that interpretations are different, which leads to incompatible design.

The goals for architecture are to reduce the number of artifacts created in an enterprise and use an approach that builds on the previous effort and not reinvent it in each new resource domain. The reduction of clutter is not an easy task as many resources have a comfort level around their view of the enterprise, but this is counterproductive. For an artifact to have true merit in the organization, it needs to pass the test of "So What." The test of "So What" is for the creators of the artifact to answer the following:

■ What purpose does this artifact serve?
■ Who is the intended audience for this artifact?
■ Do comparable artifacts exist, or is this truly a unique artifact?

If the artifact does not stand up to the above tests, then do not produce the artifact and the path of reducing clutter has begun. The artifacts of LEA exist in a table in the appendix that addresses the "So What."

Consumable

Along with testing for the use of artifacts in the previous section is the desire for usefulness by the artifacts. By passing the "So What" test, artifacts become better tools for distributing ideas throughout the enterprise, but it is not an assurance that they are easily understood or created.

Again, thinking about the artifacts created in the domain of enterprise architecture, it is paramount that the design balances the need to describe an idea, but not include too much detail such that the design becomes difficult to understand and use. The exclusion of the implementation details is often a good start, but simplicity in design is the goal.

Simplicity

The fundamental belief of LEA, restated from the beginning of this chapter, is that simplicity enhances an organization's ability to use technology more effectively. If there is less duplication of effort among resources and a better understanding of the direction of the enterprise through a simplified series of artifacts, then the likelihood of success increases.

Thus, the design of LEA as a simple framework provides the support needed for an organization to achieve some degree of simplicity. This is not to suggest that the entire domain of technology transforms into simple designs, but that diverse resources can easily communicate and share ideas for the growth of the enterprise with a minimal set of artifacts.

ROLE OF LEA

The architecture group needs to be an independent and unencumbered view of the enterprise. The architects serve best as mediators for the enterprise. This places them in the domain of reporting directly to senior leadership such as the CIO and/or CTO, or in some cases the COO and CEO. Placing them as direct reports within the technology department will influence their decisions and their designs to benefit the technology group. In contrast, placing them solely in the domain of business heading a group of analysts will influence toward the benefit of the business community at the expense of the technology group. Hence, the best position is near the leadership, which also benefits by having greater respect (gaining authority) and being better positioned to understand the vision of the business and correctly influence technology alignment.

Removing the architecture group from specific domains also has the benefit of having an unencumbered view of the organization. At a large computer manufacturer, a $70M system was still under development after three years and had not realized the initial goal of supporting a key function within the enterprise. The applications group had championed this solution and their reputations required its completion. Unfortunately, the architecture group realized that a previous effort through an external consulting firm had built the system on technology that the resources found difficult to support and develop.

The system needed to retire and further development stopped, but those in charge were afraid of the political fallout. In particular, the architecture group was an ardent supporter of finishing the system as they were in the technology department. Luckily, the CEO stepped in with input from outside influences and shut down the project. Ironically, there was only a small reorganization of leadership and those that left the organization had philosophical differences on the business strategy. The technical leadership remained intact, but significant architectural decisions shifted to the outside resources.

The 80/20 Rule

Using the common 80/20 rule, the optimal participation of architects is found close to 80 percent in the realms of LEA and 20 percent in outside activity, giving equal share to project implementations and strategy work. This is not a firm rule and upon the initial adoption of LEA, the architects will spend more time in strategic activities. Once the business strategy translates into a working Technical Charter, the focus begins to shift toward more implementation involvement and is highest during the Execution Architecture development. It will all shift back to strategy for year-end feedback and any significant new strategic planning in the enterprise.

How time allocates in the various realms will vary by the type of organization and the skill sets of the architects. If the organization has a history of transient leadership or changes in the business strategy due to volatile markets, it can require more focus on the Strategic and Conceptual realms. This depends on having strong technical resources to fill the gap in the Execution Architecture.

The other extreme for the focus of architects is a stable leadership and a persistent strategy that requires little redesign at the Strategic Architecture level once developed. However, if there are weak technology resources, then a fair amount of effort is placed on the architects in Execution Architecture and implementation activities.

Spreading the Focus

The successful adoption of any enterprise architecture requires the participation of many different stakeholders and various levels of involvement. LEA reaches a broader audience by segmenting the realms into like activities and responsibilities for the architecture group. This ensures communication to all the key stakeholders required for the successful evolution of the system landscape thus helping realize the vision of the business.

Early in Chapter 2, a model illustrated the gap often observed between the vision of a product or service and the factors of the environment that influenced the realization of the actual product. This model also showed the domain of LEA that bridged this divide by facilitating communication between the two extremes and driving toward a common shared focus on delivering a product or service. Figure 8.1 shows the three realms of LEA superimposed on the original model and the influence factors in an organization.

The model illustrates that the gaps can progressively get wider as the organization moves through a product or service realization. Hence, it becomes important for enterprise architecture to take an early role, formulate a sound Strategic Architecture, and facilitate any need for feedback from the other realms of LEA.

In addition, as the solution implements, business users should clearly understand where the solution fits within the enterprise. Thus, enterprise architecture needs to serve as a communication device to facilitate the coordination of technology resources to the requirements of the business and help set expectations for the optimal adoption of technology solutions. A well-developed Conceptual Architecture communicates to the organization the Technology Roadmap of change needed for the realization of the vision from leadership.

Finally, many resources in the organization see the architecture group as a source to solve the difficult implementation issues often associated with new system advancement. Through the Execution Architecture, LEA provides a mechanism that helps mentor new approaches. The Execution Architecture is not a means to solve low-level detail that skilled professional resources are capable of handling. This realm requires a balance of mentoring and helping break new ground so that resources can efficiently progress and the architects can provide the guidance for systems to evolve.

LEA outlines the involvement of the architect as follows:

- Interpreter in Strategic Architecture
- Creator in Conceptual Architecture
- Mentor in Execution Architecture

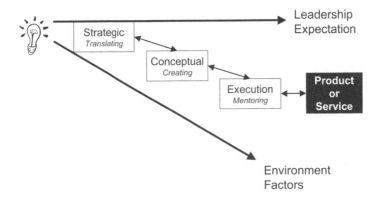

Figure 8.1. LEA in Bridging the Gap

LEA does not mandate that the realms are the charge of a single group such as the architects, as not all organizations will have available resources to fill the position(s). LEA builds the framework for the efforts of any capable resource in the enterprise as long as the activities are realized and accountable.

Often, an architect is the best match to own these activities in small to medium-sized companies. In larger companies, it becomes difficult for an organization to not have a dedicated architect or even a group, depending on technology landscape. Dedicating resources ensures that these activities complete sufficiently to meet the demands of the enterprise.

CHARACTERISTICS OF ARCHITECTS

LEA provides the framework to help organizations realize a product and/or service vision. Through a high-level multidisciplinary body of knowledge, architects are able to facilitate the technology to serve the business direction of the organization.

Good architects:

- Are great communicators
- Understand both business and technology

Good architects are not:

- Deep technical experts (e.g., programmers, DBAs)
- Senior management (i.e., the CTO or CIO)

This is not to suggest that programmers or DBAs cannot become architects, but it does mean that they need to leave the focus of those crafts behind when becoming an architect. Technical experts who still have responsibilities in their domain will have difficulty abstracting to a higher level and dedicating the appropriate amount of time to develop the enterprise architecture. Deep technical experts tend to easily go to more detail as there is a comfort level, but this does not serve the needs of the enterprise. Hence, if these resources are potential candidates to serve as an architect, then they need to commit to the role or the enterprise architecture will likely fail.

The CTO or CIO is not the best resource for the position of architect, as they will focus more of their attention on the business side and less on technical implementation. However, in smaller companies, this may not be the case; the identity of a resource as a CTO or CIO is really just a title as typically in small start-ups, resources have many roles. In larger companies, resources will have broader skills versus the smaller companies where resources tend to have deeper skills and more varied responsibilities.

The optimal (not mandatory) position for an architect in the hierarchy of an enterprise is best served in a station that is a balance between the technical and business communities. Typically, this is near the top of an organization as a direct report to senior management. Hence, this requires a balanced resource who is competent in both business and technology and not swayed too easily in either direction based on his or her background or even environment.

Architect versus Analyst

An architect's work involves analytical thinking and design, but this is often confused in organizations where architects are just analysts. Analysts typically capture detailed information that contributes toward complexity. The level of detail in the analyst's domain focuses on the "how" and "why" that support execution. These efforts are valid and help an organization become more informed, but these analytics need abstraction to a higher level before any judgment or decision can be made.

This is the real domain of architecture as the architect serves more in a leadership role for the technical community. This leadership is through the architect's technical vision in creating the conceptual designs and models. In addition, the architect needs to influence change or the technical vision is a waste of an organization's resources. Therefore, architects need to have the power to realize change and need to serve primarily as a leader and not as an analyst.

Analysts are excellent resources serving the architectural community and often provide a great service as direct reports to the architects. Ultimately, experienced analysts make great candidates for future architects as they usually have a good, broad understanding of the enterprise through the various analytical efforts and can usually make the transition easily to an architect. It also has been my experience working with some senior analysts in companies to only realize that, in fact, they were doing architectural work, but had little influence to directly make changes in the enterprise.

Democracy, Dictatorship, or Diplomacy

Another differentiator for identifying the architect is the ability to balance when to be a dictator, when to support democracy, or when to be a diplomat. The role as the enterprise architect has a complex set of responsibilities as the duty spans over the various roles (through the various realms) and this requires balancing the right character at the appropriate times. The architect needs to exhibit all of these characteristics while maintaining the position as an enterprise architect.

First, supporting the democracy is an obvious role for the architect as the field of technology is very diverse and requires the involvement of many different influential resources in the organization. This requires that consideration of all relevant resources be given in an architectural plan. In addition, for credibility of the Enterprise Architecture, there must be buy-in from the majority of these resources.

It is unlikely that there will always be consensus on new ideas and it is probably undesirable to strive for that goal. Getting unanimous support of every idea would impede the growth of any organization because this would require a great deal of effort and this is would be at the expense of the organization's profitability. Democracy refers to gaining key supporters and having a major consensus on an idea. Those who are in the minority need to consent to the majority and "agree to disagree," yet move on for the sake of the organization. The architect then takes notes on the objections and captures the issues of the minority with the intent to monitor these concerns but move forward with the majority view.

However, not all activities in the architecture require democracy, but rather the style of a dictatorship is better suited in various circumstances. First, translating the vision of leadership for the technology domain requires that the technology resources adhere to this vision and not make changes to ease system implementation. In addition, the Conceptual Architecture delivers the Technology Roadmap that achieves the goals of the enterprise, and it is the responsibility of the architects to ensure that this roadmap becomes reality. This often requires the architects to mandate resources to adhere to the timeline.

Finally, diplomacy is the most revered characteristics for the architect, even in modes of democracy or dictatorship. Diplomacy provides the best tactic to eliminate dissent from contentious resources that can affect progress. For example, acknowledging and capturing the issues of the minority in democratic forums validates to the minority that their views are important, that they are just not aligned with the majority view. The action of addressing this group is not only better diplomacy, but can later benefit the architect when help from these resources is required at another time (and it will happen).

Another area of diplomacy arises when the architect provides project oversight and notices bad judgment on the part of the resources for delivering a solution that does not meet the goals of the enterprise or affects the Technology Roadmap. It is not simply a matter of the architect pointing to the failings of the group, but rather working with the group to find an alternative approach. In addition, the architect needs to work early in projects to catch these occurrences before they are become problematic.

Take a Stance

The final and most important characteristic of the enterprise architect is the ability to present a solution early. This often means proposing a solution before all the details are known. Unfortunately, this is not a characteristic that many technical resources are competent in practicing. Often in my efforts, I term this process "placing the stake in the ground" to offer a starting point in discussions.

Many architectures fail when they do not provide a direction unless all the details are known and hence the risk is greatly reduced. Unfortunately, while this style is less risky and can provide better solutions, it comes at the expense of the enterprise because this style requires significant resources and time. These are elements that are not in abundance in any organization and, after time, the leadership will question the resolve of the architects using this approach.

To minimize risk, the architect needs to accept early criticism (even encourage it), priming the ideas from the available resources to solve a problem in the enterprise. Ego is best left behind when using this approach, and an open mind to new ideas is the requirement for true leadership. Of course, this is not to suggest that all the efforts of the architects' progress in this manner, but it is the best style when approached by the unknown in an enterprise.

At some point, the decision needs resolution and the architect needs to take a stance. The decision to move forward needs to balance collecting sufficient information and evaluating enough solutions, but a decision is imperative. My favorite quote for this process is from Theodore Roosevelt:

In any moment of decision, the best thing you can do is the right thing, the next best thing is the wrong thing, and the worst thing you can do is nothing.

Another quality of leadership for the architect is the ability to make a decision on the available information and the willingness to accept the risk. There will always be a better decision; but for the sake of the organization, the process needs to move forward. The success of LEA or any enterprise architecture necessitates that those resources in the organization regard the architect as a source of leadership.

COMMUNICATING LEA

The success of LEA is based on multiple factors in the organization, to include the strengths of the resources and the right characteristics for the architects, as outlined previously. However, how these resources interact is critical in achieving the successful coordination of the resources in an organization. The key to this coordination is through a solid communication style.

There are three main factors for a successful style:

1. Using effective tools
2. Understanding the key stakeholders
3. Delivering the right message

First, by practicing the framework of LEA, an organization will realize the effective use of the right tools from the artifacts and the deliverables in the framework. The other components —understanding the key stakeholders and delivering the right message — are indicative of knowing the audience and how to present ideas to that audience.

Defining the Key Stakeholders

Essentially, there are five types of key stakeholders in the stewardship of systems (not including the architects), including:

1. Leaders
2. Owners
3. Users
4. Creators
5. Supporters

Leaders, owners, and users of the business community are those who have the incentive for the successful delivery of functionality to the enterprise. The remaining two resources have the motivation for the design of the solution and are part of the technical community. While there are more resources than just these five, these represent the most important when considering the style for communication and who is the main audience for the architecture.

The leaders of an organization want a balance between increasing the capability of an organization and having a minimal impact on resources. This group wants ideas that present tangible solutions that deliver clear benefit to the organization. The leaders expect that all the alternatives were addressed, and that the proposed solution is the best option for the enterprise. It is best to avoid too much detail in this group.

Next are the business owners who typically budget and sponsor the system's development. The owners require an understanding of what the impact of the proposed solution is to the organization. Keeping this group informed of the progress in any effort on a regular basis is important, including the design and development of an idea. Owner support is critical for the success of any endeavor as the owners are responsible for the successful operation of the business and are the first group with which the leaders will validate any idea from the architect.

Finally, in the business domain are the users of the system whose jobs rely on the practicality of any solution. The involvement of the users in helping define the business needs and ultimately the requirements for a system enhances the chances of success. Hence, this group will want more detail, but the architect needs to constrain detail from driving design. In addition, this group's involvement improves success when allowed to frequently provide feedback in the evolution of systems.

Within the technical community, the system creator's focus is on how a solution will work. Creators help define the technical requirements for the information system and help construct and test the information system. Typically, the life cycle of the system involves different resources within the technical community.

Finally, the supporters of the system deployed are critical for the successful stewardship of any solution. Unfortunately, this group is often the last to have any input into the design of a solution. This can be a crucial mistake as these resources best understand the fit of any potential solution in the existing organization. Hence, engaging these resources early by identifying the ongoing needs of any potential solution, including reliability, growth, and the user community involved.

In organizations, I have heard many times that the supporters of systems referred to themselves as the enterprise's babysitters. These environments failed to engage these resources in the design and development of technical solutions. Unfortunately, this is a major oversight because this group often already has great insight into what works in the enterprise and what does not.

Effective Communication

Implementing architecture in an enterprise is a complex role for an architect. The architect is an interface to many different stakeholders, as seen in the previous section. This requires different skills to interact successfully with this diverse set of resources. To communicate successfully requires the architect to speak the right language to a given audience.

Table 8.1 outlines the roles the architect plays in the various realms of LEA. The style of the architect needs to shift from translator to creator to mentor, depending on the realm of effort and the audience.

Role to Senior Management

The predominant focus of communication to senior management of the enterprise (including both the leaders and the owners) is through the Strategic Architecture. The main style in this realm is as a translator, both from the vision of senior management into the Technical Charter and from the progress of the technology back to senior management.

The effective style for communicating to this group is from a more macro viewpoint of the enterprise, translating the technical issues into the resulting business impacts and not relaying the technical detail the group will likely not understand or, worse, care about. In addition, it is equally important for the architect to verify the translations of the business strategy as captured in the Technical Charter, thus validating the interpretation and avoiding any ambiguities. It also serves to confirm previous statements in strategy sessions and gets leadership to commit to previous notions that now the technology must be implemented.

Role in the Enterprise

The highest profile of the responsibilities for an architect lies within the realm of the Conceptual Architecture. When most resources think of an architect, they envision individuals focused on developing conceptual designs and models. Fundamentally, this results from the fact that the conceptual efforts provide the central mechanism to communicate to all resources. Conceptual Architecture is the creation of artifacts that all resources can rally behind to evolve the technical landscape.

The architect is the creator of these communication tools and, hence, the style of communication is the selling of these ideas to the enterprise. Mainly, the Technology Roadmap is a large "stake-in-the-ground" of what projects and what timeline will best evolve the technical landscape. The

Table 8.1. Role of the Architect

LEA Realm	Role	Stakeholders
Strategic Architecture	Interpreter	Leadership and owners
Conceptual Architecture	Owner	All
Execution Architecture	Mentor	Users, creators, and supporters

resources of the enterprise need to believe that this is the accepted path for the future development of technology.

Role to Engineering

Finally, the technology resources view the architect in the Execution Architecture as a leader of how the systems are to evolve in the enterprise. In addition, the users of the systems want a source of assurance that the progress of technology will satisfy their functional needs.

The style of the architect in the Execution Architecture is that of a mentor. This means that direct involvement is not critical to success, but rather that the architect is providing the oversight of all the resources, ensuring the systems meet the required needs from both the business community and the technical community. The architect facilitates any issues and provides suggestions, but mandating the approach of how the systems evolves needs minimal involvement of the architect in the details. Only when the issues have major influences that affect the Technology Roadmap or the Technical Charter will the architect step in and mandate a change in approach.

RESULTS OF LEA

Essentially, LEA needs to deliver to the enterprise the main three deliverables:

1. Technical Charter
2. Technology Roadmap
3. Project Scope

Through these deliverables and the activities in LEA, the architect helps evolve the system landscape. This process matures over time and improves in effectiveness as the culture begins to embrace this simple approach. Ultimately, the technology will begin to align with the needs of the enterprise and LEA will have succeeded.

LEA is Not Business Strategy

In some organizations, there may develop a blur in the vision for the future of the enterprise by the leadership. This has provided instances of the leadership approaching the architects to help drive the strategy of the business. While this may seem an obviously backward approach, this has happened to me in several instances.

First, there is no valid reason for LEA to drive the business strategy, and any attempt is a failure because LEA depends on the input from the business strategy to succeed. Often, my view on these situations is that leadership is fishing for ideas for where to take the enterprise as technology greatly influences many organizations. This is a validation of the efforts of the architect so as to provide some input into the development of the business strategy, but not set the direction.

It is paramount to not let the input from the architect make technology-centric business strategies, but rather to focus on where the enterprise's core competence lies with respect to technology and understand the potential opportunities and threats to the organization. The results must be highly probable directions the enterprise is technically capable of obtaining, thus balancing the core goals of the organization.

LEA is Not a Pristine Architecture

Another resolve of some enterprise architecture efforts is the creation of a pristine architecture. The architecture drives toward the development of the perfect architecture, void of any of the current shortcomings or resource constraints. This is not the same as in portfolio rationalization, which drives toward the target architecture, as the target can well change to accommodate better rationalization when effort is underway.

Essentially, systems are inherently inefficient, so any effort to create a pristine architecture is an effort of diminishing returns and highly unlikely. Anyone who has spent a fair amount of time developing and deploying systems knows that they never meet the original design specifications. Systems are dynamic, and any effort to force them to conform to a pristine state is an effort in futility.

Finally, most organizations have astute leadership that will intervene as soon as resources and time to market become unsatisfactory. Remember that the bottom line for any activity in the enterprise is success — that is, the profitability of any organization. Even nonprofit organizations need to adhere to the allocation of resources, as funding is limited.

As such, LEA is never to realize a finalized enterprise architecture as it evolves and grows with the needs of the enterprise. LEA matures as the organization embraces the simple framework and improves the stewardship of technology in the enterprise.

Chapter 9

THE CYCLE OF LEA

ARCHITECTURAL LAYERS

In Chapter 2, the layers of enterprise architecture consisted of three separate disciplines as shown in Figure 9.1 and relied on the business strategy for input. The success of LEA requires these disciplines to coordinate to evolve the technical landscape to deliver a product/service vision. The coordination of these disciplines primarily occurs within the Conceptual Architecture where these disciplines converge to ultimately create the Technology Roadmap.

While the business strategy is not a domain of architecture, it significantly influences the architecture. *Information architecture* takes the business strategy and builds the framework for how the organization will form and work to realize the product/service vision. *Application architecture* is then responsible for creating the software components that help shape the product/service vision. Finally, the *technical architecture* (i.e., servers, network, etc.) provides the infrastructure supporting the product/service from the initial vision of the business strategy as developed by the previous disciplines.

There is a sequence of effort between these domains as the process (information architecture) drives the design (application architecture) that determines the medium (technical architecture) of the solution. Similarly, LEA first requires a business direction before the Technology Roadmap develops; these disciplines require a logical sequence of inputs between them for the proper design of the Conceptual Architecture.

This progression is observable in various areas of LEA. Each stage within the Conceptual Architecture illustrates this sequence. In the system contracts, the first effort is the identification of areas of functionality (information architecture) within the organization. Then the next activity is the mapping of systems (combination of applications and technology architectures) against the previous functionality identified.

Figure 9.1   Enterprise Architectural Layers

In the modeling efforts, the first design is functionality-based, and also may include an application view of the functional model. The physical model that contains both the application and technical components of the enterprise then follows the functional model's activities.

However, the most apparent occurrence of the sequence of moving from the information through application to technical architecture is in the system objectives activities and is best illustrated in portfolio rationalizations efforts of the enterprise's system landscape (see Figure 6.6). The portfolio rationalization is a progression that closely adheres to the realms and provides the needed input from one layer to the next.

The progressive cycle of design through the layers is not a mandated rule, as efforts will vary depending on the domain, but they generally follow this cycle of design in LEA. If opportunities arise to rationalize a set of applications to a single platform, then the architecture can validate whether the functional needs of the enterprise are supportable by the approach. However, these are exceptions to the progress of designing the architecture in LEA.

The existence of experts in each of these disciplines would be beneficial for the architects, but the success of LEA does not require separate experts in each discipline. It is more critical that each of these disciplines is observed in the design of the Conceptual Architecture or there will be limited success realized by the organization. Very few organizations can survive long-term without the proper guidance of each of these disciplines.

LEA REVIEW CYCLES

There are three main areas where LEA interacts with project implementations:

1. Set the direction.

2. Review the design.
3. Ensure system integrity.

This does not mean these are the only times that architects involve their efforts in implementation activities, but rather that these are the minimum set of checkpoints for the architects to check the progress of implementing LEA.

Set the Direction

Initially, the activity around developing the project scope deliverable at the end of the Execution Architecture is an iterative process that is driven by the Technology Roadmap. The Technology Roadmap is generally a static document that proposes the implementation of multiple projects to evolve the system landscape. All of these projects require the development of a project scope to start these projects.

Development of the project scope is a collaborative effort with the potential project members, which usually includes the project manager and program manager. The project manager's focus is on managing the project timeline, resources, and budget. The program manager's focus is on the realization of delivering new functionality to the organization. In some organizations, a single individual performs both of these positions.

Next, the project charter maps in detail how the project will realize the solution bounded by the project scope. The project charter will create a detailed workplan, resource guide, and project templates, including communication (i.e., status updates, issue log, etc.) and project deliverables. It is important for the architect to work closely at the initiation of projects to ensure direction of the project aligns with the intent of the enterprise architecture. In addition, the architect may wish to participate in some of the early design sessions.

Joint Design Sessions

Joint Application Design (JAD) is a joint design technique pioneered in 1984 by Tony Crawford as part of the IBM development team and has ranged in technique from unstructured informal gatherings to rigid technology-driven sessions. The use of JAD became popular through the development of CASE tools, RAD approach, and the BPR approach.

Primarily, JAD is a workshop designed for people to convert opinions and abstract thought into agreement and decisions for action in less time than traditional techniques. These workshops can last anywhere from a day to several weeks, so the challenge is to secure the key resources to meet in a central location. This proves to be a logistical problem, but the benefits can be substantial for setting the right initial design to which all the key stakeholders can agree.

Some techniques to simplify the approach and increase the probability of success include:

- Preplan the meeting with an agenda, expected outcomes, talking points, and background material (i.e., project scope, initial planning, etc.) and send to all the participants to review and provide feedback before the actual session.
- Keep the design session short, from one to two days; any longer and it becomes a detailed design session.
- Limit the use of technology (as it can be a hindrance); utilize whiteboards, overheads, and a preprinted binder of handouts.
- Use a digital camera to capture whiteboard material if the whiteboard does not have print capabilities.
- E-mail the material covered in the session at the end of each day to all the participants for review.
- Keep the goal of the session simple and do not plan for detail design, but rather an agreed conceptual approach and expectations of the solution.

Review the Design

Another key point of the review by the architect is at the end of a major design phase in a project. If the methodology is an SDLC, then this is a very clear date to set. However, other approaches require that the architect keep in close communiqué when major design issues have been developed.

It is at this point that the architect then checks the designs to ensure that the direction is consistent with the Technology Charter and the Technology Roadmap. It is likely that some change has occurred to the project scope and is acceptable as long as the direction is sound.

Ensure System Integrity

The last point of review for the architect is some time during development and close to system deployment. It is at this point that the architect will check the solution to ensure that the integrity of the physical solution meets with the intended initial design as set forth by the enterprise architecture. It is the goal of LEA that this merely is a formality and only requires minor changes, if at all.

However, until the environment has matured to the design of LEA, it may be appropriate to have this review early in the development cycle.

This way, if there are changes, then it is still early enough without harming the project. It is important to note that there should be no major changes from the design review unless the project team made radical changes to the approved design. If this is the case, then there is a problem of communication, as any major issues need to reach the architect.

CHALLENGES TO LEA

Many factors can influence the success of LEA, and each environment will vary in the degrees of influence. However, any enterprise architecture must face the following three significant factors:

1. Organizational change
2. Governance
3. Cultural

Organizational change and *governance* are closely related areas of influence but affect LEA differently. Organizational change is a broader issue of aligning resources and systems that have a large impact on design of the Conceptual Architecture. However, governance is more a factor of control and influences the realization of the Conceptual Architecture. Finally, *cultural* factors can influence the implementation of LEA.

Organizational Change

Many organizations periodically change their organization and this can pose a significant challenge for system stewardship. Often, organizational changes have minimal impact on the technology landscape and require cosmetic changes only. However, when the reorganization of an enterprise is significant and the profile of the organization is radically changed, then the design of the technical landscape can become an issue.

How enterprises distribute their resources and how they share functionality influences the design of technology to support these attributes. Figure 9.2 shows a matrix that identifies four different technology profiles that best serve the various organizational designs.

Fragmented

This is potentially the worst environment to deliver an optimal technology solution for an enterprise. Having a decentralized organization and differentiated functionality offers limited ability of the technical landscape to rationalize. Hence, interconnectivity between the systems will likely not

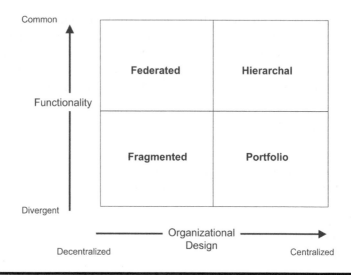

Figure 9.2 Impact of Organization on Technology Design

be a priority for the enterprise, because there is little functionality shared in the enterprise.

If an organizational change alters the profile of a company to a fragmented environment (from one of the other three), then any continuity between the systems will likely fade over time. As for enterprise architecture, there is little impact of planning on this environment as any effort produces minimal impact for the enterprise. The enterprise will be in a better position for a more efficient technology landscape if any attribute of the organization changes to move the enterprise into another quadrant.

Portfolio

In an environment that has moved toward a centralized organization but still has divergent functionality due to product constraints, there is the potential to leverage a portfolio technical profile. This is an improved situation if the organizational changes have moved the enterprise from a fragmented environment to an environment that has centralized many of the resources.

These changes provide a good opportunity to cluster systems to support the varying functions, but strive to maintain some consistency (as allowable) to minimize the number of platforms. This likely will be more effective in the technical architecture and be limited for both the information and application architectures.

However, if the organizational changes moved from a hierarchal position, then systems will likely increase in complexity and rise in cost. This is an acceptable scenario if the organization is serving distinct markets that mandate different functionality to serve these markets best. However, care must be taken to ensure that the divergent functionality is truly warranted, as this increases the cost to the organization, and there will be loss of economies of scale of platforms and resources to support these platforms.

An organizational change rarely moves from a federated state to a portfolio. This would mean that the organization centralized all the resources but now has mandated that functions become divergent. The likely cause for this scenario is through a merger of several companies or a poorly implemented business strategy.

Federated

A federated portfolio exists when functionality is common across an enterprise, but organizationally is a decentralized model. This usually occurs in enterprises that have geographic constraints on the enterprise but produce a consistent product or service. Hence, functionality is similar but resources are regionally located.

If the change of the organization placed the enterprise into this scenario from the fragmented quadrant, then there is sufficient opportunity to use technology to improve efficiencies. This will require effort of the architects in designing the technical profile of the organization to minimize replication of technology using different platforms. The success of this approach depends significantly on the ability to rationalize all the technology layers.

However, if the organization transition was from the hierarchical quadrant, then effort to maintain systems consistently is a key enforcement issue from an enterprise architecture perspective. Systems can become regionally disparate as resources are geographically dispersed, and systems will tend to evolve differently if not managed closely. The best approach is through either a collaborative design on the system from the separate resources or the development of a Center of Excellence (COE) that handles the system design across the enterprise.

Similar to an organization rarely moving from a federated state to a portfolio, the opposite is also true. Often, the scenario for this organizational change is for an organization to better serve local markets, but the architect must balance the design of an optimal technology yet not inhibit the enterprise's ability to uniquely serve its local markets.

Hierarchical

The last possible solution is the most optimal for any organization because the resources are in a centralized model and the functionality across the organization is consistent. From any quadrant, the design of the enterprise architecture is a chance to improve the system landscape.

Governance

Another factor in organizational change is the potential effect of span of control (governance). Governance is an important success factor for the realization of any effort around enterprise architecture. For systems to evolve, systems owners and the leadership must agree upon the course of the enterprise architecture. Without the buy-in from these stakeholders, there is little chance that any enterprise architecture would succeed.

The most important factor often overlooked by an architect is that governance is traceable to monies. It is the Golden Rule of "The One with the Gold Rules," as these resources have the largest influence on the fate of any system. Without the consent of these stakeholders, no system evolution will survive without a budget to support it. The architect must learn to sell to these stakeholders the needs of the enterprise architecture and convince them to buy into the Technology Roadmap.

In one multinational clothing manufacturer for which I was consulting, the CIO was on a quest to globalize the operations for better efficiency of the resources. Several key systems were identified through the enterprise architecture as best candidates for retirement, and a Technology Roadmap identified systems to rationalize into a single platform. However, the president of the European region would not relinquish control of that region's system for replacement to the new platform. Essentially, the system in that region was operating well; only several years prior, the European nation had recently successfully rationalized all the European countries' systems onto one platform.

The president of the European region was held accountable for the overall performance of the region, which included the budget and effectiveness of the core system. Until the leadership was willing to release the region, the responsibility of being accountable for that system and even the resources to provide that functionality, it was apparent that change would be unlikely. Hence, the president was not about to pay for another group to design and develop critical systems for his region.

It is important for the architect to realize that even despite good conceptual designs of the enterprise's system landscape, if the resources accountable for the affected systems are unwilling to buy in to the design, it is unlikely to succeed.

Cultural

Another challenge for the implementation of any enterprise architecture effort lies in potential cultural barriers. Not identifying these potential cultural barriers and striving to work around them will influence the implementation of any Technology Roadmap. There are many types of bad cultures, but the following seem to have the greatest effect on enterprise architecture:

- Not Invented Here (NIH) syndrome
- Group apathy
- Worked resources
- The silver bullet

Not Invented Here (NIH) Syndrome

Not Invented Here (NIH) syndrome is an expected attitude in many organizations that feel if they do not build the solutions, then the systems are not suitable for the enterprise. The common belief is that quality is not controllable and the resources in these organizations do not have access to the internals or designs of the solutions. Hence, there is a general mistrust of anything built outside the organization. This also stems from a fear of job security if solutions are obtainable from external resources.

Often, these resources seriously hinder the development of the guidelines in the Strategic Architecture. An important point to realize is that there are no companies in existence today that build their entire technical solutions from scratch. At some point, these firms build onto preexisting vendor solutions, even if it is an operating system or hardware. Not all the technical components of all solutions are internal, custom-built solutions in any organization.

Even strict government agencies that demand high levels of quality and security do not build all their solutions from scratch. Key systems are usually custom-built applications, but the supporting applications for monitoring, testing, and even building these solutions are likely vendor packages. In addition, these agencies can have administrative solutions, such as accounting or procurement, using vendor packages.

Hence, there is a balance of when to build versus buy. NIH believers have a mindset that all internal solutions are completely custom-built and an outside vendor solution is an appalling choice. This can become a hindrance when identifying best-fit solutions, as the NIH believers will place unrealistic expectations on any outside solution to attack credibility.

One organization that had very limited resources and was continually behind in providing needed functionality to the enterprise was looking to integrate several internal systems. A group was proposing to bring in a messaging vendor but the internal technical resources felt they could build a better messaging solution. Their main contention was that the external vendor's solution was unreliable and would not scale. Unfortunately, this argument had no merit because the vendor's solution was supporting solutions hundreds of times larger than the proposed system and had significant uptime in high-volume markets that would not support downtime.

Ultimately, these NIH believers were fired and the solution was implemented in less time than typical technical projects in the organization. Unfortunately, this can be an approach to deal with this behavior, but it can also be counterproductive because this is a disruptive approach as other resources will feel threatened and there is now a gap of resources in an already strained environment.

A better approach is to work with the technical resources and get them to understand that not all things technical need to be built internally. This is the reason for the existence of enterprise guidelines in the Strategic Architecture and the main benefit of developing the enterprise guidelines in LEA.

Group Apathy

Group apathy is a difficult challenge for an architect as needed resources are not likely to be vested in the success of any Technology Roadmap that may change their current environment. This can occur in organizations that are either in the fragmented or the portfolio quadrants identified in the previous section.

An organization that is very divergent in functionality will often exhibit this type of culture. This is usually the result of the divergent processes causing a lack of cultural cohesion with respect to systems. This is not to suggest that there is a lack of synergy within the organization, but rather a lack of care in coordinating the stewardship of the technology resources.

The efforts of the architect to overcome this barrier are to either gain buy-in from the needed resources or coerce them from the leadership. Obviously, gaining buy-in and the trust from the resources is the best course, but it may not be feasible in some circumstances. The final task is the enlistment of leadership to sell the need for the change to the organization, so that they either buy in to the change or believe that supporting the endeavor is a good career choice.

Worked Resources

Similar to group apathy, the worked resources culture exhibits like characteristics, but the cause of this behavior is due to overworked resources. Often, through downsizing and other shortsighted cost-cutting techniques, resources are strained to work at high productivity levels just to sustain the enterprise. Key resources are likely to be double and triple booked on meetings and are continually behind in their work.

Unfortunately, this is a very common occurrence in organizations as competition in the market has shaped these drastic measures. Typically, good resources are short-lived as high turnover rates also create a barrier for enterprise architecture. The success of any system evolution requires the attention of the key resources and these are the resources most likely to be strained.

First, the architect must concede that the resources will have to balance their time and that their involvement is limited. The architect must also factor in this limited availability of key resources and make sure the Technology Roadmap reflects this limited availability or the milestone dates will not be realized. In addition, the architect needs to optimize the use of these resources and provide sufficient reason for their involvement. The best reason for any of these resources is to produce better solutions that ease their current burden.

The Silver Bullet

The silver bullet is more of a characteristic of an environment than an actual culture, but it is a significant challenge to the architect. Environments that exhibit this behavior often believe that there exists a solution that will solve most of the key issues that an enterprise experiences. These are unrealistic expectations of what a particular solution can achieve for the organization.

Often, vendors that have the slick demonstrations that show other companies achieving amazing results from their products are the main culprits in these cases. Even though these vendors' claims can be truthful, the experience of other companies' success with a product does not guarantee success for every organization with like needs.

The goal of the architect is to balance claims from vendors and manage the expectations of the resources internal to the organization. Careful analysis of the potential solutions needs to be done, as well as the fit of the potential solution within the organization's system landscape. In addition, the resources of the organization need to assume some responsibility for the selection of the solution so as to ensure they have diligently weighed all the alternatives and have checked or tested portions of a potential solution's claims.

DEPLOYING METRICS

An additional activity that involves the architect within the enterprise is helping develop clear business cases for the new technology landscape.

It is one aspect to design a good technology; but without a solid business case that shows value for the organization, the design has little chance of becoming reality.

There are many ways to sell technology to leadership, but the most direct and usually successful approach is through tangible return on investment (ROI) or similar value metrics. Typically, a company will require that the expenditure of a given technology solution for both start-up and ongoing costs provide a higher return either through cost savings or increased revenue generation, or both.

ROI compares the lifetime profit of a project. The ROI for a project is a percentage that measures the relationship between the revenue generated from the project (over the life of the system) and the amount invested (including both start-up and ongoing costs). The lifetime ROI for a given project is calculated as follows:

$$\text{Lifetime ROI} = (\text{Est. Revenue} - \text{Est. Cost})/\text{Est. Cost}$$

The average annual ROI is calculated by dividing the lifetime ROI by the expected lifetime of the system. This is the typical figure used to evaluate projects against each other. So, the formula is as follows:

$$\text{Avg. ROI} = \text{Lifetime ROI}/\text{Years of Service}$$

Typically, companies expect to see the average annual ROI in the double digits as most money market investments can achieve these returns, so why would the business invest in technology if they yield lower results than a bond?

In some instances, the expected decrease in cost or increase in revenue cannot be estimated, so conservative numbers are used. Another potential reason is that the gain of a new technology yields a preferred value in the organization on which it is difficult to place a monetary value — such as customer satisfaction. Alternatively, it may be the case that the technology is not warranted and other options need assessment.

Not All Benefits Are Tangible

In one planning session, I was working with executive management to determine whether a potential reporting solution had a valid business case to deploy a new technology in the organization. The ROI was rather low, at around 12 to 15 percent, and there were other projects vying for funding, but reporting in the organization was in desperate need. As we were wrestling with how to better value the reporting solution, the COO finally stood up and said, "If this reporting solution really gives us better reports that we currently do not have and we cannot make at least one or two better decisions that would pay for this investment — well then, we should all just quit."

Sometimes, justification is based on an infrastructure need or other technology or functionality are plain reliant upon it. Some organizations require that all projects must pass business case criteria. This becomes extreme when resources begin spending sufficient time building the business case for every project in the enterprise. A more appropriate practice places this effort only on major projects and/or systems in the enterprise.

Intangibles to Tangible

Most intangible benefits are not beyond quantification into cost saving or revenue generation. Often, it is too easy for resources to claim that not having a particular solution would be disastrous for a company. It is all relative, and the main importance for quantifying a solution's value lies in the ability to prioritize effort in the organization, as not all potential projects can begin at the same time because money and even resources are limited. Hence, arriving at a good tangible metric is a good goal to support the Technology Roadmap, and helps illustrate to leadership the value of the effort underway.

There are several general techniques to build a measurable value from intangible benefits. Here are the more popular techniques that I have successfully used in past engagements:

- Better performance
- Improving accuracy
- Infrastructure improvements
- Resource efficiencies
- Customer satisfaction

Better Performance

Most technologists want systems that perform better than the current environment, but this is often where technologists stop when trying to sell the idea to the enterprise. Rather than trying to justify how the system is better, which business is not typically concerned with, the improvements of the proposed system need to be directed at the financial statements.

Like in the previous example of the COO, stating the reporting solution should improve decision making. One or two improved decisions from a better reporting solution can influence the operations, and a case can be made that the decision results in a benefit of 5 to 7 percent improvement in either operating costs or gross revenue. Now this seemingly intangible benefit has a measure tied to it.

Improving Accuracy

Accuracy is often a tough sell if the organization has built a system of controls and the enterprise has not experienced any need to change its current quality level. However, the controls are a cost to the organization, as they require resources and additional effort. The number of hand-offs and extended processing time also affect the cost of operations. Often, this is an effort in gathering the time spent on controls versus pure production and is a percentage of cost of operations that can be reduced by some factor for a more accurate solution.

Infrastructure Improvements

Infrastructure improvement projects typically are shelved in organizations under tight financial control. However, the cost of not being able to meet the demand of the organization can be high. For large infrastructure projects, benefits are translated into tangibles by identifying the cost of loss of operations. Loss of operations is best estimated by asking key business stakeholders if a system went down for one hour, one day, etc., how it would affect the business.

For smaller infrastructure projects, tangible benefits are realized through improved performance within the technology domain. The improved performance is similar to the first technique, but focused within the budget realm of the technology domain and likely needs only the approval from within the technology domain.

Resource Efficiencies

While resource efficiencies may seem like a simple case of reducing the number of full-time employees (FTEs) using layoffs and downsizing, it is here that one can approach this cost technique from a different perspective. First, simply reducing staff and removing them from the cost of operations is not always the best choice. If that were the case, then firing all the employees would have the biggest benefit, but then no one would be supporting the operations. Rather, it is more optimal to think of moving resources to higher value efforts within the organization.

Hence, we need to think of the number of FTEs displaced in the organization and the likely improved productivity of these resources as a percentage improvement on the operating costs. Not all resources will move to higher productivity as some resources will actually be jobless and this perspective is important for leadership to manage. In addition, the cost of hiring and retraining new resources is not trivial in many organizations.

Customer Satisfaction

Finally, customer satisfaction, often cited as a system benefit, is a truly difficult benefit to measure. Tangible measures may lie in determining the average cost to acquire a customer through the various forms of marketing (e.g., promotions, advertisement, etc.) and accordingly, a value is placed against the retention of that customer. However, the value of a customer sometimes is not a matter of simply retaining a customer, but a value of making a system more useful and thus enticing the customer toward more products or services. Then the value becomes the net worth of a potential customer through their purchases of products or services.

Finally, even with the assumptions in market share, retained customers, etc., it may become a matter of principle in the organization to be considered the best in customer satisfaction and the system plays a key role if the system is customer-facing. Then the benefits of a system are derived from analyzing usability surveys and provide a grading scale on the effectiveness and the net worth to the enterprise as a percentage of the revenue of that particular customer served.

Monitoring Metrics

After all the great effort on developing tangible measures and building solid business cases, it would be a shame if they were not monitored after the project or system went into operation. However, in many organizations, that is the case as monitoring costs the enterprise and many would rather not identify benefits not realized.

Monitoring metrics for the business will benefit the organization by learning what worked and what did not work. In addition, analyzing benefit metrics may reveal new insights into the organization, and this will then make the business cases more accurate in the future. In addition, the enterprise can be more proactive in system design and have the potential to make changes even when the solutions are operational, so that the realization of benefits becomes common.

Chapter 10

DEPLOYING LEA

GETTING STARTED

As with any major project in an organization, it requires careful planning to successfully implement the project. To make LEA a reality in an organization will require careful planning and design. This chapter provides the foundation for this activity.

Essentially, there are four milestones in deploying LEA:

1. Plan for LEA
2. Design of LEA
3. Commitment to LEA
4. Rollout of LEA

At the end of each milestone, there is a significant event. The initial milestone is realized when the stage of forming the core team is complete and success has been defined. After it has been determined how technology affects the organization and the core architecture team, then the design milestone of LEA has completed. Next, gaining the commitment of the organization to invest in LEA is critical. Finally, the success of LEA will depend on delivering quick results to the enterprise, so the initial deployment of LEA focuses on a pilot project illustrating how LEA beneficially influences future technology efforts.

Work Breakdown Structure (WBS)

Table 10.1 is the project plan for the initial cycle of LEA. This chapter discusses in detail what all these milestones, activities, and tasks entail.

Table 10.1 Project Plan for the Initial Cycle of LEA

1. PLAN FOR LEA
1.1 Identifying Core Project Team
    1.1.1.Determine the right size for success
    1.1.2. Recruit core members
1.2. Planning for Success
    1.2.1. Identify roles
    1.2.2. Determine success criteria
    1.2.3. Expand workplan
Deliverable: Core Team Manifesto
2. DESIGN OF LEA
2.1. Chronicling the Technical History
    2.1.1. Compile growth and dependence of technology
    2.1.2. Determine cost of technology
    2.1.3. Find cases of enterprise architectures
2.2. Designing the Architecture Team
    2.2.1. Define the members
    2.2.2. Determine the structure
Deliverable: LEA Draft
3. COMMITMENT TO LEA
    3.1.1. Highlighting the benefits of LEA
    3.1.2. Identify the benefits
    3.1.3. Build ROI
3.2. Identifying Stakeholders
    3.2.1. Locate key stakeholders
    3.2.2. Inform stakeholders
Deliverable: LEA Business Case
3.3. Selling LEA
    3.3.1. Build case
    3.3.2. Present case
    3.3.3. Define initial scope
Deliverable: Charter for LEA
4. ROLLOUT OF LEA
4.1. Preparing the Strategic Architecture
    4.1.1. Nail the enterprise principles
    4.1.2. Draft the enterprise patterns
    4.1.3. Outline the enterprise guidelines
Deliverable: Draft Strategic Architecture
4.2. Drafting the Conceptual Architecture
    4.2.1. Identify the key systems
    4.2.2. Develop the system models
    4.2.3. Note system objectives

Table 10.1 Project Plan for the Initial Cycle of LEA (continued)

Deliverable: Draft Conceptual Architecture
4.3. Initial Activity in the Execution Architecture
    4.3.1. Find a pilot project
    4.3.2. Develop the pilot project artifacts
Deliverable: Project Scope for Pilot

Deliverables

Several key deliverables are instrumental, as shown in the previous WBS, but more can exist that are dependent on the project culture of each organization. Organizations will also vary in their design of these deliverables, so it would be impractical to provide samples here. However, the activities and the tasks within the milestones compile to create the final product.

The variations of deliverables in organizations are diverse, but the main types include:

- Structured with formal extensive deliverables
- Staged with forms and processes
- Informal using presentation styles and social networks

The best technique would be for the architect to reach out to successful project managers and determine the best format for deliverables in the organization. It is always easier to replicate success than to rediscover it each time.

PLAN FOR LEA

Plan for LEA is the initial stage of implementing LEA, as this is the grassroots effort to make LEA a reality in the enterprise. The key deliverable in this phase is the manifesto that draws up the immediate charter of the core team and how to identify success.

Identifying Core Project Team

The core team can be the final architecture group charged with the responsibility of LEA, but this is not essential. The core team's primary task is to get LEA initiated. The identification of the core team involves determining the right size for the team and recruiting the members.

Determine the Right Size for Success

Multiple factors will dictate the right size for the core team. This is a balance between playing the right politics by having core members who can influence the right key groups and having core members who feel compelled for the success of LEA.

Recruit Core Members

It is imperative that the core team is determined to make LEA a reality and can dedicate the time for this project. Recruiting is not just a matter of convincing resources, but includes getting the commitment from management to pledge the time of these resources. In addition, it is important to get the members passionate about making change happen.

Planning for Success

Planning for success is important because every organization is different and it is key to determine how the team will know what will determine success. The process of planning for success includes identifying roles, determining the success criteria, and expanding the workplan.

Identify Roles

To ensure that everyone understands their responsibilities requires the establishment of well-defined roles. This removes ambiguity around who will do what and allows resources to be successful. The best method is to poll the core team to determine what each member would like to do and then elicit their ideas for roles and candidates for the project team.

Determine Success Criteria

What will success look like, and how will the team know when it has succeeded? This is a step that is often omitted and a source of many project failures. This is a chance for the team to agree on the project goals and unify the group.

Expand the Workplan

The final stage is to expand the WBS structure provided in this chapter with more specific detail. This can be the deletion of tasks that are irrelevant in the current environment or the addition of specifics to the organization (approval processes, documentation standards, etc.). In addition, the workplan needs timelines and resources added to become more executable.

DESIGN OF LEA

This stage of the project begins after the core team has formed and has a clear understanding of what needs to happen. Design details how LEA will fit into the organization. The milestone of this stage is achieved when LEA is drafted through the understanding of the current technology landscape and the proposed architecture group is designed. Essentially, the draft is background material for the business case that paints the current technology profile (highlighting pain points) and the proposed group to manage the future evolution of technology.

Chronicling the Technical History

Before the design of LEA, it is important to understand the history of the organization around technology. It would make little sense to build a framework for the stewardship of technology without understanding the history of technology in the enterprise. The tasks in this activity include compiling growth and dependence on technology, determining the true cost of technology, and finding cases of enterprise architectures.

Compile Growth and Dependence of Technology

Understanding how the technology landscape evolved is important in understanding why the current environment exists. This is the chance to not only gain insight and lessons learned, but also identify what has been successful. This is not a task in compiling blame, but rather a chronology of how the organization's technology has grown and determining the true dependence on and constraint of technology.

Determine Cost of Technology

Often, many organizations really do not understand the true cost of technology. Many are blinded by project costs and new technology implementations. However, the true cost also includes resources currently supporting technology and other ongoing costs (e.g., licensing, facilities, etc.). Determining the true annual costs and typical new technology project implementations will support later activities around the business case.

Find Cases of Enterprise Architectures

It is almost impossible for organizations with a significant investment in technology to not have architectural activities happening. Thus, it is beneficial to show that these activities exist and this will reinforce the case to formalize these efforts. Often, these efforts can be found through technical artifacts from technology implementation projects and key technical resources. Personally, I have witnessed companies engaging in the same architectural activities by different resources that not only created wasted effort, but also contributed to complexity in the current environment.

Designing the Architecture Team

After the implementation of LEA, it is necessary to define how to design the organization and governance of resources. This activity contains the tasks of defining the members and determining the structure.

Define the Members

This task begins by identifying the ongoing roles and responsibilities of positions within the architectural group. It is rare that an organization can effectively have a single resource dedicated to the task of LEA. Because enterprise architecture is a broad discipline, it is important to have a breadth of expertise and the stewardship of an enterprise's technology is not a simple task to own for a single resource.

After the positions have been identified, the next task is the identification of candidates. Next, the candidates need to be approached and consensus built on selecting the right candidates.

Determine the Structure

Determining how to structure the group is both a matter of matching the culture of the organization and practicality. If a company is very hierarchical and resources only respond appropriately to a chain of command model, then likely this is best reflected in the structure of the architecture group. If an organization is organizationally a matrix, then a hierarchical form may not be appropriate. However, it is imperative that it be determined how decisions will be finalized within the group.

The practicality of the structure depends on the location of technology centers in the organization. For example, it may not make sense for a multinational company to have the architecture group from only one locality. The form may either consider a distributed group that collaborates remotely or divide some of the resources through a Center of Excellence (COE) model. The COE model can separate subject matter experts by regional expertise that determines system stewardship by domain (i.e. information, application, and technical architectures). Of course, the key lies in the coordination of these resources, but this additional burden may displace any contention or distrust from other regions if one locality is used.

COMMITMENT TO LEA

Activities in this stage begin when the design of LEA is well understood by the team. This stage ends when there is sufficient sponsorship from the organization to commit to implementing LEA, either fully or on a trial basis pending review. The key deliverables in this stage include the business case and the charter for the initial cycle of LEA.

Highlighting the Benefits of LEA

This is the key activity on which to build the business case for implementing LEA. The main tasks include identification of the benefits and building the ROI model that provides the context for the business case.

Identify the Benefits

This task will take a fair amount of effort but often is paramount to gaining buy-in from the leadership. Chapter 2 provided a fair amount of detail around how to identify the benefits of enterprise architecture and these are very relevant to LEA.

In addition, it is important to enlist the support of financial resource(s) as they can provide accurate costs and shape the benefits in the following task (Build ROI). However, more importantly, this will add significant creditability to the business case. It is important that the group has done the preliminary work of gathering costs in the design stage without the dependence on the financial resources as the group should demonstrate competence and optimize resources.

Build ROI

It has not been my experience that an organization will commit major resources to any project without understanding the financial impact of the project. This can be through exact financial models (ROI, cost basis, etc.) or an informal agreement of budgetary constraints. Essentially, this equates to how much this will initially cost, what the ongoing costs are, and how this will either save the organization money and/or increase revenue. It is also important to consider the tolerance level of the organization on distributing capital on internal projects and the expected returns on these investments.

Identifying Stakeholders

Often, many projects fail because key resources were not considered in the design of the project and/or resources do not understand (or worse, care) about the success of a project. This activity is about increasing the chance of gaining buy-in from key resources and making any unforeseen adjustments in the design that could derail the project.

Locate Key Stakeholders

Before presenting the business case, it is important to understand the influencers of the decision to implement LEA. Key stakeholders that can influence this decision include:

- LEA champion
- LEA experts
- Key stakeholders
- Key groups

Inform Stakeholders

After the key stakeholders have been identified, it is important to meet with these stakeholders to understand how they will respond to the project and to tailor the presentation to best influence these resources positively. In addition, this is a chance to do some pre-selling of the project. Finally, if there are any serious objections, then it is prudent for the team to address them and find a good compromise if warranted.

Selling LEA

This activity is the most important in setting the initial expectation of what LEA will accomplish. After communicating with the key stakeholders and knowing the benefits of LEA, the team should now be in a position to sell the idea to the organization. This is accomplished by building a solid business case and presenting this case to key stakeholders.

Build Business Case

This task is straightforward, as the effort in the previous activities should have provided sufficient material to compile the business case. However, it is very important that the previous activities were diligently executed, because any key stakeholders not consulted can influence this project negatively if they feel threatened. In addition, the benefits need to be well developed and verified or the entire case could unravel and then the creditability of the team is lost.

Present Case

Most likely, presenting this case is not a one-time affair as there are usually very diverse stakeholders who will require varying levels of detail and interaction. In addition, it is important to polish the style of the presentation by presenting the most significant stakeholders last and gaining confidence from previous presentations and stakeholder feedback.

Define Initial Scope

After sufficient feedback from the stakeholders, the team should have a clear understanding of the expectations of the organization. This will lead to defining the scope of the initial cycle of LEA.

ROLLOUT OF LEA

Once the organization has committed to deploying LEA, it will become important to show success early and gain creditability. This means that the initial cycle of LEA is not the full development of all the artifacts of LEA, but a limited set to realize short-term results. The deliverables of this stage include drafts of the Strategic Architectures (Technology Charter) and Conceptual Architectures (Technology Roadmap). However, the artifacts of the Execution Architecture need full development, thus resulting in a project scope as this demonstrates one of the benefits from LEA.

Preparing the Strategic Architecture

Most likely, the leadership of the organization has had significant interaction with the team, so they expect results. The best tactic is the immediate involvement of this group to set the direction of LEA through the development of the principles. Then the following tasks within the Strategic Architecture would include drafting the enterprise patterns and outlining the enterprise guidelines.

Nail the Enterprise Principles

This task is critical and if not successful will most assuredly cause LEA to fail. It is my intention to scare future LEA practitioners and to gain respect for this effort. Without the agreement from leadership on how to drive technology, no amount of effort can effectively evolve the technology landscape and leadership needs to understand this before committing to LEA.

The best technique I have employed in the past was to interview every key leader (do not miss any) and get his or her view of the key success factors of the organization. Then the architecture group needs to translate these factors into technical principles and map the variations from these stakeholders. Next, rank and organize the principles and set a meeting with all key resources (if possible) to build the key five to seven principles that will set the foundation for LEA.

This can be a significant effort, but once complete the architecture group will have the key drivers of technology that no one in the enterprise will dispute. In addition, this may be a major revelation of the different expectations for technology from the leaders of the organization and how this might influence the current environment. This will be the first tangible result of LEA and the standard of success for the stewardship of technology.

If there is disagreement and dissention among the leadership, then there needs to be a contingency plan implemented. Success is not likely when leaders cannot agree on what technology should do for the enterprise.

Draft the Enterprise Patterns

This task is the beginning of the development of the enterprise patterns and mainly the introduction of how to view the current environment. This will be refined in future iterations, but an initial draft needs to be created and communicated to key stakeholders. This is another key activity that can greatly influence the success of LEA; so if there are not sufficient sources for this task, then look outside the organization to find suitable material. Appendix B provides a very detailed source that can provide a potential start for many organizations.

Outline the Enterprise Guidelines

This task is not critical in the initial deployment of LEA. Only after LEA has gained success in the organization can the architecture group focus on the development of this artifact. The initial cycle will rely on current informal guidelines, so as not to create any potential obstacles in the early development of LEA.

Drafting the Conceptual Architecture

After the effort around the Strategic Architecture is complete, the team can draft the Conceptual Architecture. Again, this is not a full development of all the artifacts, but rather a focus on short-term success.

Identify the Key Systems

The key in the development of this artifact is to simply identify the key systems in the enterprise. Only the key functional systems and some of the minor functional systems need identification at this point. Then, only basic functionality is mapped to these systems — mainly to help develop the next task of developing the system models.

Develop the Initial System Models

These should not be detailed models, but rather very simple representations of the current environment that resources can agree on for accuracy. These models will help bound where future activity occurs in the technology landscape and serve as a common communication source in later activities. Some forethought on the potential initial projects should help limit the scope of these models and thus limit the time to develop them.

Note System Objectives

During this initial cycle, this artifact is not critical and should only be lightly addressed to set the stage for later interactions. A skeleton of how this artifact is later developed is sufficient, so that resources can understand when LEA matures how this can best serve the technical community.

Initial Activity in the Execution Architecture

After the completion of the Strategic and Conceptual Architecture activities, the project team can begin the activities around the Execution Architecture. This is the last set of activities for the initial cycle of LEA and includes the identification of a pilot project and the development of the artifacts.

Find a Pilot Project

At this point in the project, the project team should have several projects that are considerations for a pilot project. Now the team must finalize the candidate project and secure the right resources to initiate the project.

Develop the Artifacts

Upon successful selection of a pilot project and the induction of the resources to execute this pilot, the project team now needs to develop all the artifacts of the Execution Architecture to best demonstrate the level of quality and detail that future efforts will produce. The project team should interact with the pilot resources to best refine these artifacts and to ensure usefulness of these artifacts.

PROJECT CLOSURE AND HANDOFF

After the pilot project has been initiated, the project team needs to begin the closure of this initial cycle of LEA by reviewing the performance of the project, reporting to leadership, and hopefully handing over control of LEA to the architecture group. Following the closure of this initial effort is the gradual release of the extra resources required in the initial cycle of LEA.

This initial cycle of LEA from a methodology perspective is similar to an SDLC or even a Waterfall project. However, the next steps will really recycle through the previous stages and mature the design of LEA within the organization. The intent of the next phase is to fully develop both the Strategic and Conceptual Architectures.

These cycles will continue to reiterate over time until the Technology Roadmap is well-defined. Hence, the entire LEA life cycle resembles the spiral model more closely than any other methodology. However, it may be more efficient to handle the initial cycle of LEA as an SDLC project. This also may be required if this was a trial period as mandated by leadership.

The LEA life cycle will fully mature when the focus is more upon the Execution Architecture and managing the projects to realize the Technical Roadmap.

Chapter 11

DYSFUNCTIONAL ENTERPRISE ARCHITECTURES

WHAT IS DYSFUNCTIONAL BEHAVIOR?

Over the course of my career, I have had the opportunity to experience hundreds of environments as a consultant and have seen many different styles of enterprise architecture (or what appeared as such). Most interesting were the environments in which the architect's behavior posed a significant challenge to the well-being of the enterprise. Unfortunately, in many organizations architects by their background tend to have a lot of control over the design and fate of technology in their organizations. If the architectures from these architects are ineffective, their stewardship of technology is a problem for the enterprise.

Dysfunctional behavior is any counterproductive characteristics from architects or leaders serving the needs of architecture that influence the stewardship of technology. This behavior stems from the practice of the architects and their beliefs in the architectural style they practice.

Identifying Dysfunctional Behavior

The largest challenge to LEA can occur when there already exists an enterprise architecture in the organization. If the enterprise architecture is fulfilling the needs of the organization, then there is little need to implement LEA if the business and technical communities are well conversant between themselves, but this is not common. Even if the enterprise architecture has established guidance for the technology, LEA can still provide some improvements in design to an already successful program.

However, this is not the case in many organizations and thus the topic of this chapter. This chapter provides the characteristics, scenarios, effect on the organization, and potential solutions to dysfunctional behaviors observed in many organizations. There are many dysfunctional behaviors in organizations today, but the following are the most common and ineffective forms of enterprise architecture:

- The "ivory tower"
- Prima donnas
- War campaigns
- Tribal lore
- Diagrams are for sissies
- Happy analysts
- Absent leaders
- Technology is cool
- Circling vultures
- Seagull management

While the style of this chapter is different from the other chapters in this book, this topic is not descriptive of LEA. My intention is to lighten up what probably many organizations experience and not only find fault, but rather identify the problem, understand the potential cause, and find a solution to fix this behavior in the enterprise. The goal of this chapter is to make this an enjoyable read and give any future practitioners of LEA a good laugh and proceed with a successful means (and a positive mental frame) to solve a potentially serious issue in the organization.

THE IVORY TOWER

In some organizations, the architecture group is a removed body in the enterprise. Essentially, the group is very accomplished in its domain, but the problem is that there is a large disconnect from the rest of the organization. Not only is there a gap between this group and business, but also the technology community has trouble following their direction.

The communications from this group are rarely understood by anyone outside of the group. Often, the architecture consists of a defined process with complicated documentation specifications that this group mandates.

Symptoms

A common quote from this group is, "Bring us a problem to solve and provide us with the business case and we will help design the solution." Characteristics of the "ivory tower" dysfunctional behavior include:

- Arrogance
- Poor communication skills

- Intimidate even technology folks
- Unsympathetic

Typical Scenario

Project Mgr: The goal for this meeting is to review the initial design specification for our customer Web portal.

Architect: Was the SBC [System Business Case] and the Technology Impact form RFT102 filled out for this project?

Project Mgr: Yes we were getting to that — it's in the handout, but let's look at the agenda for this meeting. As you will...

Architect: This is the old RFT102 version 19.2; we are now on version 21.5. You need to do these over in the right format.

[Architect leaves the meeting.]

Project Mgr: That's just great! Now we have to reschedule this meeting and we're already behind schedule.

User: Can't we just continue and redo the forms later?

Project Mgr: No, because I have to submit a resource justification that is part of the SBC; and without the architect's sign-off, I can't proceed.

Causes

- Past successes
- Very intelligent architects
- Architects are aware of their intelligence
- Limited practical communication skills

Enterprise Impact

- Solutions are difficult to implement.
- Enterprise architecture is easily misaligned with business needs.
- This behavior promotes rift between business and technology community and sometimes between architects and technologists.

Solutions

- Make the architects accountable:
  - Tie compensation to project success.
  - Tie compensation to internal customer satisfaction (survey to project resources).

PRIMA DONNAS

Prima donnas are architects who either got into the position because of past success or already have a great network, but offer little service to the organization. A prima donna rarely will provide direction or guidance for system stewardship. Prima donnas lack accountability for anything tangible, so getting results from them is difficult.

Many confuse prima donnas with the "ivory tower" folks, but the truth is that the main difference is that the "ivory tower" folks usually work very hard on their architecture (it is just that no one understands it). The prima donna, however, avoids effort like the plague and has a plethora of prior meetings, conflicts of interest, and other diversion tactics to avoid being an architect who makes things happen.

Symptoms

An organization may have a prima donna for an architect if the following symptoms are noted:

- The architect is noncommittal.
- The architect always has a meeting to attend.
- No one is sure what the architect really does in the organization.
- The architect is always ready to criticize or defend, but rarely offers new solutions.

Typical Scenario

Project Mgr: The agenda for this meeting is to review the initial design specification for our customer Web portal. We want to leave this meeting with a consensus on the design captured thus far. We are on an aggressive schedule to catch up to our competitors. Finally, we would like to leverage the Web capabilities of the AQRT system.

Analyst: As you can see in the design specifications, we have a reasonable number of requirements. Also, we attached some use cases that we have worked with a focus group and the business users. We've tried to keep the specification light so that we can move forward quickly with this project.

Developer: This looks great; I just have a few questions. First, the users don't have the ability update the schedule, do they?

Analyst: No. I'm sorry we lumped the use cases together so that we wouldn't have too many. Besides, we thought the customer service agents…

[Prima donna architect arrives late to the meeting.]

Architect: Is this the portal meeting and, if so, can someone provide me with the details later?

Project Mgr: We would like your help in developing the new customer Web portal.

Architect: Why?

Project Mgr: We feel that you can provide us with insight on the current Web solution in the organization and how we can use the existing technology and not have to reinvent a new one.

Architect: Well, you can talk with our current Web developers and get them to implement the system. This does not require any effort from me.

Project Mgr: We have Steve and Cindy from the Web development group here but they need direction on how this solution will fit into the current hosting model for the company.

Architect: Just use the current solution and place it on a separate box. Why does this require my time? I have to work with the CFO on the budgets for next year.

Project Mgr: Isn't that for the division heads to decide?

Architect: No. If we let everyone decide on their own budget, then this company will go broke. I've got to go now. E-mail me if there are any issues.

Causes

- Lost faith in organization
- In learning mode versus applying knowledge to organization
- Successes in the past (not now)

Enterprise Impact

- Essentially, the enterprise does not have an architect, so enterprise-wide planning is a challenge.
- The prima donna can harm needed projects.

Solutions

- Define enterprise architects' role:
  - Weekly status updates of existing projects to senior management
- Find new role for prima donna

WAR CAMPAIGNS

War campaigning is a behavior that exists when there are distinct divisions in approach within the organization. This does not mean that the division derives from separate values because, most often, they are consistent; rather, these groups believe in obtaining the goals of the enterprise in different ways. Sometimes, the values of these divisions are different and then the organization has a real dilemma, as this is more difficult to solve and the organization needs to regroup at the strategic level.

The behavior identified here deals with the division at the approach level as groups are divided as to how to obtain the needs of the enterprise. Typical divisions in the technology department are akin to solutions such as:

- UNIX versus Microsoft
- Open source versus commercial vendor
- Java versus C++

Symptoms

War campaigning environments exhibit the following attributes:

- Tense environment
- Heated meetings
- Feuding groups
- Mistrust

Typical Scenario

Project Mgr: The goal for this meeting is to review the initial design specification for our customer Web portal.

Group A: Have we decided to build this portal on a UNIX platform?

Group B: We thought this was going to be an ASP application!

Project Mgr: We are still in the initial planning session and need to first understand the business needs.

Group B: Yeah, but if we use a Microsoft solution, then we can easily add functionality because we know the requirements are going to change anyway.

Group A: We need a UNIX platform so we can scale.

Project Mgr: That's to decide later, first…

Group B: That's hogwash! MSN is on the Microsoft platform and it scales way beyond our needs.

Group A: But we don't want the solution to continually crash, so it needs to be built on a UNIX platform.

Group B: We have an excellent uptime record.

Project Mgr: Let's get back to...

Group A: Right, your systems have three to four times as many boxes to support the same solution as ours.

Group B: We're not going to keep arguing with you. Let us know when the decision on the platform is made so that we can begin planning.

Group A: Well, if it's an ASP solution, don't call us.

[Groups A and B leave — the meeting is essentially over.]

Causes

- Federated technology community
- Different skills and philosophies in the technology communities
- Enterprise depends on both UNIX and Microsoft solutions

Enterprise Impact

- Solutions are difficult to implement.
- There is poor interoperability among systems.
- There is inefficient deployment of resources.

Solutions

- Segment camps into relevant solutions (through Guidelines in Strategic Architecture).
- End the war:
  - Cross-train resources.
  - Consolidate the technical departments.
- Prove or disprove claims, as appropriate:
  - Run internal tests.
  - Bring in vendors.
  - Find industry benchmarks.

TRIBAL LORE

Tribal lore is an interesting phenomenon usually found in a highly effective technology community. Tribal lore usually has grown from grassroots activities and the technology resources have banded together to provide solid solutions for difficult business needs at the time. However, time has passed and the heroic efforts of the past are vague memories and now it is difficult to determine who are the responsible resources for any given system.

Essentially, the only way to understand the environment is through conversations with the old-timers, as there is little to no documentation for the systems. This is a dangerous position for any organization because knowledge of these systems is slipping away from the organization slowly over time.

Symptoms

Warning signs that your organization exhibits tribal lore include:

- Informal processes
- Clannish behavior
- Limited documentation
- Unclear who does what

Typical Scenario

Project Mgr: The goal for this meeting is to review the initial design specification for our customer Web portal.

Architect: Is this project an extension of the AQRT system?

Project Mgr: Yes.

Architect: Then we should have a resource from that development team here at the meeting. I believe it was Jeff who developed the Web capabilities of that system.

Project Mgr: I'll see if Jeff is available as he's just a floor away from us. [Project Mgr leaves to get Jeff.]

Project Mgr: Jeff, I heard that you were responsible for creating the Web capabilities of AQRT.

Jeff: No. I helped in building the messaging solution to the Web site. I believe it was Cindy who was in charge of the Web development. [Project Mgr leaves to see Cindy.]

Project Mgr: Cindy, I heard that you developed the Web capabilities of AQRT.

Cindy: No, I'm the Webmaster. Actually, I prefer Webmistress.

Project Mgr: Well, can you help us with the design of the proposed Web portal?

Cindy: Oh, I think I've heard of that. Actually, my tasks involve updating content to the site and ensuring that the system is available. You want Bob, as he was the developer who built the Web site. [Project Mgr leaves to find Bob and stops to ask a programmer.]

Project Mgr: Excuse me, can you tell me were Bob is located?

Programmer: Bob is gone. He left about a month ago.

Project Mgr: Can you tell me who is responsible for Web development for AQRT?
Programmer: I'm not sure, but you should ask the architect!
[Project Mgr leaves in frustration and everyone in the meeting has left.]

Causes

- Close technical community
- Many heroes in the technical community
- No documentation standards or requirements

Enterprise Impact

- Enterprise at risk when key resources are lost
- Development difficult for new and outside resources
- Slow system evolution

Solutions

- Document current critical systems (use external resources if necessary).
- Create design and review sessions into development.
- Create standard documentation templates and repository.
- Rotate staff.

DIAGRAMS ARE FOR SISSIES

This dysfunctional behavior stems from the traditionalist views of system development. These architects likely began their careers in the early days of the mainframe and have very traditional education around information systems. Typically, these architects are also very quality centric and value verbose specifications.

Proponents for "diagrams are for sissies" have not embraced any of the agile approaches or any of the object-oriented languages. These proponents are likely ex-COBOL programmers and are baffled as to why these systems need replacing. In some respects, this group is correct in that these old systems are still viable. However, often the platform on these solutions is no longer supported and the current development community has moved on to more progressive tools — and hence the need for change and the cause of friction.

Symptoms

- Big documentation (thud factor)
- Snobbish environment
- Frequent over-explanations
- Very formal environment
- Process-heavy environment

Typical Scenario

Project Mgr: The goal for this meeting is to review the initial design specification for our customer Web portal.

Architect: The design specifications seem a bit light, so is this the session to determine how to develop this document?

Project Mgr: No, we are here to gain buy-in to the design and begin development as we're on an aggressive timeline.

Architect: Well, that is nice that you are responsive to an eager business community, but we are an ISO-compliant organization and this is unacceptable documentation.

Project Mgr: I understand, but this is just an extension of a system that is already in production. We just need to add some functionality.

Architect: Nothing is as simple as it seems and we cannot lower our quality of work just to get something out the door. Besides, these diagrams look like something my five-year-old granddaughter would draw. They are stick figures.

Project Mgr: These are UML diagrams developed with the business community.

Architect: I cannot accept these, so either you use the right documentation or build and support this yourself.

[Architect leaves and meeting ends]

Causes

- Rigid, old-school approach
- Critical systems are on legacy platforms
- Architects require detailed understanding

Enterprise Impact

- Progress is slow and labor intensive.
- Not everything can be descriptive; hence, innovation is inhibited.

- Documentation efforts provide limited value as few resources will read through the documentation.

Solutions

- Demonstrate effective diagramming.
- Create comparative documentation and survey organization.
- Run a sissy diagram project and measure effectiveness.
- Ignore the architects and work directly between business users and technologists; then use successes for change.

HAPPY ANALYSTS

Happy analysts behavior occurs when architects function as analysts in the guise of architecture. Essentially, the determination of these architects is the modeling of the entire organization in detail. The belief is that increased detail captured in the right modeling tool will make future development easier and create reuse of effort. While this is a noble goal, the reality is that no organization can really afford to model the organization into the detail required because this necessitates significant effort, broad acceptance of these tools, and coordination of various resources.

Ultimately, this results in an abstracted view of the organization that few resources can use, and this is just another level of effort to add to an already strained environment. While certain modeling techniques are very valid and well used throughout organizations today, this particular dysfunctional behavior has the effort of the analyst placed above all other needs of the organization. The architect/analyst believes the organization will reach a state of nirvana after everything has been captured.

Symptoms

Organizations that have architect/analysts have the following symptoms:

- System documentation is cryptic.
- Every aspect of the business is modeled.
- System's details rarely resemble documentation.
- When architect/analyst speaks, you feel sleepy.

Typical Scenario

Project Mgr: The agenda for this meeting is to review the initial design specification for our customer Web portal.
Architect: Do we have a use case model for the portal?

Project Mgr: Yes, we were getting to that — it's in the handout, but let's look at the agenda for this meeting. As you will...

Architect: Who created these use case diagrams?

Analyst: I created those after working extensively with the user community to ensure that the system functions consistently with the expectations of the users.

Architect: You lumped use cases together, and there's a problem with functional entitlements in these diagrams!

Analyst: What do you mean?

Architect: Well, in this use case you have different types of actors who have different entitlements. It appears as if the actors can look up the schedule and make changes (this is a separate flow). Only the customer service agents have those entitlements, not the customer.

Analyst: I thought that would be well understood and wanted to limit the number of use cases for the sake of brevity.

Architect: They are wrong, and we need to have corresponding sequence diagrams to support these use cases so that the designs are not random. You need to do these use cases correctly before we can review the design. [Architect leaves and meeting is over.]

Causes

- Architect/analysts have too much freedom.
- Architect/analysts focus on understanding versus action.
- Architect/analysts are smart and very detailed oriented.

Enterprise Impact

- Separate version of systems and enterprise that requires sufficient resources
- Creates complex and detailed system specifications that few resources can use
- Requires very skilled resources
- Extra analytics usually increase implementation cycle

Solutions

- Limit effort on analytics.
- Determine minimum set of analytics for development.
- Survey internal comprehension on current artifacts.

THE ABSENT LEADERS

Absent leader behavior is unfortunately a common dysfunctional behavior in many organizations. This is not to suggest that there are no leaders, but rather that leaders are rarely available for input in technology evolution because the focus of their attention is elsewhere in the organization. Typically, this stems from the top of the organization where the direction of leadership is poorly communicated down through the organization. This has the effect of creating an environment where resources are unsure of what the organization needs.

This is an environment that is left to fend for itself and the functional needs of various departments compete through informal networks. In addition, this environment is typically very federated as each department vies for their own needs.

Symptoms

An organization has absent leaders when the following occurs:

- Decision making is slow and usually consensual.
- There is no coordination of resources.
- There is a need to make friends with developers to have solutions implemented.
- Failure is severely punished.
- Environment feels like the Wild West.

Typical Scenario

Project Mgr: The agenda for this meeting is to review the initial design specification for our customer Web portal.

Developer: Who is sponsoring this effort?

User: This is for Jane's department.

Developer: What cost center should I charge this meeting for my time? Our manager is constantly getting on everyone's case to document our time better.

Project Mgr: I believe that is WST86.

User: Can we leverage the AQRT system for this portal?

Developer: No, that's the sales department's system and they won't allow any modifications. I need to create this system from scratch.

Project Mgr: We have a limited budget. Is this going to be a problem?

Developer: No, we've been playing with a WebLogic server that we could easily put into production.

Project Mgr: Great! When can we get started?

Developer: We've been using a demo copy of the software, so we need to secure a runtime license.

Project Mgr: Who is in charge of getting the license?

Developer: I don't know, but we can start development while you work that out.

Project Mgr: Do you want to go over the design specification?

Developer: Nah, these look OK. I'll holler if we have any questions.

Causes

- Leadership characteristics are missing (including senior management)
- Limited accountability from architects
- Resources unsure of business direction

Enterprise Impact

- High incidence of wasted effort
- Systems rarely provide true enterprise value
- High resource turnover, due to frustrating environment
- Resource use not optimal

Solutions

- Engage leadership:
  - Work with leadership for buy-in on technology strategy plan
  - Have regular project lead meetings
  - Status reporting with issues to leadership
- Create direction:
  - Gain buy-in with Technology Roadmap

TECHNOLOGY IS COOL

It is rare to find anyone in technology who is not in love with technology. This passion has driven these resources to this profession, so it is common for these resources to blindly use technology for the sake of technology. In other words, technologists will often try to find situations to fit new technologies.

The problem with this approach is that technology really is only secondary to the needs of the enterprise. An organization must first realize its needs and if there is a technology fit to help, then this is a good match. However, the organization does not exist for the experimentation of technology, so the first priority is an understanding of the business need and then finding the appropriate solution. Often, this is not the latest and greatest technology.

Symptoms

An organization that is exhibiting the dysfunctional behavior of "technology is cool" has the following signs:

- Long delivery cycles for functionality
- System failures are common
- Architects talk in techno-babble
- Large rift between business and technology communities

Typical Scenario

Project Mgr: The agenda for this meeting is to review the initial design specification for our customer Web portal.
Architect: What communication modes are we going to offer our customers?
Project Mgr: This is just a Web portal.
Developer: Yeah, but what about wireless access?
Project Mgr: We have not determined that the customer base wants wireless access.
Architect: We need to build that up-front if we should need it later.
Project Mgr: How much will that cost, and how much longer will it take?
Developer: We just need the right platform and it shouldn't take too much longer.
Architect: Plus, we then have the capability for message alerting and we could possibly tie our IVR system using speech recognition.
Project Mgr That's great but we need to have this system in production within four months.
Developer: Not a problem! Some great platforms out there will get us up and running quickly.
Project Mgr: What are the costs?
Architect: What will be the cost if we don't and then need it later! Give us the specifications and we see what vendor can do this for us.
[The Project Mgr feels that the control of the design session is lost and the technology community is going to build what they want… again!]

Causes

- Architects are enamored with technology.

- Architects and technologists are very skilled.
- Architects thrive on challenges.
- Architects have limited accountability for business performance.

Enterprise Impact

- Common system failures
- Functional requirement not always realized
- Strain on operational resource
- High technology costs

Solutions

- Think need first, technology second:
  - Have technologist repeat the mantra, "first understand what and why; then last is how."
  - Provide compensation on functionality deployed and user satisfaction.
- Limit technology budget.

CIRCLING VULTURES

Circling vulture behavior can be a very disruptive dysfunctional behavior in any organization. Vultures are those devil's advocates in meetings who rarely (if ever) provide helpful insight, but are quick to criticize. These resources always find fault in other people's efforts and rarely give positive feedback. It would seem these resources hate almost everything and are generally not happy with the current environment.

The main reason for these vultures is their limited accountability in the given environment and hence, they have no stake in new successful approaches. Essentially, these resources have nothing to lose and nothing to gain, but have a large boost in ego when they have successfully found a flaw in something. Hence, it is this behavior that manifests itself and breeds vultures in the enterprise.

Symptoms

- Many devil's advocates
- Intimidation is a revered quality
- Slow progress on anything
- Not clear who is accountable

Typical Scenario

Project Mgr: The agenda for this meeting is to review the initial design specification for our customer Web portal.

Vulture 1: How long is this meeting?

Project Mgr: We have scheduled this for an hour.

Vulture 2: What is the intent of this meeting?

Project Mgr: I'm passing out the agenda and the design specifications that we going to review.

Vulture 1: Where is this portal going to reside?

Project Mgr: We anticipate that the AQRT system can accommodate our needs.

Vulture 2: You've got to be kidding! That system is already at capacity and it is continually going down.

Project Mgr: Yes we are aware, but there's another project that is reviewing those issues and looking for a solution.

Vulture 2: They won't be done in time; so what is your alternative?

Project Mgr: Well, our organization needs a solution that scales and is reliable. What's your recommendation?

Vulture 1: You called this meeting and are charged with this project. We need to resolve the AQRT system first and then we can entertain additional functionality.

Project Mgr: But we need this functionality for the organization as all our competitors offer this functionality.

Vulture 1: Well, I've got another meeting; I'm double and triple booked all day.

[Vultures leave and Project Mgr is baffled as to how to proceed.]

Causes

- Existence of many power fiefdoms
- Accountability based on department performance
- Very smart resources within their domains

Enterprise Impact

- Consensus is rare and new solutions are often seen as failures.
- System implementation is slow.
- Innovation and significant evolution are rare.

Solutions

- Work with vultures:

- Build a culture in which criticism is healthy.
- Create a rule that criticism is acceptable only if a vulture can provide a reasonable alternative.
■ Work around vultures:
  - Do not invite them to meetings.
  - Limit vultures' condemnation.
  - Ask vultures to leave if uncooperative.

SEAGULL MANAGEMENT

Similar to the disruptive nature of the vultures is another bird, the *seagull*, someone who is an architect/manager in the organization. However, unlike the vulture who waits for opportune moments to cause havoc, the seagull flies in with little interest in the environment, but rather serves an entirely different need. The seagull's interest is only with his own agenda, with no regard for others and only sees them as competition against their own goals.

Essentially, a seagull flies into a situation, squawks loudly, craps over everything, and then flies away. This often disorients many resources and is very disruptive if these seagulls are senior architects with political power. It is rare that a seagull is someone who is not influential and hence this is a serious dysfunctional behavior in the organization.

Symptoms

An organization has potential seagulls when the following observations exist:

- This is a fear of the architect/manager.
- The architect/manager is unsympathetic.
- Networking (social — not technology) with senior management is a quality revered by the architect/manager.
- Scope change is expected.

Typical Scenario

Project Mgr: The agenda for this meeting is to review the initial design specification for our customer Web portal. We want to leave this meeting with a consensus on the design captured thus far. We are on an aggressive schedule to catch up to our competitors. Finally, we would like to leverage the Web capabilities of the AQRT system.

Analyst: As you can see in the design specifications, we have a reasonable number of requirements. Also, we attached some use cases that result from working with a focus group and the business users. We've tried to keep the specification light, so that we can move forward quickly with this project.

Developer: This looks great; I just have a few questions. First, the users don't have the ability update the schedule, do they?

Analyst: No. I'm sorry we lumped the use cases together; we did that so that we wouldn't have too many. Besides, we thought the customer service agents...

[Seagull architect shows up.]

Architect: Has this meeting already started?

Project Mgr: Yes, we just started going over the design specifications. Also, I mentioned that there is an aggressive timeline and we want to use the AQRT system, if possible.

Architect: Well, that's not possible and I don't know why you are using these developers for this project. Bill, I thought you were working on debugging the AQRT system!

Developer: We are working on that this afternoon.

Architect: Well, we need you to work on it now, because we can't afford another crash. I've got a tiger team on that now. Please join them; they are in the server room.

[Developer leaves.]

Project Mgr: What are we going to do? We are on an aggressive timeline.

Architect: That's not my problem. You shouldn't be grabbing critical resources for these types of projects.

[Architect leaves and the Project Mgr is unsure of the next steps.]

Causes

- There is fragmented management with many architect/managers.
- Typical architect/manager's focus is departmental, not enterprise.
- Architect/manager not accountable for project failures and often interferes with projects.

Enterprise Impact

- Project cost over-runs
- Unproductive and tense environment
- Difficulty in meeting business needs

Solutions

- Deal with seagulls:
  - Gain buy-in to Technology Roadmap and project scope.
  - Identify project champions.
  - Provide for weekly status updates that include next week's goals.
- Avoid seagulls:
  - Plan meetings that conflict with their schedule.
  - Stick to the project charter and get management involved.

CONCLUSION

There are many dysfunctional behaviors in enterprises today, and having them all disappear is unrealistic. Hence, these solutions provide some hedge to best realize an effective enterprise architecture. Remembering that LEA is really only a framework with a basic philosophy of keeping architecture simple should provide a suitable practice for many organizations.

It is my hope that the readers have gained some valuable techniques to use in their organizations. It is my sincere hope that many will embrace the simplicity of this framework and easily deploy parts and perhaps even the entire framework successfully. Often in organizations today, the technology landscape is getting more complex and the activities of the architect are difficult tasks and often misunderstood by the enterprise. LEA sets a possible practice for an individual or groups to regain control of the system stewardship of their enterprise and also gain a sense of purpose.

Finally, simpler does not mean ineffective or even easy, but it does often paint a better picture for the organization and that is the key for success. It is my hope that you have found this book a valuable resource.

Good luck and great architecting!

SECTION 4

APPENDICES

Our life is frittered away by detail... Simplify, simplify, simplify!...

— Henry Thoreau

Appendix A

LEA ARTIFACTS

This appendix includes the description and relationship of all the artifacts as identified by LEA. Tables A.1, A.2, and A.3, respectively, show the artifacts for the Strategic Architect, Conceptual Architect, and Execution Architect. Of significant importance is to note that all the artifacts of LEA have inputs to influence their design and have outputs. The significance of each artifact having an output is that all these artifacts build into other efforts and hence illustrate that LEA has identified important artifacts that lead to less wasted efforts in the design of enterprise architecture.

Table A.1 Strategic Architecture Artifacts Mapping

Artifact ID	Responsibility	Artifact	Description	Inputs	Outputs	Primary Audience
S1	Enterprise principles		Creation of 5 to 7 statements for the adoption of technology, forming a set of values or goals translated from the business strategy	Business Strategy	S3.1, S3.2, S3.3, S, E1	Leadership
S2	Enterprise patterns		Determination of where functionality resides in the enterprise	S2.1, S2.2, S2.3, S2.4	S	Leadership, business owners, technology owners
			Compilation of S2.1, S2.2, S2.3, and S2.4 artifacts			
S2.1	Enterprise patterns	Functional boundaries	Identification of where functionality resides in the organization	Business analyst docs. (i.e. value chain, work flow models, functional decomposition diagram (FDD), etc.)	S2, S2.2, S2.3, S2.4, C2.1, E2.1, E3.3, C1.2, C1.3	Architects
S2.2	Enterprise patterns	Internal users	Identification of where the functions and sub-function reside within the organization	S2.1	S2, S2.4, C2.1, E2.1	Architects
S2.3	Enterprise patterns	Customer access	Identification of what channels the organization interacts with the customer base	S2.1	S2, S2.4, C2.1, E2.1	Architects

ID	Artifact	Type	Description			Role
S2.4	Enterprise patterns	Management	Interpretation of where technology can best reside in the enterprise to support the patterns identified	S2.1, S2.2, S2.3	C1.1, C2.2, C3.1, C3.2, E2.2, S3.3, S2, C2.1	Architects
S3	Enterprise guidelines		Setting technology policies for the enterprise Compilation of S3.1, S3.2, and S3.3 artifacts	S3.1, S3.2, S3.3	S	Leadership, business owners, technology owners
S3.1	Enterprise guidelines	Construction	Develop policy of how best to construct technology within the enterprise	S1	S3, C3.1, C3.2, S3.3	Architects
S3.2	Enterprise guidelines	Resource	Develop policy of when to deploy technology in-house or when to outsource technology	S1	S3, C3.1, C3.2, S3.3	Architects
S3.3	Enterprise guidelines	Control	Develop policy of who will govern specific technologies	S1, S2.4, S3.1, S3.2	C3.2, E3.1	Architects
S	Technical charter		Compilation of all the artifacts in the Strategic Architecture published for the enterprise	S1, S2, S3	C, E	All

Table A.2 Conceptual Architecture Artifacts Mapping

Artifact ID	Responsibility	Artifact	Description	Inputs	Outputs	Primary Audience
C1	System contracts		Determination of what each system of the enterprise is doing A compilation of C1.1, C1.2, and C1.3	C1.1, C1.2, C1.3	C	Business owners, technology owners
C1.1	System contracts	Categorization of systems	Accessing the impact of the systems on the enterprise	S2.4	C1, C1.2, C2.2, C3.1, C3.2, C2.1	Architects
C1.2	System contracts	Map systems to functionality	Identify the functional uses of the systems in the enterprise	C1.1, S2.1	C1, E1, E3.3, C2.1	Architects
C1.3	System contracts	Supporting principles	Determine the adherence of the principles to the systems in the enterprise	S1, S2.1	C1, C2.2, E1, C3.1, C3.2	Architects
C2	System models		Conceptualization of the systems of the enterprise A compilation of C2.1 and C2.2	C2.1, C2.2	C	Business owners, technology owners
C2.1	System models	Functional	Capturing how the functions of the systems interrelate throughout the enterprise	S2.1, S2.2, S2.3, S2.4, C1.1, C1.2	C2, E2.3, E3.1, E2.2, E3.3, C2.2, C3.1, C3.2, C3.1	Architects
C2.2	System models	Physical	Capturing where the major system resources reside within the enterprise	S2.4, C1.1, C1.3, C2.1	C2, E2.3, E3.1, E2.2, C3.2	Architects

C3	System objectives	Determination of the plan to evolve the system landscape	C3.1, C3.2	C	Business owners, technology owners
C3.1	System objectives / Portfolio rationalization	A compilation of C3.1 and C3.2 / Identifying the minimal technology footprint for the organization	S2.4, S3.1, S3.2, C1.1, C1.3, C2.1, C2.1	C3, E1, E3.3, C3.2	Architects
C3.2	System objectives / Preferred solutions	Determine the best fit for solutions from vendors	S2.4, S3.1, S3.2, S3.3, C1.1, C2.1, C2.2, C3.1	E3.2, C3	Architects
C	Technical Roadmap	Compilation of all the artifacts in the Conceptual Architecture published for the enterprise	C1, C2, C3	E	All

Table A.3 Execution Architecture Artifacts Mapping

Artifact ID	Responsibility	Artifact	Description	Inputs	Outputs	Primary Audience
E1	Requirements		Outlining the system needs for a project	S1, C1.2, C1.3, C3.1	E, E3.2, E2.3, E3.1, E2.1, E2.2, E3.3	Users, creators, supporters
E2	Project diagrams		Capturing key system's design for the project. A compilation of E2.1, E2.2, and E2.3	E2.1, E2.2, E2.3	E	Users, creators, supporters
E2.1	Project diagrams	User interaction	Providing the design of where functionality should reside for both internal and external users	S2.1, S2.2, S2.3, E1	E2, E2.3, E3.1	Architects
E2.2	Project diagrams	Interfaces	Providing the design of the key messaging streams for the proposed solution with the existing systems	S2.4, C2.1, C2.2, E1	E2, E2.3, E3.1	Architects
E2.3	Project diagrams	Logical	Providing the design of where business logic and physical logistic is best located and how the solution fits within the enterprise	C2.1, C2.2, E1, E2.1, E2.2	E2, E3.2, E3.1	Architects
E3	Project vision		Capturing of all the prevalent information for the project. A compilation of E3.1, E3.2, and E3.3	E3.1, E3.2, E3.3	E	Users, creators, supporters
E3.1	Project vision	Impacted systems	Assessment of how this solution affects these current systems in the organization	S3.3, C2.1, C2.2, E1, E2.1, E2.2, E2.3	E3, E3.2	Architects

E3.2	Project vision	Potential solutions	Discovery of potential solutions that can offer the needed functionality to the enterprise	C3.2, E1, E2.3, E3.1	E3, E3.3	Architects
E3.3	Project vision	Business logic	Determination of what functionality the solution provides and critical business practices that characterize how the organization operates	S2.1, C1.2, C2.1, C3.1, E1, E3.2	E3	Architects
E	Project scope		Compilation of all the artifacts in the Execution Architecture related to a specific project for the stakeholders of that project	E1, E2, E3	Project charter, workplan, etc.	Project staff

Appendix B

REFERENCE MATERIALS

AUTHOR'S COMMENTS

Why This Is Here

One of the most difficult activities in starting any enterprise architecture is for the architect to determine what the artifacts should look like and know how much detail to provide. This was always a complaint that I had against many of the architecture books currently on the market. Essentially, where does one start to successfully deploy enterprise architecture?

In LEA, perhaps the most difficult part of this framework is the early creation of the enterprise patterns in the Strategic Architecture. The enterprise patterns as shown in Appendix A, Table A.1, illustrate that these artifacts have the most input to later artifacts created in LEA. In addition, many organizations do not have a standard definition of their functional processes and that is usually the case for many complex environments.

Thus, the inclusion of this reference material is provided for the following reasons:

- This material provides a "stake-in-the-ground" for the enterprise patterns in the Strategic Architecture.
- This material can serve as a source for project diagramming (especially the interfaces).
- This material can illustrate the level of detail necessary for LEA.
- Just providing a link to a Web site is often not enough.

Some of the most important activities in LEA are the determination of what the organization does and for the architect to build consensus around a standard view of the enterprise's functionality. Without a common understanding of an organization's functionality, there is no amount of effort that can evolve the system landscape to meet the needs of the enterprise in the future. If the architect does not understand what the enterprise does at a fundamental level, then how can the architect evolve the systems to meet the needs of business requirements?

Often, the difficulty in getting to a common understanding is in beginning the process of reconciliation. Using this material as a starting point is a solid strategy even if it does not properly define the organization. It is very effective in determining where it does not represent the current environment and making the appropriate changes rather than trying to create a functional view of the enterprise from scratch. Again, many organizations suffer from not creating a standard view of functionality, so how can the leadership expect the enterprise to streamline its processes and meet new future functional needs if the basics are unknown? This is why creating enterprise patterns is an early activity in LEA.

Another key development need in LEA is the creation of the Interaction artifacts in the project diagrams. One of the tenets of LEA is the realization that systems will remain diverse in most organizations, so there is a need to integrate these federated systems. This is the domain of the messaging infrastructure in the system landscape and the identification of how systems should interact. Again, it is far easier to start with reference material and determine how the current environment compares and make the appropriate changes.

Starting with this reference material will also control the quality and level of detail for both the enterprise patterns and the project diagrams. Not only is it easier to begin these activities with this reference material, but it also serves as a model of what is required from resources in developing LEA. It is not the sole responsibility of the architect to create these artifacts, but rather to reach out to the various resources in the enterprise to get their input into these artifacts. On many occasions, it was far easier for me to show clients what I was looking to develop by first starting with a solid "stake-in-the-ground." Next, it was simply a matter of determining the gaps, assigning resources to track down the definitions, and then finalizing the artifacts through some consensus building.

Finally, just pointing to reference material on the Internet through a link is not enough. Many books that I own now have dead links and some resources no longer exist, so the reference is arcane and the original intent of the author is lost. In addition, it is my belief that there is a need to provide some context around this material that would help the reader understand how this material is useful in deploying LEA. Thus, I have rewritten some pieces, cut out irrelevant material, and compiled the reference material into a better format for LEA.

Why Use Standards

Standards provide creditability to the activities in LEA, which is an important factor in gaining consensus among the various resources in the organization. It has been a frequent observation of mine that resources often cannot see past their current environment and the existing processes. This makes any new concept to these resources very suspect as it is unfamiliar and potential change is often met with resistance. However, using creditable material usually gave me the advantage to gain buy-in from resources that may have objected to anything other than a current process view of the organization.

Standards are often the result of very talented resources who are passionate about their domain. This usually results in material that is well-defined and accepted by the organization's industry. In addition, standards are more beneficial in today's environment as more companies need to integrate their systems with business partners to effectively compete in the marketplace. Using standards to model the enterprise provides a more acceptable approach for multiple companies to interact, as proprietary solutions will only make a company appear less open to other organizations.

Finally, while this section is long, all the material is very relevant for the development of LEA. It was not my intention to only provide a snippet of information and then leave the reader to scramble to find more documentation. It is my belief that less information in this instance would have been more of a hindrance than help for the reader. Some of this material may not be relevant to some organizations, but breadth will likely provide useful material for many.

Source of This Material

The source for this reference material is the Open Applications Group Integration Specification (OAGIS) developed by the Open Applications Group. The following is a clip from their Web site:

> The Open Applications Group is a non-profit consortium focusing on best practices and process based XML content for eBusiness and Application Integration. It is the largest publisher of XML based content for business software interoperability in the world. Open Applications Group, Inc. members have over 6 years of extensive experience in building this industry consensus based framework for business software application interoperability and have developed a repeatable process for quickly developing high quality business content and XML representations of that content.[1]

It is my belief that the material around this standard is one of the better sources and a great start for most organizations. However, the material is centric to collaborative companies focused on products rather than service. Some of the material is generic enough as to be useful to most organizations, but this is not the only source. There are many vertical industry consortiums and standards that could provide a similar starting point for an organization. Some other useful standards include:

- Rosetta Net
- Interactive Financial eXchange (IFX)
- Society for Worldwide Interbank Financial Telecommunication (SWIFT)
- Association for Retail Technology Standards (Arts)
- Health Level Seven (HL7)

How to Use This Material

The reference material is broken down into the following sections:

- Notice
- Overview
- Application Area in OAGIS
- Verbs in OAGIS

The Notice is part of the agreement to include this agreement, but also to show the reader that this material is an open license and royalty free if usage follows the terms of the notice. Next, the Overview provides the structure for the material and shows the depth of this standard. It is important to note for the development of LEA that the Application Area and the Verbs are relevant, while the remaining portions are more for implementation and out of scope for LEA (too much detail). The Application Area is a great source for the enterprise patterns, and the Verbs provide excellent material for potential project diagrams.

Please note that the following documentation is solely the work of the OAG and has not been edited for reprint in this book.

OAGIS 8.0 DOCUMENTATION

Notice

Copyright © 1998-2002 Open Applications Group, Inc. All Rights Reserved Documents and resource files on the Open Applications Group, Inc. Internet site are provided under the following license. By obtaining, using, and/or copying this file, or any related file obtained from this site, you agree that you have read, understood, and will comply with the following terms and conditions:

Permissions to use, copy, and distribute the contents of this file, in any medium for any purpose and without fee or royalty is hereby granted, provided that you include the following on ALL copies of the file that you use:

- A reference to the original Open Applications Group resource
- A notice of the form "Copyright © Open Applications Group. All Rights Reserved"

Please Note: This file is a work in process, and may be modified or enhanced at the discretion of the Open Applications Group without notice, at any time.

Please contact the Open Applications Group at www.openapplications.org with any questions or comments regarding the usage of this material.

Overview

To achieve interoperability between disparate systems, disparate companies, and disparate supply chains, there must be a common horizontal message architecture that provides a common understanding for all.

Once a horizontal messaging architecture has been agreed upon, these messages can be sequenced together to form scenarios. Scenarios can provide the detailed step-by-step exchange of information needed to perform specific tasks. These tasks can be simple or complex. As such, the scenarios describing them may be simple or complex. Complex scenarios may reuse one or more simple scenarios.

OAGIS provides example scenarios that can be used as a starting point for integration. By identifying a scenario that most closely matches your needs, it is possible to identify the messages needed to satisfy those needs.

The remainder of this appendix describes the architecture of the Open Applications Group Integration Specifications, Business Object Document (BOD). The BOD is a common horizontal message architecture. BODs are the business messages or business documents that are exchanged between software applications or components, between companies, across supply chains, and between supply chains.

To do this, the BOD must be able to inform the receiving system what kind of message to expect in the data area. Often there is a two-way interaction between a sender and receiver; for this reason, the BOD must be able to communicate status and error conditions. It is also necessary to provide for multiple actions on a common business object (Noun). For this reason, the OAGIS BODs have been designed to make use of a common Noun to which a given action (Verb) can be applied. As different industries have different needs, OAGIS must be extensible in order to allow industry verticals to plug in information that is needed in their industry. For this reason, the BODs have been designed to be extensible, while providing a common architecture and content for integration.

The BOD Message Architecture is independent of the communication mechanism. It can be used with simple transport protocols such as HTTP and SMTP, and also in more complex transport protocols such as SOAP, ebXML Transport and Routing, or any other Enterprise Application integration system.

A BOD graphically consists of the following in Figure B.1.

These areas are defined as follows:

- The outermost layer of the BOD identifies the Verb, Noun, revision and runtime environment (Test or Production in which the BOD instance is to be used).
- The Application Area communicates information that can be used by the infrastructure to communicate the message.
- The Data Area carries the business-specific payload or data being communicated by the BOD.
- Verbs identify the action being performed on the specific Noun of the BOD.

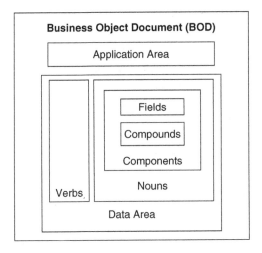

Figure B.1 BOD Architecture

- Nouns identify the business-specific data that is being communicated (i.e., PurchaseOrder, SalesOrder, Quote, Route, Shipment, etc.). They are comprised of Components, which are described below. Nouns are extensible in order to support the needs of specific vertical industries.
- Components are extensible building blocks of a Noun (i.e., Purchase-Order Header, PurchaseOrder Line, Address, etc.). They are comprised of Compounds and Fields, which are described below. Components are extensible.
- Compounds are basic, shared building blocks that are used by all BODs (i.e., Quantity, Amount, etc.). They are extensible through contextual use but not with additional fields (i.e., OrderedQuantity, ShippedQuantity, BackOrderedQuantity).
- Fields are the lowest-level elements defined in OAGIS. Fields are fundamental elements that are used to create Compounds and Components. (i.e., Description, Name, etc.).

Note: The graphics within this document are from XML Spy. They are shown here as a way for the reader to visually see the constructs being defined. The Open Applications Group does not recommend individual tools. However, it does recommend using an XML Integrated Development Environment (IDE) when working with complex XML Schema languages such as OAGIS.

Business Object Document

The Verb identifies the action that the Sender application wants the Receiver application to perform on the Noun. OAGIS defines a standard list of Verbs and Nouns that are needed in most supply chain and manufacturing integration scenarios.

The general structure for all Business Object Documents is shown in Figure B.2.

For a given Business Object Document, the generic names (Business-ObjectDocument, Verb, Noun) are replaced by specific names (ProcessPurchaseOrder, Process, and PurchaseOrder) as shown in Figure B.3.

The child elements of a BusinessObjectDocument are:

- ApplicationArea
- DataArea

The ApplicationArea and DataArea separate the application-specific information common to all BODs from the information that is specific to each BOD. Each is discussed in more detail in the following sections.

In addition to these child elements, each BOD contains three attributes: the BOD's revision, its environment, and language.

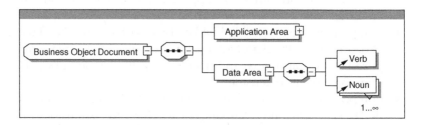

Figure B.2   Business Object Documents

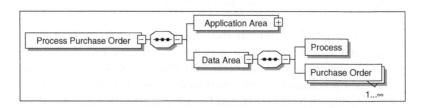

Figure B.3   ProcessPurchaseOrder Structure

Revision

Revision is used to identify the version of the Business Object Document. Each BOD has its own revision number to specifically identify the level of that BOD, not just the release version of OAGIS. The specific BOD revision number is documented in each chapter of OAGIS. The outermost element name no longer includes the revision number; it is instead now carried as a required attribute of the BOD.

Environment

Environment is used to identify whether this particular BOD is being sent as a result of a test or as production-level integration. Often times as new systems are brought online, testing must be performed in a production environment in order to ensure integration with existing systems. This attribute allows the integrator to flag these test messages as such. The environment attribute is an optional attribute of the BOD.

Language

The lang (language) attribute indicates the language of the data being carried in the BOD message. It is possible to override the BOD level language for fields that may need to carry multilingual information. Examples of this are Notes and Description.

XML supports only one encoding for an XML message; as such, the languages carried within a BOD are limited to the set that XML encoding can support.

Application Area

The ApplicationArea carries information that an application may need to know in order to communicate in an integration of two or more business applications. The ApplicationArea is used at the applications layer of communication, while the integration framework's Web services and middleware provide the communication layer that OAGIS operates on top of.

As indicated in Figure B.4, each BOD contains one unique ApplicationArea. The ApplicationArea serves four main purposes:

1. To identify the sender of the message
2. To identify when the document was created
3. To provide authentication of the sender through the use of a digital signature, if applicable
4. To uniquely identify a BOD instance; the BODId field is the Globally Unique Identifier for the BOD instance

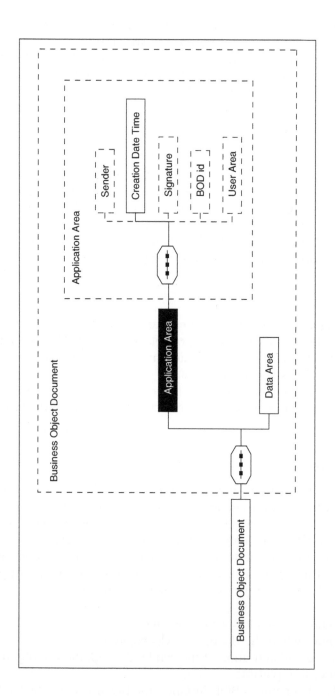

Figure B.4 Each BOD Has a Unique ApplicationArea

The ApplicationArea is comprised of the following elements:

- Sender
- Creation (date and time)
- Signature
- BODId
- UserArea

Sender

The Sender identifies characteristics and control identifiers that relate to the application that created the Business Object Document. The Sender area can indicate the logical location of the application and/or database server, the application, and the task that was processing to create the BOD (see Figure B.5).

The Sender area also provides the ability to create an audit trail to allow users to drill down from their Receiving business application to the information used to complete the business transaction being communicated in the BOD.

In today's business environments and advanced technology frameworks, a single BOD may be routed to multiple destinations or receivers. For this reason, it is not feasible for the sending system to "know" all of the possible destinations of a BOD. For this reason, the Open Applications Group has made a conscious decision NOT to include a Receiver in the ApplicationArea. This is left to the middleware or infrastructure framework to ensure delivery to all locations that are interested in the content of the BOD.

The Sender is comprised of the following information:

- LogicalID
- Component
- Task
- ReferenceID
- Confirmation
- AuthorizationID

Logical Identifier

The Logical Identifier element provides the logical location of the server and application from which the Business Object Document originated. It can be used to establish a logical to physical mapping; however, its use is optional.

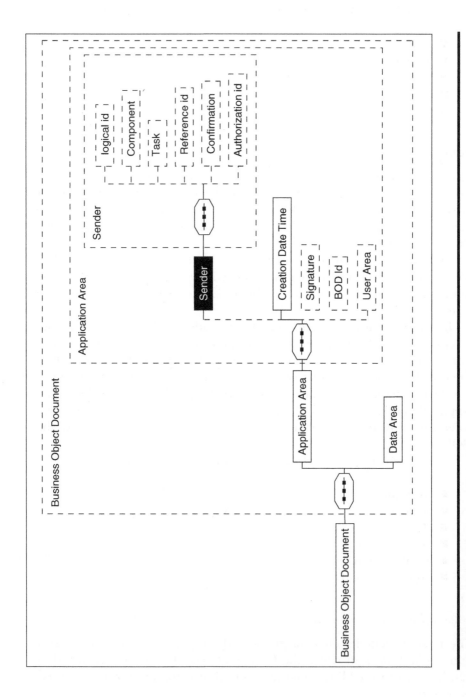

Figure B.5 Sender Relation to the BOD

Each system or combination of systems should maintain an external central reference table containing the logical names or logical addresses of the application systems in the integration configuration. This enables the logical names to be mapped to the physical network addresses of the resources needed on the network.

> *Note:* The technical implementation of this Domain Naming Service is not dictated by this specification.

This logical to physical mapping can be done at execution time by the application itself or by a middleware transport mechanism, depending on the integration architecture used.

This provides for a simple but effective directory access capability while maintaining application independence from the physical location of those resources on the network.

Component

The Component provides a finer level of control than the Logical Identifier and represents the business application that issued the Business Object Document. Its use is optional.

The Open Applications Group has not constructed the list of valid Component names. A suggestion for naming is to use the application component names used in the scenario diagrams in Section Two of OAGIS. Example Components would be "Inventory" or "Payroll."

Task

The Task describes the business event that initiated the need for the creation of the Business Object Document. Its use is optional. Although the Task may differ, depending on the specific implementation, it is important to enable drill-back capability. Example Tasks would be "Receipt" or "Adjustment."

Reference Identifier

ReferenceId enables the sending application to indicate the instance identifier of the event or task that caused the creation of the BOD. This allows drill-back from the BOD message into the sending application. This may be required in environments where an audit trail must be maintained for all transactions.

Confirmation

The Confirmation request is an option controlled by the Sender business application. It is a request to the receiving application to send back a confirmation BOD to the Sender. The confirmation Business Object Document may indicate the successful processing of the original Business Object Document or return error conditions if the original Business Object Document was unsuccessful.

The Confirmation request has the valid values shown in Table B.1.

Authorization Identifier

The Authorization Identifier describes the point of entry, such as the machine or device the user uses to perform the task that caused the creation of the Business Object Document.

The Authorization Identifier is used as a return routing mechanism for a subsequent BOD, or for diagnostic or auditing purposes. Valid Authorization Identifiers are implementation specific. The Authorization Identifier might be used for authentication in the business process. As an example, in the case of Plant Data Collection, the Authorization Identifier is used to fully define the path between the user of a hand-held terminal, any intermediate controller, and the receiving application.

In returning a BOD, the receiving application would pass the Authorization Identifier back to the controller to allow the message to be routed back to the hand-held terminal.

CreationDateTime

CreationDateTime is the date/time stamp when the given instance of the Business Object Document was created. This date/time must not be modified during the life of the Business Object Document. The OAGIS Date Time type supports ISO Date Time format.

Table B.1   Confirmation Request Values

0	Never	No confirmation Business Object Document requested
1	OnError	OnError send back a confirmation Business Object Document only if an error has occurred
2	Always	Always send a confirmation Business Object Document

Signature

If the BOD is to be signed, the signature element is included; otherwise it is not.

Signature will support any digital signature that may be used by an implementation of OAGIS. The QualifyingAgency identifies the agency that provided the format for the signature.

This element supports any digital signature specification that is available today and in the future. This is accomplished by not actually defining the content, but by allowing the implementation to specify the digital signature to be used via an external XML Schema namespace declaration. The Signature element is defined to have any content from any other namespace.

This allows the user to carry a digital signature in the XML instance of a BOD. The choice of which digital signature to use is left to the users and their integration needs.

For more information on the W3C's XML Signature specification, refer to: http://www.w3.org/TR/xmldsig-core/.

BODId

The BODId provides a place to carry a Globally Unique Identifier (GUID) that will make each Business Object Document uniquely identifiable. This is a critical success factor to enable software developers to use the GUID to build the following services or capabilities:

- Legally binding transactions
- Transaction logging
- Exception handling
- Re-sending
- Reporting
- Confirmations
- Security

How to obtain a GUID:

- Sun's iPlanet Application Server provides the ability to generate a GUID; see http://docs.iplanet.com/docs/manuals/ias/60/sp3/JavaProgGuide/jpgdeplo.htm
- The following link provides example VisualBasic code to create a GUID generating component: http://www.aspzone.com/articles/john/GUIDGen/BuildaGUIDGeneratingComponent.asp

- The following link shows a simple VisualBasic generator: http://www.vbaccelerator.com/codelib/tlb/guid.htm
- The following link provides an example of how to generate a GUID in Delphi: http://www.delphifaq.com/fq/q2104.shtml

Data Area

The DataArea of the Business Object Document contains the instance(s) of data values for the business transaction. For example (see Figure B.6), to send a Purchase Order or Orders to a business partner, the DataArea will contain the Verb (the action) and the Noun (the object) on which the action is to be performed.

The DataArea contains a single verb and one or more occurrences of a noun. This is shown in the examples above where the repeating PurchaseOrder element indicates that "1" or more instances of the "PurchaseOrder"s are to be "Process"ed.

Verb

The Verb is the action to be applied to the object (the Noun). Examples of Verbs include Cancel, Add, Process, and Synchronize. Any additional information that is exclusively related to the action is also stored with the Verb. For example, a Process verb indicates that it is acknowledgeable and confirmable.

Noun

A Noun is the object or document that is being acted upon. Examples include PurchaseOrder, RequestForQuote, and Invoice. Nouns are extensible within OAGIS, meaning that they can include content that was not originally designed by OAGI.

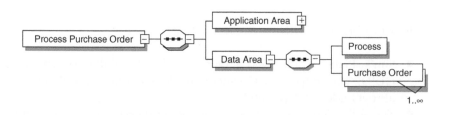

Figure B.6 Sample DataArea

There are different types of verbs or actions that can be performed on a PurchaseOrder; as such, the base Noun (e.g., PurchaseOrder) contains all of the information that might be present on a PurchaseOrder. The instantiation of each of the possible verb and noun combinations then further defines what must be provided to perform the intended transaction. For example, in a ProcessPurchaseOrder transaction, business partners and line item data must be provided; whereas in a CancelPurchaseOrder, only the order identifier needs to be provided.

Nouns are extensible within OAGIS, meaning that additional content (fields, compounds, and components) can be added to an existing Noun. This additional content can be defined external to OAGIS and added through the use of In-Line extensions. In-Line extensions are discussed later in this appendix.

Components

Components are the large-grained building blocks of a Noun. Components are extensible within OAGIS. Components consist of other Components, Compounds, and Fields. Examples of Components include PurchaseOrder Header, Party, and Address.

Components are extensible within OAGIS, meaning that additional content (Fields, Compounds, and Components) can be added to an existing Component. This additional content can be defined external to OAGIS and added through the use of *In-Line extensions*. In-Line extensions are discussed later in this appendix.

The instantiation of the Component identifies the OAGI recognized fields, compounds, and other components that must be present to support the intended business transaction on a BOD-by-BOD basis.

Compounds

Compounds are a logical grouping of Fields (low-level elements) that are used across all BODs. Examples include Amount, Quantity, DateTime, and Temperature. Unlike Components, Compounds cannot be extended to include new data content.

Fields

Fields are the lowest-level elements used in OAGIS Components and Compounds. These Fields can be based on either an OAGIS-defined type or a user-defined type.

Fields versus Compounds

In the instantiation of OAGIS in XML Schema, the distinction between Fields and Compounds becomes less defined. This is due to the fact that XML Schema provides a richer type system than that offered by DTDs; in fact, a type system did not exist prior to the approval of the W3C XML Schema Recommendation (May 2001). This allows the expression of dates and quantities in lower-level elements. With the XML Schema type system, the need for Fields and Compounds is replaced by the combination of:

- Built-in datatypes, based on ISO standards (e.g., for dates, times, and decimal numbers)
- Simple user-definable types, which are user-constrained versions of the standard types
- Complex user-definable types, which are user-defined structures built up from other simple and complex types

Because OAGIS is independent of the language used to instantiate it, the concepts of Compounds and Fields remain constant. However, they are both derived from Types in XML Schema. The XML Schema instantiation of OAGIS defines both Compounds and Fields as types. For this reason, they are both defined in a single file "Types.xsd," whereas the XML DTD instantiation defines them in separate files.

Extensions

While it is important to clearly define the messages to be passed between business partners and between business applications, it is not possible to identify all of the possible information that may be needed in every given situation. It is also not possible to completely identify the unique characteristics that may provide value for a given customer's implementation.

In other words, there are always going to be extensions needed such that a company can communicate its unique needs. These may be in the form of additional fields or in the form of additional values for a given field(s). For this reason, OAGIS is designed to be extended. OAGIS can be extended in the following ways:

- *UserArea extensions.* UserArea extensions provide an optional element within each OAGIS defined component that may be used by an implementer to carry any necessary additional information. For example, it may be necessary to carry field XYZ in the Header of a ProcessPurchaseOrder BOD in order to meet the unique customer demands. This can easily be accomplished by defining the field XYZ in a XML Schema file and reference this file via a namespace in the XML instance of the BOD and carrying the extended field in the UserArea of the ProcessPurchaseOrder's Header. As long as this additional XML Schema file is referenceable, the extension can be validated.

■ *Overlay Extensions.* Overlay extensions provide users with the ability to have their extensions appear within OAGIS-defined components. To add elements, a user must extend the OAGIS types within their own namespace. This is accomplished by creating a series of files that are similar to the OAGIS resource files. By doing this it is possible for users to enforce additional restrictions and/or add additional elements to OAGIS-defined Nouns or Components. It is also possible for users to provide additional constraints in their own XSL constraints, which may then be applied to OAGIS.

For more on how to extend OAGIS, see the OAGIS XML Schema Extensions white paper.

Note: Regardless of whether the extensions are inline or in the UserArea, they must use namespace qualified element names. Unqualified elements based on namespace types are not allowed.

UserArea Extensions

A UserArea is a special field that identifies where the user's unique data for a particular implementation may be provided. For example, it may be necessary to carry customer, vendor, or project extensions. The UserArea is provided as a place to carry these additional elements.

The UserArea is defined by embedding XML tags for each new Field Identifier, new Compound, or new Component needed within this area. When a new Field Identifier or a new Compound is determined to be necessary but was not included in the OAGIS specification, the project team for the specific integration project can develop new tags. These new tags can be used to describe the fields and compounds within the UserArea. The UserArea may contain multiple Fields, Compounds, or Components coded in this way.

The UserArea is implemented as an unrestricted ANY element, allowing any content to appear in the UserArea.

The optional UserArea is specified in all Components. It always appears after any OAGIS-defined Components, Compounds, or Fields in a Component. The only things that will appear after the UserArea are Overlay extensions. XML Schema requires that any extensions be appended to the end of the currently defined type.

Overlay Extensions

To provide the additional functionality required by vertical industries, the XML Schema instantiation of the OAGIS Message Architecture supports In-Line extension of OAGIS. This is accomplished through the use of the XML Schema ability for types to extend other types and through the use of Substitution Groups.

It is possible to extend the content of any OAGIS Noun or Component. Doing so appends new element content to an existing Noun or Component. Table B.2 shows how a ProcessPurchaseOrder BOD can be extended by a fictitious vertical industry, IndustryA, to include additional fields that may be needed within the vertical.

> *Note:* These extensions, while providing new elements in OAGIS, are distinguished from core OAGIS content by the presence of a namespace identifier. In this case, the default namespace is used to identify Industry A extensions prefix. OAGIS-defined elements are identified by the "oa:" namespace.

A detailed explanation of how to accomplish this and how it works can be found in the OAGIS XML Schema Extension white paper.

While it is possible to carry externally defined elements within the UserArea, OAGI recommends using Overlay extensions to add additional information to OAGIS.

Constraints

While XML Schema provides a powerful mechanism for validating types and structures, it does not provide a good mechanism for applying rules and constraints that may differ from implementation to implementation. For this reason, the decision was made to separate the type and structure validation from the rules and constraint validation, with the structure and type being provided by XML Schema and the rules and constraints being provided by XSL — more specifically, XPath. But because there are many different XSL processors available and no simple XPath processors, XPath is a part of XSL.

This allows OAGI to define the required fields that our constituency agrees must be present but a given implementation can also apply their own requirements fields, compounds, or components by simply populating an XSL and applying the additional constraints. This is explained further in the OAGIS 8.0 Users Guide.

Table B.2   Extending ProcessPurchaseOrder BOD

```
<ProcessInvoice xmlns="http://www.oagi.net/oagis/ia"
xmlns:oa="http://www.openapplications.org/oagis"
xmlns:xsi="http://www.w3.org/2001/XMLSchema-instance"
xsi:schemaLocation="http://www.oagi.net/oagis/ia
../BODs/ProcessInvoice.xsd" revision="001" environment="Production"
 lang="en-US">
<oa:ApplicationArea>
     <oa:Sender>
        <oa:LogicalId>String</oa:LogicalId>
        <oa:Component>String</oa:Component>
        <oa:Task>String</oa:Task>
        <oa:ReferenceId>String</oa:ReferenceId>
        <oa:Confirmation>0</oa:Confirmation>
        <oa:AuthorizationId>String</oa:AuthorizationId>
     </oa:Sender>
        <oa:CreationDateTime>2001-12-17T09:30:47-
05:00</oa:CreationDateTime>
        <oa:Signature qualifyingAgency="String"/>
        <oa:BODId>String</oa:BODId>
        <oa:UserArea/>
     <oa:ApplicationArea>
     <DataArea>
         <oa:Process/>
         <Invoice>
           <Header>
             <oa:DocumentIds>
                <oa:CarrierDocumentId>
                    <oa:Id/>
                </oa:CarrierDocumentId>
             </oa:DocumentIds>
             <oa:Status>
                <oa:Code/>
             </oa:Status>
             <TimeCard/>
           </Header>
           <oa:Line/>
           <GrandTotal/>
         </Invoice>
     </DataArea>
</ProcessInvoice>
```

Error Handling

OAGIS facilitates error handling at the application layer through the ConfirmBOD.

If an error occurs in the processing of a BOD in the receiving application and the Sender sets the Confirmation to either OnError or Always, Then the receiving application must provide a ConfirmBOD that references the original BOD's BODId. This ConfirmBOD indicates that there was an error in the original BOD and carries the error messages from the receiving system.

Once the original sending system receives the ConfirmBOD indicating an error has occurred in the original BOD, OAGIS leaves what happens next up to the integrator.

It is possible for the sending system to re-send the BOD or to attempt to correct any missing information through advanced error correction mechanisms. It is important to consider the effect of the time that has lapsed on the information that is being communicated.

The OAGIS ConfirmBOD is in addition to any communication layer error handling that may be provided by the infrastructure framework, Web service, or middleware.

APPLICATION AREAS IN OAGIS

BillOfMaterial

When included in a hierarchy, the Components are position dependent for their meaning and applicability to the Bill of Material. The Bill of Material structure is broken down into three classifications or ways to represent the Item. An Item may be included by itself as in the first sub-grouping, or an Item may be represented as part of a set of options or as an option within a class of options. An example of an option would be a CD-ROM for a laptop computer. Then each of the types of CD-ROMs for the option would be a separate Item. An example of an option class would be memory for a laptop. The options could then be 128, 256, or 512 megabytes of RAM. Each of these options would then have separate Item identifiers for memory modules that make up the appropriate amount of memory. For 256 megabytes of RAM, this could be two 128-megabyte memory modules or one 256-megabyte module.

BOD

The outcome of processing a specific BOD describes overall/summary outcome, plus the outcome of processing each noun of the BOD. This includes noun-specific error and/or warning messages encountered during processing, and may include summary and/or roll-up messages at the BOD level.

ChartOfAccounts

ChartofAccounts represents the accounting structure of a business. Each account represents a financial aspect of a business, such as its Accounts Payable, or the value of its inventory, or its office supply expenses. Typically, each account consists of a character string representing various elements such as major account code and department code.

Consumption

This is the process whereby a certain amount or quantity of inventory, resources, or product is utilized that is likely to lead to the need for some form of replenishment.

CostingActivity

For Dual Cycle accounting applications, Activity is used to communicate the details of the activities in the Manufacturing Application that caused the entries in the journal.

Credit

Credit represents customer credit information, and is used in the context of credit checking new sales orders.

CreditStatus

CreditStatus represents the credit approval status of a customer or a specific customer order.

DeliveryReceipt

DeliveryReceipt represents a transaction for the receiving of goods or services. It can be used to indicate receipt of goods in conjunction with a purchase order system.

The Delivery document contains Charge and Distribution elements at various levels to support the assessment of receiving service or compliance penalty charges. Several large retailers that demand receiving efficiency commonly assess penalty charges for supplier deliveries that are not compliant with the retailer's policies. Charges may be incurred for deliveries, ship units, or items that contain discrepancies from what was ordered or electronically manifested, for improper labeling of items and ship units, and the incorrect packing or loading of ship units.

DispatchList

A DispatchList shows the manufacturing or production supervisor or foreman a *prioritized* detail status of orders and operations scheduled or in-process at a specific work center.

ElectronicCatalog

ElectronicCatalog is a list of items or commodities. The items can be arranged according to a classification scheme. The catalog can identify the classification scheme it uses, as well as the classifications and features that are defined within that scheme. Within the catalog, each item can be classified into one or more categories, and the specifications of each item can be identified. A catalog has at least one publisher and one or many suppliers for the items in the catalog.

EmployeeTime

EmployeeTime refers to time sheet information for an employee. This information can be collected in an external source and then transferred to an HRMS or Payroll application.

EmployeeWorkSchedule

EmployeeWorkSchedule represents data related to the planned work-hours for an employee. A work schedule typically includes relatively static employee information, such as employee ID and name. It will also include schedule-specific information such as dates and amount of time to be worked.

EngineeringChangeDocument

An EngineeringChangeDocument can be used to request a change to a manufactured item. This document allows the change to progress through the different states from being a request and going through the review process to becoming an approved EngineeringChangeOrder.

ExchangeRate

ExchangeRate is information that applies to the exchange rate ratio.

Field

Field represents any element of user data that is to be synchronized across databases. The specific field name and value are specified in the Business Object Document.

Inspection

Inspection reports the inspection of items and identifies the source document.

InventoryBalance

InventoryBalance includes all stocked items and primarily represents the quantities of each item by location. Other item-by-location information, such as serial numbers or lot numbers, can also be included. The use of this Noun does not include basic item master data that is independent of location, such as item description and dimensions.

InventoryCount

InventoryCount represents the results of a physical inventory or cycle count of the actual on-hand quantities of each item in each location. Compare to the Noun InventoryBalance, which represents system-maintained on-hand quantities.

InventoryIssue

The InventoryIssue can be used to request an application to process an issue or request information about an issue.

InventoryMovement

InventoryMovement allows organizations to do quantity movement between locations, whether they are located in the same plant or across the country, or between countries.

InventoryReceipt

The Inventory Receipt is intended for use in Unplanned Receipt scenarios.

Invoice

The Invoice is use to invoice the customer.

ItemCrossReference

ItemCrossReferences describe both alternate and related items. Alternate items could specify items that have alternative universal identifiers such as EAN and UPC, or party-specific identifiers such as supplier part number or customer part number. Related items could be spares, accessories, or substitutes. Substitute items could be items that were validated by a development department for use as a substitute for the regular item.

ItemMaster

ItemMaster represents any unique purchased part or manufactured product. Item, as used here, refers to the basic information about an item, including its attributes, cost, and locations. It does not include item quantities. Compare to the Noun InventoryBalance, which includes all quantities and other location-specific information. Item is used as the ItemMaster.

JournalEntry

A Journal represents a change in the balances of a business' financial accounts. Many tasks or transactions throughout an enterprise will result in the creation of a Journal. Some examples are creating a customer invoice, paying a vendor, transferring inventory, or paying employees. A Journal consists of a header with general information, and two or more lines specifying what accounts will be affected. A Journal typically includes balanced debit and credit lines.

LedgerActual

LedgerActual represents actual amounts by account within ledger within company or business area. Actual amounts may be generated in a source application and then loaded to a specific ledger within the enterprise general ledger or budget application.

LedgerBudget

LedgerBudget represents budget amounts by account within ledger within company or business area. Budget amounts can be generated in a source application and then loaded to a specific ledger within the enterprise general ledger or budget application.

MaintenanceOrder

A MaintenanceOrder is an order for a machine, building, tooling, or fixed asset to be repaired or for preventive maintenance to be performed.

MatchDocument

MatchDocument identifies an internal document containing matching information. Essentially, it holds cross-reference information among the customer PurchaseOrder and the SupplierInvoice. It supports N-way matching.

MatchFailure

MatchFail represents notification that purchasing lines have failed in matching to a supplier invoice. The matching of a purchase order to an invoice is used to determine the amount paid to the vendor.

Party

This allows for communication of party information between business applications within a given integration. These Parties may play different roles within an integration from Supplier, Customer, to Carrier, and many more.

Payable

Payable is a transaction that represents an invoice from a supplier. A Payable is an open item, approved and ready for payment, in the Accounts Payable ledger. In some systems it might be called a voucher. Compare to PurchaseLedgerInvoice, which represents a not-yet-approved supplier invoice.

Personnel

Personnel information is the human resource information maintained for each employee. It includes such data as job code, employee status, department or place in the organization, and job-related skills. Although generally maintained in a Human Resource Management System (HRMS), this information may also be needed and updated by manufacturing applications (workforce scheduling) or project management (resource allocation).

PickList

A Pick(ing) List is a document that lists material to be retrieved ("picked") from various locations in a warehouse in order to fill a production order, sales order, or shipping order. A picking list includes general identifying information (header information), as well as line-item details. Depending on the Verb used, PickList may refer to header information only, or both header and detail information.

PlanningSchedule

PlanningSchedule indicates a demand forecast sent from a customer to a supplier, or a supply schedule sent from a supplier to a customer.

PriceList

PriceList defines a list of items with their base price, price breaks, discounts, and qualifiers. For each item, price breaks can be defined, above which certain discounts or overriding prices might apply. Price breaks can be defined in volume or in dollar amount. PriceList qualifiers specify for which catalog, customer, and/or effective dates this price list applies.

ProductAvailability

ProductAvailability represents information on the availability of a specified item at a specified inventory location for a specified date. Product availability is typically needed in the processing of customer sales orders. It is used in this context as the object of an inquiry function.

ProductionOrder

ProductionOrder is a document requesting the manufacture of a specified product and quantity.

ProductRequirement

ProductRequirement is a request to reserve or allocate a specified quantity of a specified item. Typically, this requirement would is received by an inventory or production system.

ProjectAccounting

ProjectAccounting is used to enable all relevant sub-systems that submit single-sided transactions to send information to a Project Accounting

Application. This would include, but not necessarily be limited to, Accounts Payable, Accounts Receivable, Budget, Order Management, Purchasing, Time and Labor, Travel and Expense. ProjectAccounting is a synonym for Project, and the LoadProjectAccounting BOD has the effect of populating the Project's TotalCost field or the ProjectActivities' Cost fields.

PurchaseLedgerInvoice

A PurchaseLedgerInvoice represents a not-yet-approved for payment purchase ledger invoice or debit memo. A PurchaseLedgerInvoice uses an InvoiceReference to reference the original supplier's invoice.

PurchaseOrder

The purpose of the PurchaseOrder Business Object Document is to communicate an order to purchase goods from a buyer to a supplier. The PurchaseOrder carries information to and from the buyer and supplier. The PurchaseOrder is a legally binding document once both Parties agree to the contents and the specified terms and conditions of the order.

The Process PurchaseOrder sends the electronic form of a purchase order document from a customer to a supplier in order to purchase n-number of Lines, each of which contains an Ordered Item.

Quote

A Quote is a document describing the prices of goods or services provided by a vendor. The Quote includes the terms of the purchase, delivery proposals, identification of goods or services ordered, as well as their quantities. The Quote noun is used in conjunction with the RFQ noun to form a business-to-business negotiation dialogue concerning the goods or services specified.

Receivable

Receivable is a transaction representing an invoice, credit memo, or debit memo to a customer. A receivable is an open (unpaid) item in the Accounts Receivable ledger.

RequestForQuote

RequestForQuote (RFQ) is a document describing goods or services desired from a vendor. The RFQ includes the terms of the purchase, delivery requirements, identification of goods or services ordered, as well as their quantities. The RFQ noun is used in conjunction with the Quote noun to form a business-to-business negotiation dialogue concerning the goods or services specified.

Requisition

Requisition is a request for the purchase of goods or services. Typically, a Requisition leads to the creation of a PurchaseOrder to a specific supplier.

ResourceAllocation

ResourceAllocation identifies the resources needed for a ProductionOrder and indicates where they are to be assigned.

Routing

Routing is the description of all the resources, steps, and activities the path associated with a manufacturing or production process. Typically, a Routing contains people, machines, tooling, operations, and steps.

SalesOrder

The SalesOrder is an order or customer order; it is a step beyond a PurchaseOrder in that the receiving entity of the Order also communicates SalesInformoration about the Order, along with the Order itself. The SalesOrder is intended to be used when an order needs to be communicated between business applications and the PurchaseOrder terms and conditions and quantities have been agreed to. This agreement may occur electronically or by other means.

SequenceSchedule

A ShipTo Partner is required to represent to the business partner that the goods or services are shipped to that partner. Optionally, partner types SoldTo, BillTo and ShipFrom, and Supplier can be used.

Shipment

A Shipment document identifies and describes a specific collection of goods to be transported by a carrier and delivered to one or more business partner destinations. A Shipment document represents the extent and content of "transportation work" to be done by the carrier. For transportation efficiency, a Shipment document typically consolidates deliveries to multiple destinations within a certain geographic region and may provide carrier routing instructions to each delivery stop.

ShipmentSchedule

Commonly, the ShipmentSchedule is generated by a material planning application and transmitted to an order or material planning application.

UnitOfMeasureGroup

UnitofMeasureGroup is a set of related Units-of-Measure (UOMs). A UOM-Group is typically defined by inventory control systems and assigned to many different Items that otherwise share common handling, packaging, or other physical inventory attributes.

WIPConfirm

Work-in-Progress confirmation (WIPConfirm) represents confirmation of the movement of WIP materials. The Noun refers to general information about the entire WIP transaction, as well as line-item detail about the specific WIP operation or routing step. This may apply to the movement of raw materials or finished products.

WIPMerge

WIPMerge is used to notify a Manufacturing Application of the creation of a single production lot from multiple production lots of a product being made on a ProductionOrder.

WIPMove

WIPMove is used to communicate which processing step the product is coming from and which step it is being moved to, along with the quantity moving and the time this event occurred.

WIPRecover

WIPRecover is used to notify a Manufacturing Application of the creation of usable production materials from material previously considered unsuitable for production use. This is most often likely to represent a return to production of scrap material.

WIPSplit

WIPSplit is used to notify a Manufacturing Application of the creation of multiple production lots from a single production lot of a product being made on a ProductionOrder.

WIPStatus

WIPStatus is used to notify a Manufacturing Application of the progress of a ProductionOrder at a point in time.

VERBS IN OAGIS

BillOfMaterial (BOM)

GetBillOfMaterial

The purpose of the GetBillOfMaterial (Figure B.7) is to enable an application to request specific Item Bill of Material information from another

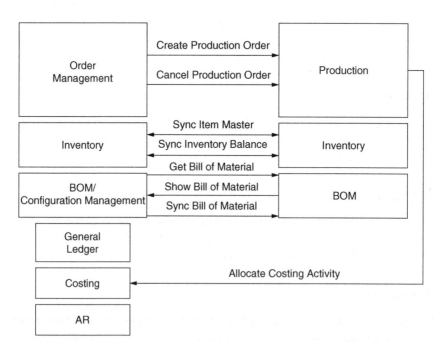

Figure B.7   Context Map 1

business application module. The response to the GetBillOfMaterial is the ShowBillOfMaterial (Figure B.7).

GetListBillOfMaterial

The purpose of the GetListBillOfMaterial (Figure B.7) is to enable an application or component to request a summary list of Bill of Material information from another business application or component. The response to the GetListBillOfMaterial is the ListBillOfMaterial (Figure B.7). The GetListBillOfMaterial also enables the retrieval of information across several documents using selection fields. An example of this could be requesting all Bills of Material for a specific Item.

ListBillOfMaterial

The purpose of the ListBillOfMaterial is to communicate one or more summary listings of BOM information to another business application component. This may be the result of a GetList request or it may be initiated by some other business event.

ShowBillOfMaterial

The purpose of the ShowBillOfMaterial is to supply ItemBillofMaterial information to another business application module. This BOD can also be initiated by the sending system upon some event occurring.

SyncBillOfMaterial

The purpose of the SyncBillOfMaterial (Figure B.7) is to communicate to a business application module or system the need to initiate the creation of a Bill of Material structure. This BOD may be necessary to address the Make to Order, Assemble to Order, or Mixed Mode business ordering scenarios in the Order Management to Manufacturing application integration scenario.

BOD

ConfirmBOD

ConfirmBOD (Figure B.8) reports on the outcome of processing a BOD. Only one BODOutcome noun will be returned, corresponding to a previously transmitted BOD that was earmarked for returning outcome notification. Summary BOD-level outcome is reported in the Header, with

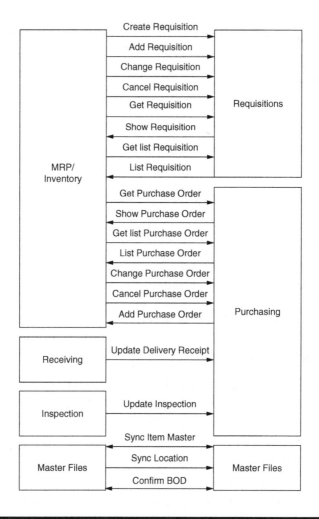

Figure B.8   Context Map 2

noun-specific errors or warnings reported for each noun instance that accompanied the original BOD.

ChartOfAccounts

SyncChartOfAccounts

The purpose of the SyncChartOfAccounts (Figure B.9) is to distribute general ledger chart of accounts code identifiers to other applications to store for validation purposes.

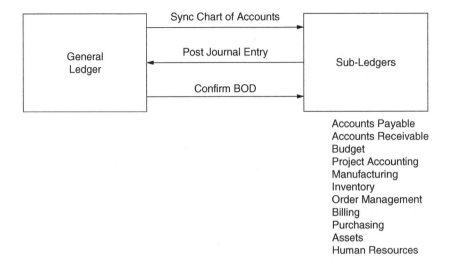

Figure B.9   Context Map 3

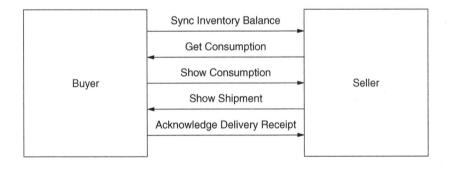

Figure B.10   Context Map 4

Consumption

GetConsumption

The most common use of GetConsumption (Figure B.10) is to request a buyer's usage information about an item or product for the supplier of such item or product. This BOD will not create or update either the buyer's or supplier's inventory records. The receiver of the request is responsible for making effective use of this information. The BOD can be used in the following ways:

- For a supplier of goods to request from the buyer the consumption status of goods
- For a vendor to request from the retailer if retail sales of goods have been made
- For inventory systems to request consumption status from plant data collection and warehouse management systems

This is an outline of the business flow that this BOD supports:

- Overall purchase, replenishment, or vendor-managed inventory agreement is in place and/or a GetConsumption message is sent by the supplier.
- ShowConsumption message is returned to the supplier, distributor, or third-party logistics provider that material has been consumed. This is done in response to events such as these (and/or the Get message), depending on implementation context:
  - Material is replenished to line side at manufacturing facility
  - Material is assembled into final product
  - Material is purchased and removed from facility by customer
- Supplier, distributor, or third-party logistics provider replenishes material, using information provided in the ShowConsumption message, the demand and shipment forecasts, and the terms of the overall purchase or vendor-managed inventory agreement.

ShowConsumption

The most common use of ShowConsumption (Figure B.10) is to share a buyer's usage information about an item or product with the supplier of such item or product. This BOD will not create or update either the buyer's or supplier's inventory records. The receiver of the request is responsible for making effective use of this information. The BOD can be used in the following ways:

- For a buyer of goods to inform the supplier that goods have been consumed, and replenishment will likely be required
- For a retailer to inform the vendor that retail sales of goods have been made
- For plant data collection systems and warehouse management systems to inform inventory systems that goods have been consumed and inventory records should be adjusted accordingly

This is an outline of the business flow that this BOD supports:

- Overall purchase, replenishment, or vendor-managed inventory agreement is in place.
- Message is sent to supplier, distributor, or third-party logistics provider that material has been consumed. This is done in response to events such as these, depending on implementation context:
  - Material is replenished to line side at manufacturing facility
  - Material is assembled into final product
  - Material is purchased and removed from facility by customer
- Supplier, distributor, third-party logistics provider replenishes material, using information provided in the ShowConsumption message, the demand and shipment forecasts, and the terms of the overall purchase or vendor-managed inventory agreement.

CostingActivity

AllocateCostingActivity

The purpose of the AllocateCostingActivity (Figure B.11) BOD is to enable the update of Activity information from a production or manufacturing application to a costing application. This is necessary for applications that are based on a Dual Cycle Accounting model. This Dual Cycle Accounting model does not capture the details of the Activities that caused entries to

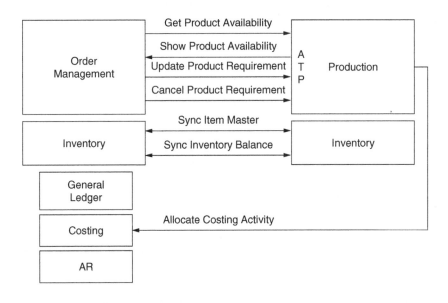

Figure B.11   Context Map 5

be made in the general ledger application, but instead captures them in a separate overall costing application.

This BOD commonly causes updates to occur and may be used as part of a large integration scenario or as a single tool for updating data. For Single Cycle Accounting systems, the PostJournalEntry BOD will be used to ensure that the costing information flows from the Manufacturing Application to the Financial Application. In most cases, either PostJournal or AllocateActivity will be used when the Financial Applications are included with Logistics, but both Business Service Requests will not be used in the same integration scenario.

Credit

GetCredit

The purpose of GetCredit (Figure B.12) is for the Order Management Application to request credit data for a trading partner from the credit management function. The GetCredit does not imply any update; it is only an inquiry function. The ShowCredit will be the response back to the Order Management Application. The UpdateCredit can be used in both directions between the Order Management and the Accounts Receivable Applications. Its purpose is to keep order, shipment, and open item amounts current. Finally, the ChangeCreditStatus is used to update the Order Management Application with any changes in business status for a particular trading partner.

ShowCredit

The purpose of ShowCredit (Figure B.12) is to provide credit information concerning a trading partner. The ShowCredit is the reply required by the GetCredit BOD. This BOD type can also be used as an information mechanism that is triggered by a business event and not a GET request.

UpdateCredit

The purpose of UpdateCredit (Figure B.12) is to update the Credit Management functionality within the Customer Order Management or the Accounts Receivable Application. The UpdateCredit will also transmit changes in the Accounts Receivable open item balances to the Credit Management function of the Customer Order Management Application.

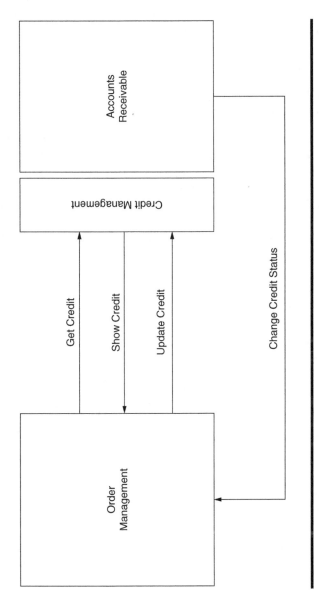

Figure B.12   Context Map 6

CreditStatus

ChangeCreditStatus

The purpose of ChangeCreditStatus (Figure B.12) is to notify the Customer Order Management Application that the overall credit status of a trading partner has changed or that the status on specific order(s) is to be changed.

DeliveryReceipt

AcknowledgeDeliveryReceipt

The AcknowledgeDeliveryReceipt (Figure B.13) can be used to notify the shipping business partner that the shipment has been received by the customer or consignee destination, and alert them to any discovered discrepancies. The acknowledgment may contain the full detail of the receipt as created by the receiving party or just the discrepancies and other exception conditions. The AcknowledgeDeliveryReceipt BOD supports receipt acknowledgments at either the line-item level and/or the ship unit level. Intermediate transportation/logistics providers or freight forwarding partners can use this document to acknowledge the receipt of entire shipping units without detailing the corresponding contents.

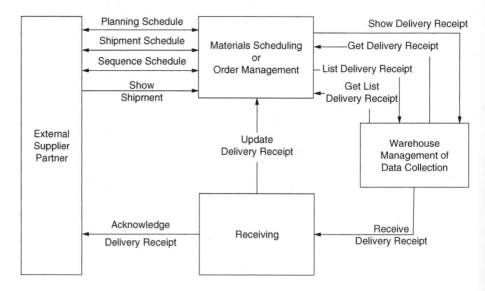

Figure B.13   Context Map 7

GetDeliveryReceipt

The GetDeliveryReceipt (Figure B.13) can be used to request information about a specific expected (unreceived) or previously received goods delivery. The response to the GetDeliveryReceipt request is ShowDeliveryReceipt. For expected deliveries, the ShowDeliveryReceipt document content may act as a receiving template or checklist to identify the quantity and shipping configuration of the expected goods. The ShowDeliveryReceipt supports describing shipment content at either the line-item level and/or the ship unit level. Intermediate transportation/logistics providers or freight forwarding partners can use this document to acknowledge the receipt of entire shipping units without detailing the corresponding contents.

GetListDeliveryReceipt

The GetListDeliveryReceipt (Figure B.13) can be used to request information about a set of expected (unreceived) or previously received goods deliveries meeting certain selection criteria. The response to the GetListDeliveryReceipt request is ListDeliveryReceipt.

ListDeliveryReceipt

The ListDeliveryReceipt (Figure B.13) document can be used to obtain a limited information listing about expected (unreceived) or previously received goods deliveries that match certain selection criteria in a GetListDeliveryReceipt request. Additional information about a specific DeliveryReceipt can be obtained through ShowDeliveryReceipt using the listing information to populate a GetDeliveryReceipt request.

ReceiveDeliveryReceipt

The ReceiveDeliveryReceipt (Figure B.13) can be used to update the receiver's internal receiving and order management business applications to indicate that the requested material has arrived, including any unexpected quantity, condition, or other exception discrepancies. The ReceiveDeliveryReceipt supports receiving at either the line-item level and/or the ship unit level. Intermediate transportation/logistics providers or freight forwarding partners can use this document to acknowledge the receipt of entire shipping units without detailing the corresponding contents.

ShowDeliveryReceipt

The ShowDeliveryReceipt (Figure B.13) can be used to obtain information about specific expected (unreceived) or previously received goods delivery. The ShowDeliveryReceipt can be issued in response to a GetDeliveryReceipt request, or emitted asynchronously for notification upon some business event. For expected deliveries, the ShowDeliveryReceipt document content may act as a receiving template or checklist to identify the quantity and shipping configuration of the expected goods.

UpdateDeliveryReceipt

The UpdateDeliveryReceipt (Figure B.14) can be used to update the receiver's internal receiving and order management business applications to indicate that the requested material has arrived, including any unex-

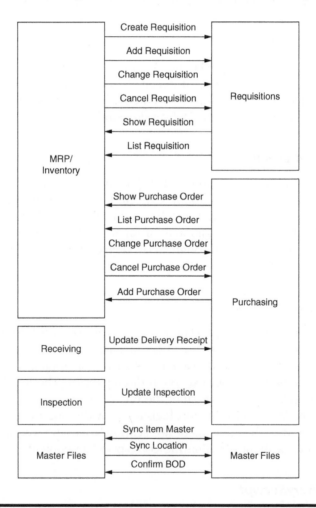

Figure B.14 Context Map 8

pected quantity, condition, or other exception discrepancies. There exist many other possible business applications in several environments that can use this capability. For example:

1. A Purchasing application can use this BOD to notify an Accounts Payable application of a specific delivery. This will enable the Accounts Payable application to accurately calculate the amount it needs to pay a business partner.
2. A Purchasing application could use this to notify an MRP, Inventory, or Manufacturing business application that a delivery has occurred and the goods are available for use or inspection, etc.

An MRP/Inventory system could use this BSR to communicate changes on a physical receipt in inventory to the Purchasing system. The UpdateDeliveryReceipt supports receipts at either the line-item level and/or the ship unit level. Intermediate transportation/logistics providers or freight forwarding partners can use this document to acknowledge the receipt of entire shipping units without detailing the corresponding contents.

DispatchList

GetDispatchList

The purpose of the GetDispatchList (Figure B.15) is to enable a business application module to request this information from another business application. The reply to this BOD is the ShowDispatchList.

ShowDispatchList

The purpose of the ShowDispatchList (Figure B.15) is to communicate to a business application module or system the sending system's representation of dispatch list (finite schedule) information. This request can be used as a response to a GetDispatchList request or as a push notification of an event.

SyncDispatchList

The purpose of the SyncDispatchList (Figure B.15) is to update dispatch list (finite schedule) information.

UpdateDispatchList

The purpose of the UpdateDispatchList (Figure B.15) is to update dispatch list (finite schedule) information.

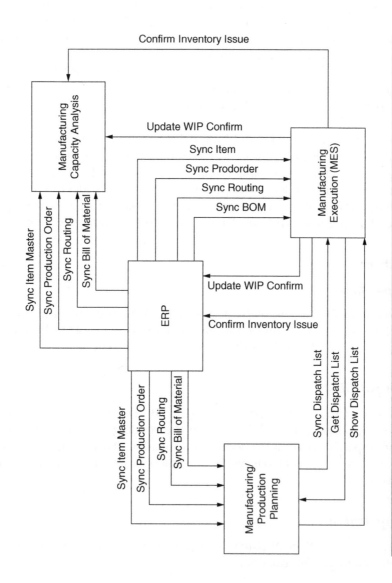

Figure B.15 Context Map 9

ElectronicCatalog

GetElectronicCatalog

The purpose of the GetElectronicCatalog (Figure B.16) is to enable a business application module or system to request catalog information. The catalog information that is requested by the GetElectronicCatalog may include:

- Item identifiers
- Specifications
- Pricing information agreed on either
- Purchase agreements
- Price lists
- Availability and delivery information
- Related items and accessories

ShowElectronicCatalog

The purpose of the ShowElectronicCatalog (Figure B.16) is to supply a business application module or system with requested catalog information. In communicating catalog information, the ShowElectronicCatalog may cause other information to be coordinated.

SyncElectronicCatalog

SyncElectronicCatalog (Figure B.16) is the synchronization of all the items within the ElectronicCatalog between the OrderManagement and Purchasing systems.

EmployeeTime

UpdateEmployeeTime

The purpose of the UpdateEmployeeTime (Figure B.17) is to update work time information for an employee from a data collection application to an ERP Human Resources application.

EmployeeWorkSchedule

SyncEmployeeWorkSchedule

The purpose of the SyncEmployeeWorkSchedule (Figure B.17) is to enable the synchronization of Employee Work Schedule data that exists on

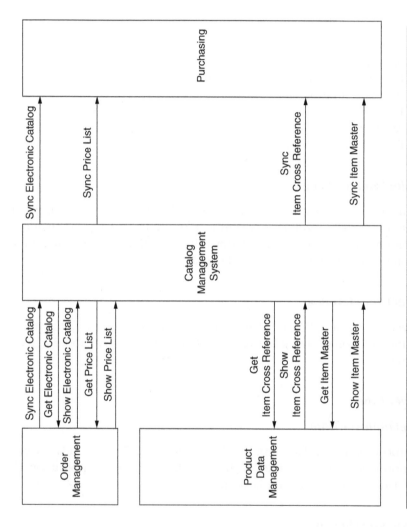

Figure B.16 Context Map 10

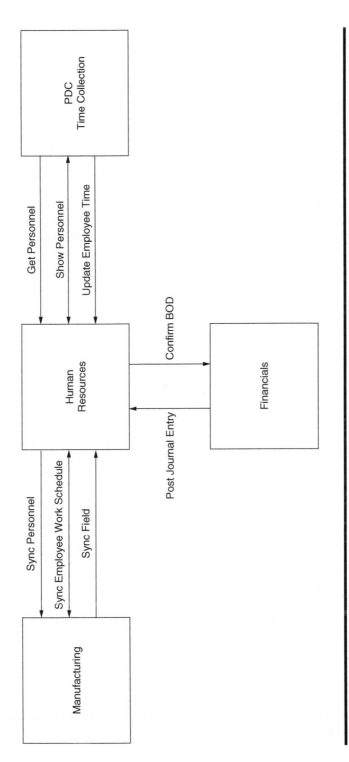

Figure B.17 Context Map 11

separate databases. The SyncEmployeeWorkSchedule allows the adding of new Employee Work Schedules as well as the modification of previously established Employee Work Schedules.

EngineeringChangeDocument

ConfirmEngineeringChangeDocument

The purpose of the ConfirmEngineeringChangeDocument (Figure B.18) is to communicate to a business application module or system that the synchronization of a specified engineering change document has been completed successfully. This BOD may be necessary to address the Make to Order, Assemble to Order, or Mixed Mode business ordering scenarios in Order Management to Manufacturing application integration scenarios.

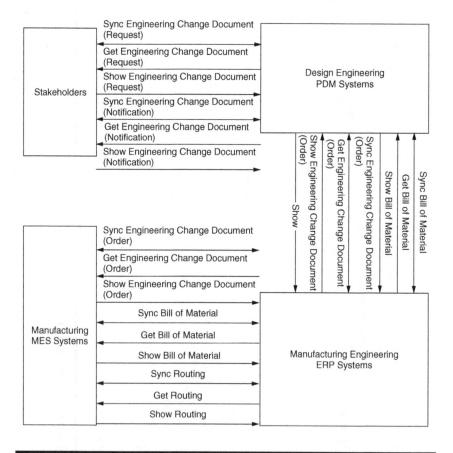

Figure B.18   Context Map 12

GetEngineeringChangeDocument

The purpose of the GetEngineeringChangeDocument (Figure B.18) is to communicate to a business application module or system the need to request a ShowEngineeringChangeDocument for the Engineering Change Document specified in the Message.

ShowEngineeringChangeDocument

The purpose of the ShowEngineeringChangeDocument (Figure B.18) is to communicate to a business application module or system the sending system's representation of a specified Engineering Change Order. This request is a response to a Get request or as a push notification of an event.

SyncEngineeringChangeDocument

The purpose of the SyncEngineeringChangeDocument (Figure B.18) is to communicate to a business application module or system the need to initiate the creation of an Engineering Change Document.

ExchangeRate

SyncExchangeRate

The purpose of the SyncExchangeRate is to enable the passing of updates of currency exchange rates to other applications that have exchange rate tables.

Field

SyncField

The purpose of the SyncField (Figure B.19) is to enable the validation of data that exists on separate application databases. This BOD can cause online validation to occur or may be a single tool for synchronizing data.

Inspection

UpdateInspection

The purpose of the UpdateInspection (Figure B.14) is to supply Inspection information for goods or services to another business application module.

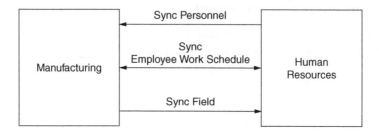

Figure B.19   Context Map 13

This BOD may be initiated by the sending system upon some event occurring. For example;

1. A Purchase Order application could use this to send information to a Plant Data Collection application, or vice versa.
2. An MRP, Inventory, Purchasing, or Manufacturing business application could use this to communicate inspection information.
3. A Laboratory Information System could send quality information to an Inventory application.
4. A Quality Control application could send information to an MRP, Inventory, or Purchasing application.

InventoryBalance

SyncInventoryBalance

The purpose of the SyncInventoryBalance (Figure B.11) is to enable the synchronization of InventoryBalance data that exists on separate Item Master databases. This data is not the master data that describes the attributes of the item such as dimensions, weight, or unit of measure. Rather, this is data that describes the Item as it exists at a specific location. The primary focus of this BOD is to synchronize the quantity of an Item by stocking location.

UpdateInventoryBalance

The purpose of the ChangeInventoryBalance (Figure B.11) is to enable the communication of a Change in the InventoryBalance data that exists on separate Inventory databases.

InventoryCount

Get InventoryCount

The purpose of the GetInventoryCount (Figure B.20) is to request occurrences of InventoryCount information from an ERP system. This count may be a cycle count or a physical count.

GetListInventoryCount

The purpose of the GetListInventoryCount (Figure B.20) is to enable a business application to request several occurrences of summary InventoryCount information from an ERP system. This count may be a cycle count or a physical count.

ListInventoryCount

The purpose of the ListInventoryCount (Figure B.20) is the response to the GetListInventoryCount request for several occurrences of summary InventoryCount information from an ERP system. This count may be a cycle count or a physical count.

ShowInventoryCount

The purpose of the ShowInventoryCount (Figure B.20) is the response to the Get request for occurrences of InventoryCount information from an ERP system. This count may be a cycle count or a physical count.

UpdateInventoryCount

The purpose of the UpdateInventoryCount (Figure B.20) is to transmit an inventory count to ERP from the actual physical inventory location. This count may be a cycle count or a physical count.

InventoryIssue

ConfirmInventoryIssue

The purpose of the ConfirmInventoryIssue (Figure B.21) is to notify a Manufacturing Application of the issue of required material to a production order for making a product. This BOD is also used to notify a Manufacturing Application of the return of material from a production order back into inventory. The business environments most likely to require this

Figure B.20   Context Map 14

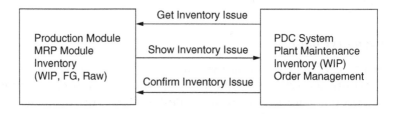

Figure B.21   Context Map 15

capability include any type of manufacturing scenario. This BOD communicates what the Item is that is being issued, where it is being issued from, which processing operation it is being issued to, what quantity was issued, and at what time this event occurred. In the case of a return, this BOD communicates what the Item is that is being returned, which processing operation it is being returned from, which inventory location it is being returned to, the quantity being returned, and the time at which this event occurred.

GetInventoryIssue

The purpose of the GetInventoryIssue (Figure B.21) is to request inventory issue information against an order, from an ERP system into a PDC system to confirm the InventoryIssue transaction (BOD).

ProcessInventoryIssue

The purpose of the ProcessInventoryIssue is to reflect an unplanned issue of an Item to a miscellaneous location. Possible reasons for this include:

1. Somebody broke the material.
2. The material is defective and needs replacing.
3. The material is used up and needs replenishment.

ShowInventoryIssue

The purpose of the ShowInventoryIssue (Figure B.21) is to supply InventoryIssue information against an order, from an ERP system into a PDC system, to confirm the InventoryIssue transaction (BOD).

InventoryMovement

IssueInventoryMovement

The purpose of the IssueInventoryMovement (Figure B.22) is to give the organization the ability to do a quantity movement of materials from one organizational unit to another organizational unit.

ReceiveInventoryMovement

The purpose of the ReceiveInventoryMovement (Figure B.22) is to give the organization the ability to do a quantity movement of materials from one organizational unit to another organizational unit.

InventoryReceipt

ProcessInventoryReceipt

The purpose of the ProcessInventoryReceipt is to give the organization the ability to do a quantity movement of materials from one organizational unit to another organizational unit.

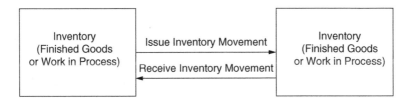

Figure B.22   Context Map 16

Invoice

GetInvoice

The purpose of the GetInvoice (Figure B.23) is to enable a request of an invoice. This BOD can be used as a request by a customer to its supplier. The ShowInvoice BOD would be the expected response.

ProcessInvoice

The purpose of the ProcessInvoice (Figure B.23) is to transmit an invoice from a supplier to a customer indicating that the receiver of the invoice is to process the invoice for payment.

ShowInvoice

The purpose of the ShowInvoice (Figure B.23) is to transmit an invoice from a supplier to a customer. This BOD can be used as a response to a GetInvoice request or as a push notification of an event.

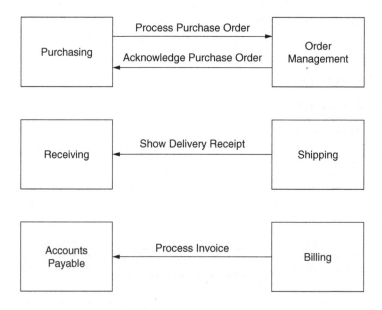

Figure B.23   Context Map 17

SyncInvoice

The purpose of the SyncInvoice (Figure B.23) is to transmit an invoice from a supplier to a customer. This information is passed in order to keep customers updated on the number of invoices they have.

ItemCrossReference

GetItemCrossReference

The purpose of the GetItemCrossReference (Figure B.16) is to enable a business application module or system to request information concerning an Item cross-reference. Cross-references can be to other item identifiers, to the same form fit and function, as well as references to item identifiers of other items (form fit and function).

In this document item relationships is used to refer to where the "to item" identifier, identifies a different form, fit and function to the "from item" identifier. It should be noted that the item identifier that is "primary" in one system may be a "secondary" identifier in another system. For example, in the Application Integration space, the Manufacturing System may regard the "Item Number" as the primary identifier. The Order Management System may regard the Catalog number as the primary identifier. A company that manufactures hand-held multimeters may identify a given item in manufacturing with a 12-digit numeric code, 5432 123 12345. The marketing and sales department may refer to the same item by its catalog number, FL 30/4.

ShowItemCrossReference

The purpose of the ShowItemCrossReference (Figure B.16) is to supply a business application module or system with information concerning an Item cross-reference.

SyncItemCrossReference

The purpose of the SyncItemCrossReference (Figure B.16) is to communicate to a business application module or system the need to synchronize an Item cross-reference. Cross-references may be to other item identifiers, to the same form, fit, and function, as well as references to item identifiers of other items (form, fit, and function).

ItemMaster

GetItemMaster

The purpose of the GetItemMaster (Figure B.24) is to enable a business application module to request information concerning a specific Item from another business application. The reply to this BOD is the ShowItemMaster.

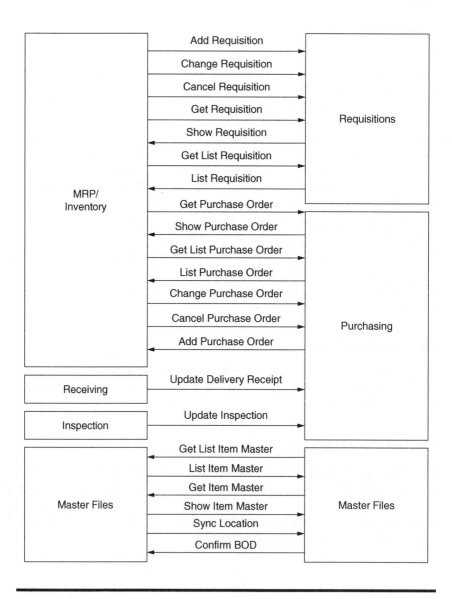

Figure B.24   Context Map 18

GetListItemMaster

The purpose of the GetListItemMaster (Figure B.24) is to enable a business application module to request summary information concerning an Item-Master or Items from another business application. This type of function-ality is limited to the capabilities of the responding application and needs to be determined during the implementation project. The response to this request is the ListItemMaster. This BOD does not usually cause updates to occur.

ListItemMaster

The purpose of the ListItemMaster (Figure B.24) is to enable a business application module to respond to a GetListItemMaster request or to pro-actively send a listing of summary information about Items to one or more other applications. There are many possible business applications in several environments that may use this capability. For example, an MRP, Inventory, or Manufacturing business application could use this to request item information. The picture below visualizes a possible use of this BOD.

ShowItemMaster

The purpose of the ShowItemMaster (Figure B.24) is to supply Item information to another business application module. This request can be used as a response to a GetItemMaster request or as the result of some other business event.

SyncItemMaster

The purpose of the SyncItemMaster (Figure B.11) is to supply Item information for goods or services to another business application module. This BOD can also be initiated by the sending system upon some event occurring. This BOD is not for synchronizing Item quantities at each inventory location. The SyncInventoryBalance Business Object Document is used for this purpose.

JournalEntry

PostJournalEntry

The purpose of the PostJournalEntry (Figure B.9) is to transmit data necessary to create a journal entry from any sub-ledger business applica-tion to a general ledger application. Many applications in the enterprise environment create data that causes changes in the account balances of a general ledger application. Some components that have activity that will be reflected in a general ledger application include:

- Benefits
- Costing
- Human Resources
- Inventory Control
- Manufacturing
- Payroll
- Production
- Treasury

This is not a complete list of all the components that create activity that generates a journal entry. Many tasks that occur within the enterprise applications cause the creation of a general ledger journal entry. Tasks relate directly to the Component. For example, the adjustment of Inventory value is a task that occurs within the InventoryControl Component. Some of the tasks that would be catalysts for changes in a general ledger include:

1. Receiving Inventory
2. Issuing Inventory
3. Transferring Inventory
4. Adjusting Inventory Value
5. Adjusting Inventory Count
6. Calculating Material Variances
7. Calculating Labor Variances
8. Calculating Overhead Variances

LedgerActual

GetLedgerActual

The purpose of the GetLedgerActual (Figure B.25) is to enable an enterprise application to request detailed accounting ledger actual data.

GetListLedgerActual

The purpose of the GetListLedgerActual (Figure B.25) is to request information containing summary information for one or more ledgers. The response to this request is ListLedgerActual.

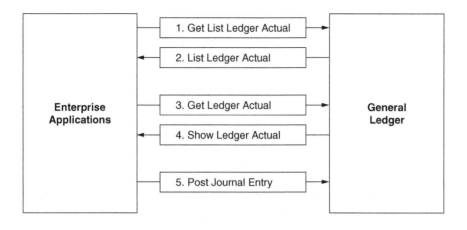

Figure B.25   Context Map 19

ListLedgerActual

The purpose of the ListLedgerActual (Figure B.25) is to publish one or more summary listings of ledger information. This may be in response to a GetListLedgerActual request or to proactively publish a listing of summary ledger information for a business event.

ShowLedgerActual

The purpose of ShowLedgerActual (Figure B.25) is to communicate to an enterprise application the sending system's representation of the ledger information specifically requested. This may be in response to a GetLedgerActual request or to proactively publish a listing of ledger information for a business event.

LedgerBudget

LoadLedgerBudget

The purpose of the LoadLedgerBudget (Figure B.26) is to transmit budget amounts from all possible source applications throughout an enterprise to a general ledger or budget application.

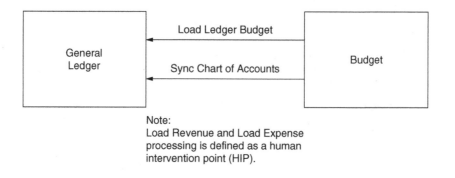

Figure B.26　Context Map 20

Location

SyncLocation

The purpose of SyncLocation (Figure B.8) is to enable a mechanism to ensure that the physical location identifiers are synchronized between the business applications that require this to communicate clearly. This is particularly critical when only the codes that identify locations are used. Without the meaning of the codes clearly communicated, the integration is not effective. This BOD enables the Location codes to be synchronized among business applications. This BOD can also be initiated by the sending system upon some event occurring.

MaintenanceOrder

CancelMaintenanceOrder

The purpose of the CancelMaintenanceOrder (Figure B.27) is to publish to a business application or system the need to cancel a Maintenance Order or one or more of its operations. One possible scenario is the cancellation of Maintenance Order from field devices, service trucks, production system, etc.

CreateMaintenanceOrder

The purpose of the CreateMaintenanceOrder (Figure B.27) is to publish to a business application component or system the need to create or update a Maintenance Order. One possible scenario is the synchronization of a Maintenance Order between field devices, service trucks, etc., with a CMMS system.

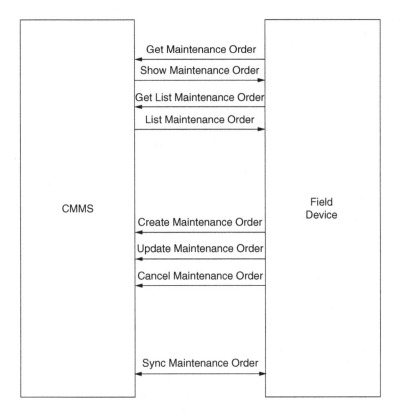

Figure B.27   Context Map 21

GetMaintenanceOrder

The purpose of the GetMaintenanceOrder (Figure B.27) is to enable one business application module to request this information from another business application. The response to this BOD is the ShowMaintenance-Order.

GetListMaintenanceOrder

The purpose of the GetListMaintenanceOrder (Figure B.27) is to enable a business application module to request information containing summary information. The GetListMaintenanceOrder enables the retrieval of information across several documents using selection fields. An example of this could be requesting all Resource Component occurrences for a specific Maintenance Operation.

ListMaintenanceOrder

The purpose of the ListMaintenanceOrder (Figure B.27) is to publish one or more summary listings of Maintenance Order information to other business application components. This may be in response to a GetList-MaintenanceOrder request or to proactively publish a listing of summary Maintenance Order information for a business event. When a receiving application receives this BOD, the information can be used as is or it can be used to initiate the selection of a specific Maintenance Order through the GetMaintenanceOrder request. The processing is designed to provide multiple occurrences of summary data.

ShowMaintenanceOrder

The purpose of the ShowMaintenanceOrder (Figure B.27) is to communicate to a business application module or system the sending system's representation of Maintenance Order information. This request can be used as a response to a GetMaintenanceOrder request or as a push notification of an event.

SyncMaintenanceOrder

The purpose of the SyncMaintenanceOrder (Figure B.27) is to ensure that all business software components in a specific integration instance have the current Maintenance Order information. This BOD is commonly used to publish the need to create or update a Maintenance Order in a publish-and-subscribe integration environment. One possible scenario is the synchronization of a Maintenance Order between field devices, service trucks, etc., with a CMMS system.

UpdateMaintenanceOrder

The purpose of the UpdateMaintenanceOrder (Figure B.27) is to publish to a business application component or system the need to create or update a Maintenance Order. One possible scenario is the synchronization of a Maintenance Order between field devices, service trucks, etc., with a CMMS system.

MatchDocument

GetMatchDocument

The purpose of the GetMatchDocument (Figure B.28) is to enable a business application module to request information concerning invoice

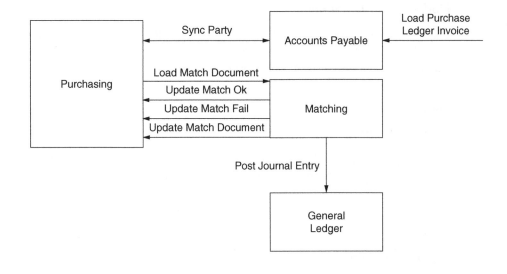

Figure B.28   Context Map 22

matching from another business application. The reply to this BOD is the ShowMatchDocument. This BOD does not usually cause updates to occur.

The invoice matching process may include several document types, including the following:

- *Two-way match* — Purchase Order and the Invoice
- *Three-way match* — Purchase Order, Invoice, and Receipt
- *Four-way match* — Purchase Order, Invoice, Receipt, and Inspection Results

LoadMatchDocument

The LoadMatchDocument (Figure B.28) is for use both by the Accounts Payable application and the Purchasing application in exchanging the transactions that are required to be matched. The purpose of Update-MatchDocument is for the Accounts Payable application to send successful matching notification or a match fail notification to a Purchasing application.

ShowMatchDocument

The purpose of the ShowMatchDocument (Figure B.28) is to enable the Accounts Payable application and the Purchasing application to exchange information required either by request or initiated by some business event.

UpdateMatchDocument

The purpose of UpdateMatchDocument (Figure B.28) is for the Accounts Payable application to send successful matching notification or a match fail notification to a Purchasing application.

MatchFailure

UpdateMatchFail

The purpose of the UpdateMatchFail (Figure B.28) is to notify the Purchasing application of a matching failure such as a tolerance failure.

MatchOk

UpdateMatchOk

The UpdateMatchOk (Figure B.28) is used for the Accounts Payable application to send successful matching notification to a Purchasing application. The LoadMatchDocument is discussed elsewhere. The LoadMatchDocument is used to keep invoice, purchase order, goods receipt note, and inspection ticket information current. In the model here, invoice matching functionality exists in the Accounts Payable application, the invoice is entered into Accounts Payable, and Purchasing publishes matching document information to which Accounts Payable subscribes.

Party

GetParty

The purpose of the GetParty is to facilitate keeping Party information synchronized that exists on separate databases. The GetParty request allows a business application to request information about a given Party. The ShowParty command is the response to this request providing the specific information requested.

ShowParty

ShowParty allows the communication of Party information between business applications within a given integration. These Parties may play different roles within integration from Supplier, Customer, to Carrier and many more.

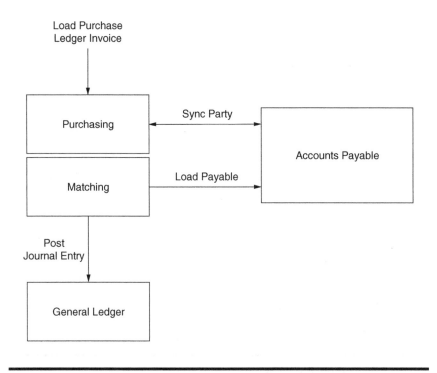

Figure B.29   Context Map 23

SyncParty

The purpose of SyncParty (Figure B.29) is to facilitate keeping Party information synchronized that exists on separate databases. The SyncParty allows for adding a new Party and modification of previously established Parties.

Payable

LoadPayable

The purpose of the LoadPayable (Figure B.30) is to transmit data to create a payable open item in a Payables application from the purchasing information generated in a Purchasing application. The LoadPayable can also update the General Ledger, depending on the specific architecture of the Financial applications. The scope of the LoadPayable indicates that the supplier's invoice is ready to be paid and has already been approved before the information moves to the Accounts Payable application. An approved invoice is also known as the voucher.

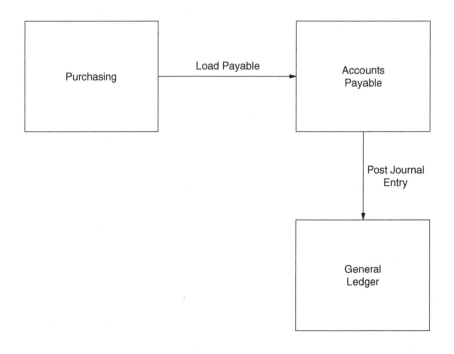

Figure B.30 Context Map 24

Personnel

GetPersonnel

The purpose of the GetPersonnel (Figure B.17) is to request Personnel data for a worker.

ShowPersonnel

The purpose of the ShowPersonnel (Figure B.17) is to provide Personnel data for a worker to a requesting business application. This BOD may be in response to a Get Personnel request, or it may be triggered by a business event.

SyncPersonnel

The purpose of the SyncPersonnel (Figure B.17) is to enable the synchronization of employee data that exists on separate databases between Manufacturing and Human Resources applications. The SyncPersonnel allows the adding of new employees and their relevant data, as well as the modification of previously established employees. The SyncPersonnel is used to facilitate the maintenance of human resources data in a manufacturing workforce planning module. This enables the workforce planning module to use current personnel information when creating finite production schedules. The SyncPersonnel can also be used by a Project Accounting application or a Work Order Management application to assign qualified personnel or to perform resource planning.

PickList

GetPickList

The purpose of the GetPickList (Figure B.31) is to enable a request for the retrieval of a single Pick(ing) List from an ERP system. The reply to this request is the ShowPickList. Individual lines from a Pick(ing) List are not selectable with this BOD; only the complete document is selected and returned.

GetListPickList

The purpose of the GetListPickList (Figure B.31) is to enable a business application to request summary information for one or more Pick(ing) Lists from an ERP system. If a List of documents is requested, that List will be used so a selection and Get request of a specific Pick(ing) List can be made, if necessary.

ListPickList

The purpose of the ListPickList (Figure B.31) is to provide a list of Pick(ing) Lists from an ERP system to another application. This BOD can be initiated in response to a GetListPickList request or upon some business event. When a receiving application receives this BOD, the information can be used as is or it can be used to initiate a selection of a specific PickList

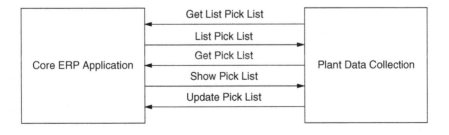

Figure B.31   Context Map 25

through the GetPickList request. The processing is designed to provide multiple occurrences of summary data. This BOD will not usually cause updates to occur.

ShowPickList

The purpose of the ShowPickList (Figure B.31) is to show the details of an individual Pick(ing) List from an ERP system. This BOD can be sent in response to a GetPickList or it can be initiated upon some business event.

UpdatePickList

The purpose of the UpdatePickList (Figure B.31) is to update the details of an individual Pick(ing) List from a plant level to an ERP system. This BOD will usually cause updates to occur.

PlanningSchedule

GetPlanningSchedule

The purpose of the GetPlanningSchedule (Figure B.32) is to enable a business applications module to request this Planning Schedule information from another business application. The response to this BOD is ShowPlanningSchedule.

ShowPlanningSchedule

The purpose of the ShowPlanningSchedule (Figure B.32) is to communicate to a business application module or system the sending system's representation of PlanningSchedule information. This request can be used as a response to a GetPlanningSchedule request or as a push notification of an event.

SyncPlanningSchedule

SyncPlanningSchedule (Figure B.32) allows for adding new requirements and the modification of previously established requirements. Customers can use this PlanningSchedule to communicate demand requirements in three different ways. It can be as specific as the Item level or at the Commodity code level, which is higher than Item.

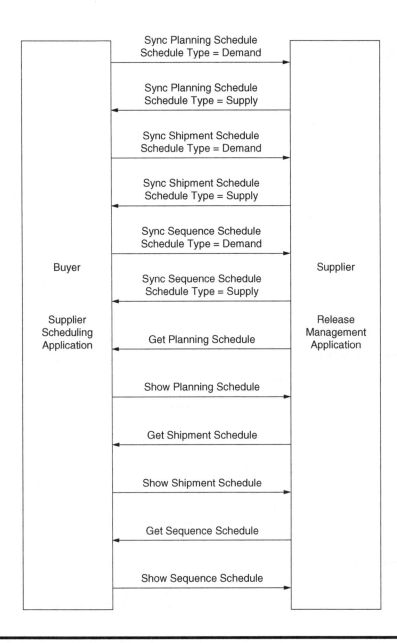

Figure B.32   Context Map 26

PriceList

GetPriceList

The purpose of the GetPriceList (Figure B.16) is to enable a business application module or system to request information concerning new or existing product price lists.

ShowPriceList

The purpose of the ShowPriceList (Figure B.16) is to supply a business application module or system with information concerning new or existing product price lists.

SyncPriceList

The purpose of the SyncPriceList (Figure B.16) is to communicate to a business application module or system the need to initiate the creation of product price list information as well as to update existing price lists.

ProductAvailability

GetProductAvailability

The purpose of the GetProductAvailability (Figure B.11) is to enable requests of product availability data by an Order Management business application to an Available to Promise (ATP) or Production business application. The business process scenario is the Order Management application interacting with the Available to Promise or Production application in order to determine the availability of a product for the customer. This scenario is commonly referred to as Make to Order or Build to Order. The response to this request is the ShowProductAvailability.

ShowProductAvailability

The purpose of the ShowProductAvailability (Figure B.11) is to respond to a GetProductAvailability request or to initiate the passing of product availability data from a Production or Available to Promise (ATP) business application to an Order Management business application. The business process scenario is the Order Management application interacting with the Available to Promise or Production application in order to determine availability of a product for the customer. This scenario is commonly referred to as Make to Order or Build to Order.

ProductionOrder

CancelProductionOrder

The purpose of the CancelProductionOrder (Figure B.7) is to notify a Manufacturing application of the need to cancel a previous order to make a product in a specific quantity, for a specific need, by a specific date. This BOD can be used to cancel an entire Production Order, or a specific line on the Production Order.

> *Processing Note:* This Cancel must refer to the original document and/or item ordered. To Cancel the entire order, include only the Header information for the instance of the Production Order you wish to cancel. To cancel a line or several lines, each line to be Cancelled must be included in the request.

CreateProductionOrder

The purpose of the CreateProductionOrder (Figure B.7) is to notify a Manufacturing application of the need to make a product in a specific quantity, for a specific need, by a specific date. The business environments most likely to require this capability include an Engineer to Order or a Configure to Order manufacturing scenario. This BOD communicates what the product configuration is and what choices have been made from the configuration.

GetProductionOrder

The purpose of the GetProductionOrder (Figure B.33) is to enable a business application module to request specific Production Order information from another business application module. The reply to this is the ShowProductionOrder.

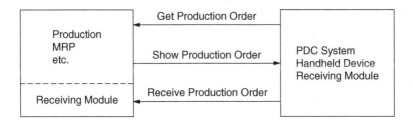

Figure B.33   Context Map 27

GetListProductionOrder

The purpose of the GetListProductionOrder (Figure B.33) is to enable a business software component to request summary Production Order information from another business application module. The response to this request is the ListProductionOrder. The GetListProductionOrder also enables the retrieval of information across several documents using selection fields. An example of this could be requesting all ProductionOrder Lines for a specific Item. This type of functionality is limited to the capabilities of the responding application and needs to be determined during the implementation project.

ListPurchaseOrder

The purpose of the ListPurchaseOrder (Figure B.33) is to send information relative to demand for goods or services to another business application. This may be in response to a GetListPurchaseOrder request, or it may be a notification vehicle, initiated upon an event in a business application. These listings of information may be supplied for Purchase Orders (PO), PO Lines, or PO Sub-Lines.

ReceiveProductionOrder

The purpose of the ReceiveProductionOrder (Figure B.33) is to supply information that the ERP system requires to do receipt posting against a Production Order.

ShowProductionOrder

The purpose of the ShowProductionOrder (Figure B.33) is to supply Production Order information to another business application module.

SyncProductionOrder

The purpose of the SyncProductionOrder (Figure B.34) is to ensure that all business software components in a specific integration instance have the current Production Order information. This BOD is commonly used in a publish-and-subscribe integration environment.

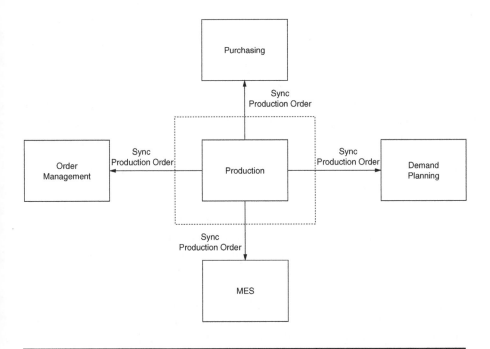

Figure B.34   Context Map #28

ProductRequirement

CancelProductRequirement

The purpose of the CancelProductRequirement (Figure B.11) is to com-municate from one business application to one or more other business applications that a previously requested Item is no longer required.

UpdateProductRequirement

The purpose of the UpdateProductRequirement (Figure B.11) is to enable a business application such as Order Management to reserve a quantity of goods or services for a specific date and time. The business process scenario is the Order Management application interacting with the Avail-able to Promise or Production application in order to determine availability of a product for the customer. This scenario is commonly referred to as

Make to Order or Build to Order. The UpdateProductRequirement accomplishes this task in a two-step process within this one request:

1. The receiving business application checks to see if an Item is available in sufficient quantity by a specific date and time.
2. The receiving business application then reserves that quantity of inventory for that specific date and time combination if the product is available.

If the product requested is not available, the responding application can send one of two responses:

1. A ConfirmBOD to confirm the denial of the request.
2. A ShowProductAvailability to communicate an alternative product availability; this may be OrderItem, Date, or Quantity, or a combination of these.

This may also be accompanied with a message in the Note field Identifier stating that this is an alternative. If the product requested is available, then the responding application may send a ConfirmBOD to confirm the execution of the request.

Project

SyncProject

The purpose of the SyncProject (Figure B.35) is to enable all relevant subsystems that submit transactions to the Project Accounting application to maintain valid values for the key project fields. The target applications for this update would include, but are not necessarily be limited to:

- Accounts Payable
- Accounts Receivable
- Budget
- Order Management
- Purchasing
- Time and Labor
- Travel and Expense

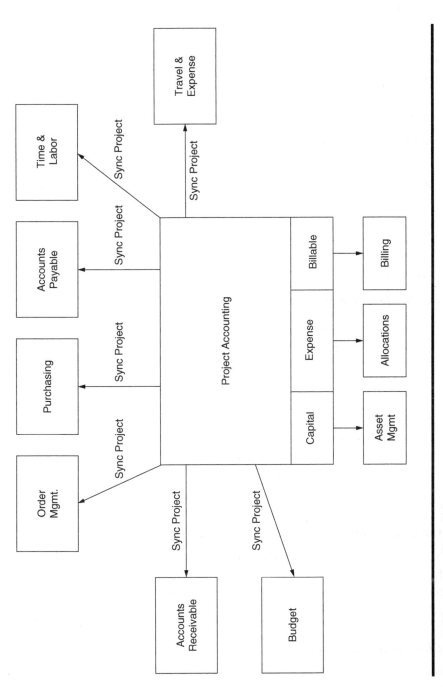

Figure B.35 Context Map #29

ProjectAccounting

LoadProjectAccounting

The purpose of the LoadProjectAccounting (Figure B.36) is to enable all relevant sub-systems that submit single-sided transactions to send information to a Project Accounting application.

PurchaseLedgerInvoice

LoadPurchaseLedgerInvoice

The purpose of the LoadPurchaseLedgerInvoice (Figure B.29) is to transmit data to create an unapproved open item in either a Payables application or a Purchasing application. The scope of the LoadPurchaseLedgerInvoice indicates that the supplier's invoice has not yet been approved and the invoice is to be used as part of the invoice matching process.

PurchaseOrder

AcknowledgePurchaseOrder

The purpose of AcknowledgePurchaseOrder (Figure B.37) is to acknowledge receipt of the Purchase Order and to reflect any changes. Commonly, the acknowledgment is generated by an Order Management application and transmitted to a Purchasing or Procurement application.

AddPurchaseOrder

The purpose of AddPurchaseOrder (Figure B.14) is to communicate from one business application to one or more other business applications that a Purchase Order has been added or needs to be added, depending on the business case.

CancelPurchaseOrder

The purpose of the CancelPurchaseOrder (Figure B.14) is to communicate from one business application to one or more other business applications that a previous Purchase Order or Purchase Order Line is no longer needed.

ChangePurchaseOrder

The purpose of the ChangePurchaseOrder (Figure B.14) is to request another business application to make changes to an existing Purchase Order.

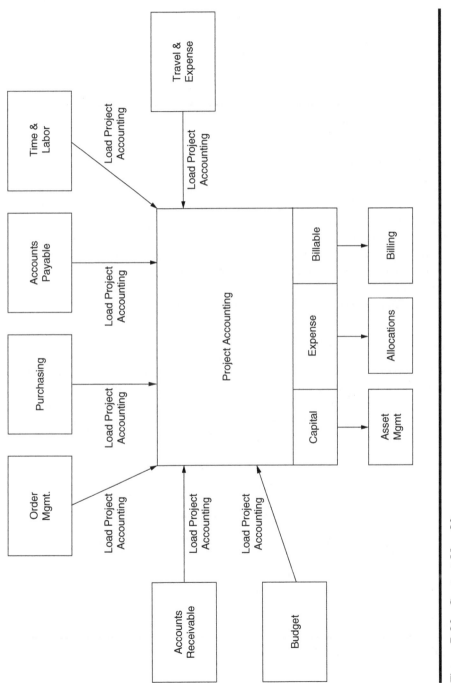

Figure B.36 Context Map 30

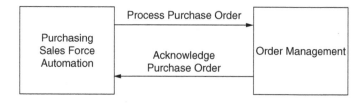

Figure B.37   Context Map 31

GetPurchaseOrder

The purpose of the GetPurchaseOrder (Figure B.38) is to enable a business application module to request information concerning a specific Purchase Order from another business application. The reply to this BOD is the ShowPurchaseOrder. There are several environments that can use this capability. For example, an MRP application can use this BOD to ask for information from an Order Management application, and a Plant Data Collection application can also use this BOD to request information from an Order Management application. This can also happen across business parties.

GetListPurchaseOrder

The purpose of the GetListPurchaseOrder (Figure B.38) is to enable a business application to request information containing summary information for one or more Purchase Orders from another business application. The GetListPurchaseOrder also enables the retrieval of information across several documents using selection fields.

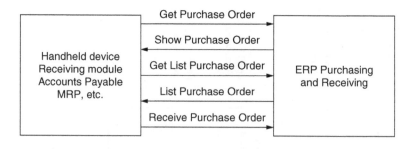

Figure B.38   Context Map 32

ListProductionOrder

The purpose of the ListProductionOrder (Figure B.38) is to enable a business software component to respond to a GetListProductionOrder request or to proactively send a listing of summary information about Production Orders to another business software component.

ProcessPurchaseOrder

The purpose of the ProcessPurchaseOrder (Figure B.37) is to transmit a Purchase Order to a supplier's Order Management application.

ReceivePurchaseOrder

The purpose of the ReceivePurchaseOrder (Figure B.38) is to supply the information that a business application module requires to do receipt posting against a Purchase Order.

ShowPurchaseOrder

The purpose of the ShowPurchaseOrder (Figure B.38) is to supply Purchase Order information to another business application module. This request can be used as a response to a GetPurchaseOrder request or as a push notification of an event. There are many possible business applications in several environments that can use this capability. Examples include:

- An Order Management application could use this BOD to send information to a Plant Data Collection application.
- An MRP, Inventory, or Manufacturing business application could use this BOD to obtain order information.
- An Order Management application can notify the MRP/Inventory application when a vendor gives or changes a promise day.

SyncPurchaseOrder

The purpose of the SyncPurchaseOrder is to facilitate keeping Purchase Order information synchronized on separate databases throughout an enterprise. The SyncPurchaseOrder allows for adding new purchase orders and for the modification of previously established purchase orders.

Quote

AddQuote

The purpose of the AddQuote (Figure B.39) is to communicate from one business application to one or more other business applications that additional data related to a Quote has been added or needs to be added, depending on the business case.

CancelQuote

The purpose of the CancelQuote (Figure B.39) is to publish to a business application or system the need to cancel an entire Quote or one or more of its line items.

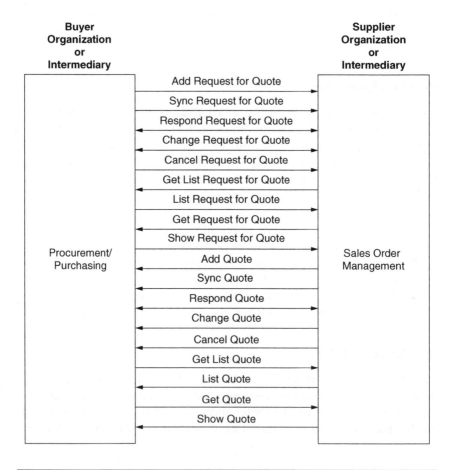

Figure B.39   Context Map 33

ChangeQuote

The purpose of the ChangeQuote (Figure B.39) is to request that another business application component make changes to an existing Quote.

GetQuote

The purpose of the GetQuote (Figure B.39) is to enable a business application module to request this Quote information from another business application. The response to this BOD is ShowQuote.

GetListQuote

The purpose of the GetListQuote (Figure B.39) is to enable a business application module to request information containing summary information for one or more Quotes. The response to this request is ListQuote. The GetListQuote also enables the retrieval of information across several documents by using selection fields. An example of this could be requesting all SalesInformation Component occurrences for a specific Quote line.

ListQuote

The purpose of the ListQuote (Figure B.39) is to publish one or more summary listings of Quote information to other business application components. This may be in response to a GetListQuote request or to proactively publish a listing of summary Quote information for a business event.

RespondQuote

The purpose of the RespondQuote (Figure B.39) is to communicate from one business application to one or more other business applications that additional data related to a Quote has been added or needs to be added, depending on the business case.

ShowQuote

The purpose of the ShowQuote (Figure B.39) is to communicate to a business application module or system the sending system's representation of Quote information. This request can be used as a response to a GetQuote request.

SyncQuote

The purpose of the SyncQuote (Figure B.39) is to ensure that all business software components in a specific integration instance have the current Quote information. This BOD is commonly used to publish the need to create or update a Quote in a publish-and-subscribe integration environment.

Receivable

LoadReceivable

The purpose of the LoadReceiveable (Figure B.40) is to transmit data to create a receivable open item in a Receivable application from the billing information generated in an Order Management application.

The LoadReceiveable can also update the General Ledger, depending on the specific architecture of the Accounting application. The scope of the LoadReceiveable is to create a BOD to recognize customer obligation (Accounts Receivable asset). Specific transactions include:

- Sales Invoice
- Credit Memo
- Debit Memo
- Charge-Back

The LoadReceiveable can also be used for transactions that do not originate from an Order Management application. The following two models illustrate that the LoadReceiveable may, in some cases, be adequate to update the Financial applications (i.e., Receivables and General Ledger) and in other cases, will also require the PostJournal to ensure that the General Ledger account balances are updated.

RequestForQuote

AddRequestForQuote

The purpose of the AddRequestForQuote (Figure B.39) is to communicate from one business application to one or more other business applications that additional data related to a Request for Quote has been added or needs to be added, depending on the business case.

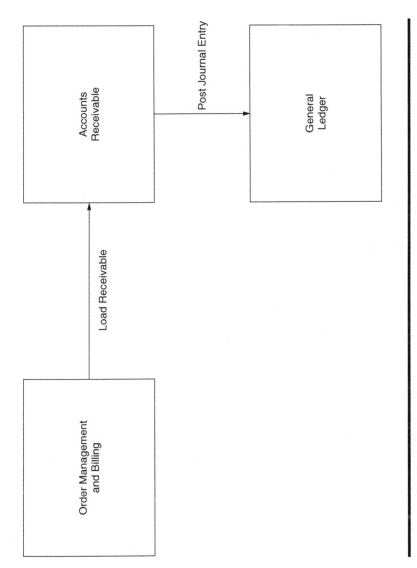

Figure B.40 Context Map 34

CancelRequestForQuote

The purpose of the CancelRequestForQuote (Figure B.39) is to publish to a business application or system the need to cancel an entire Request for Quote or one or more of its line items.

ChangeRequestForQuote

The purpose of the ChangeRequestForQuote (Figure B.39) is to request that another business application component make changes to an existing Request for Quote.

GetRequestForQuote

The purpose of the GetRequestForQuote (Figure B.39) document is to enable a business application module to request Request for Quote information from another business application. The response to this BOD is ShowRequestForQuote.

GetListRequestForQuote

The purpose of the GetListRequestForQuote (Figure B.39) is to enable a business application module to request information containing summary information for one or more Requests for Quotes. The response to this request is ListRequestForQuote. The GetListRequestForQuote also enables the retrieval of information across several documents using selection fields.

ListRequestForQuote

The purpose of the ListRequestForQuote (Figure B.39) is to publish one or more summary listings of Request for Quote information to other business application components. This may be in response to a GetListRequestForQuote request or to proactively publish a listing of summary Request for Quote information for a business event.

RespondRequestForQuote

The purpose of the RespondRequestForQuote (Figure B.39) is to communicate from one business application to one or more other business applications that additional data related to a Request for Quote is available.

ShowRequestForQuote

The purpose of the ShowRequestForQuote (Figure B.39) is to communicate to a business application module or system the sending system's representation of Request for Quote information. This request can be used as a response to a GetRequestForQuote request.

SyncRequestForQuote

The purpose of the SyncRequestForQuote (Figure B.39) is to ensure that all business software components in a specific integration instance have the current Request for Quote information. This BOD is commonly used to publish the need to create or update a Request for Quote in a publish-and-subscribe integration environment.

Requisition

AddRequisition

The purpose of the AddRequisition (Figure B.14) is to send demand for goods or services to another business application for consideration of buying or in some way obtaining the requested items.

CancelRequisition

The purpose of the CancelRequisition (Figure B.14) is to communicate from one business application to one or more other business applications that a previous requisition or requisition line item is no longer needed.

ChangeRequisition

The purpose of the ChangeRequisition (Figure B.14) is to communicate changes to an existing request for goods or services. This change must refer to the original document and/or item requested. The change processing assumes replacement of fields sent, with the exception of: the key fields for the Order and Line. If any of the Field Identifiers above require changing, that constitutes a cancellation of the request and/or the addition of another Requisition.

CreateRequisition

The purpose of the CreateRequisition (Figure B.14) is to notify another business application of the need to order parts in a specific quantity, for a specific need by date.

GetRequisition

The purpose of the GetRequisition (Figure B.14) is to enable a business application to request information concerning a specific requisition from another business application. The reply to this BOD is the ShowRequisition.

GetListRequisition

The purpose of the GetListRequisition (Figure B.14) is to enable a business application to request summary information for one or more requisitions from another business application. The GetListRequisition also enables the retrieval of information across several documents using selection fields. An example of this could be requesting all Requisition Lines for a specific OrderItem.

ListRequisition

The purpose of the ListRequisition (Figure B.14) is to send information relative to demand for goods or services to another business application. This may be in response to a GetListRequisition request, or it may be a notification vehicle, initiated upon an event in a business application. The List verb describes the behavior of supplying one or several documents in a summary format to the requesting business application. These listings of information may be supplied for requisition documents, or requisition lines, and/or requisition sub-lines.

ShowRequisition

The purpose of the ShowRequisition (Figure B.14) is to send information relative to demand for goods or services to another business application. This may be in response to a GetRequisition request, or it may be a notification vehicle, initiated upon an event in a business application.

ResourceAllocation

ProcessResourceAllocation

The purpose of the ProcessResourceAllocation (Figure B.41) is to notify a Manufacturing application of the use of required labor or machine time on a production order making a product. The business environments most likely to require this capability include any type of manufacturing scenario. This BOD communicates what machine was utilized or which person performed the work and their labor skill class, along with the amount of time worked and at what time this event occurred.

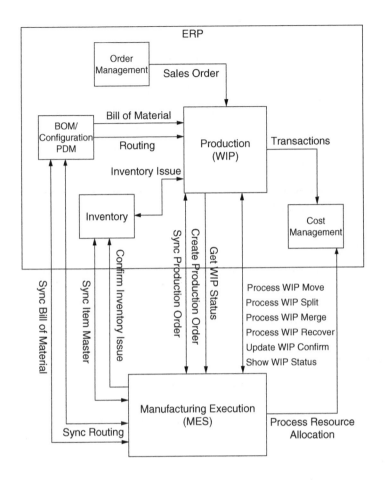

Figure B.41   Context Map 35

Routing

GetRouting

The purpose of the GetRouting (Figure B.42) is to communicate to a business application module or system a request for an existing Routing structure to be returned in a ShowRouting.

GetListRouting

The purpose of the GetListRouting (Figure B.42) is to communicate to a business application component or module a request for a summary list of a Routing structure or structures to be returned in a ListRouting.

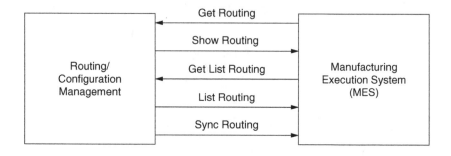

Figure B.42   Context Map 36

ListRouting

The purpose of the ListRouting (Figure B.42) is to communicate one or more summary listings of Routing information to another business application component. This may be the result of a GetList request or it may be initiated by some other business event.

ShowRouting

The purpose of the ShowRouting (Figure B.42) is to communicate to a business application module or system the relevant information about a specific Routing. The ShowRouting is in response to a GetRouting request.

SyncRouting

The purpose of the SyncRouting (Figure B.42) is to communicate to a business application component or system the need to create a new Routing or to update an existing Routing structure. This BOD may be necessary to address the Make to Order, Assemble to Order, and Finished Goods business ordering scenarios in a Logistics to Manufacturing application integration scenario.

SalesOrder

AddSalesOrder

The purpose of the AddSalesOrder (Figure B.43) is to communicate from one business application to one or more other business applications that a Sales Order has been added or needs to be added, depending on the business case.

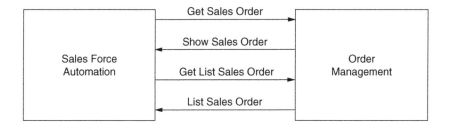

Figure B.43   Context Map 37

CancelSalesOrder

The purpose of the CancelSalesOrder (Figure B.43) is to communicate from one business application to one or more other business applications that a previous Sales Order, line, or schedule is no longer needed.

ChangeSalesOrder

The purpose of the ChangeSalesOrder (Figure B.43) is to request that another business application component make changes to an existing Sales Order.

GetSalesOrder

The purpose of the GetSalesOrder (Figure B.43) is to enable a business application module to request information concerning a specific Sales Order from another business application. The reply to this BOD is the ShowSalesOrder. There are several possible business applications in several environments that can use this capability. For example, a Sales Automation application might use this BOD to ask for information from a Customer Order application.

GetListSalesOrder

The purpose of the GetListSalesOrder (Figure B.43) is to enable a business application module to request information containing summary information for one or more Sales Orders from another business application. The response to this request is the ListSalesOrder. The GetListSalesOrder also enables the retrieval of information across several documents using selection fields.

ListSalesOrder

The purpose of the ListSalesOrder (Figure B.43) is to enable a business application module to respond to a GetListSalesOrder request or to proactively send a listing of summary information about Sales Orders to one or more other applications. This BOD does not usually cause updates to occur. It may be used as part of a large integration scenario or as a single tool for sending information concerning existing demands for goods or services. For example, a Customer Order application might use this BOD to respond to a request for information from a Sales Automation application.

ShowSalesOrder

The purpose of the ShowSalesOrder (Figure B.43) is to supply Sales Order information to another business application module. This request can be used as a response to a GetSalesOrder request or as a push notification of an event.

SyncSalesOrder

The purpose of the SyncSalesOrder (Figure B.44) is to facilitate keeping sales or customer order information synchronized on separate databases throughout an enterprise. The SyncSalesOrder allows the adding of new sales orders and the modification of previously established sales orders.

SequenceSchedule

GetSequenceSchedule

Commonly, the GetSequenceSchedule (Figure B.32) is generated by a Work In Process application and transmitted to an Order or Material Planning application. The purpose of the GetSequenceSchedule is to enable a business application module to request this SequenceSchedule information from another business application. The response to this BOD is ShowSequenceSchedule.

ShowSequenceSchedule

Commonly, the ShowSequenceSchedule (Figure B.32) is generated by a Work In Process application and transmitted to an Order or Material Planning application. The purpose of the ShowSequenceSchedule is to

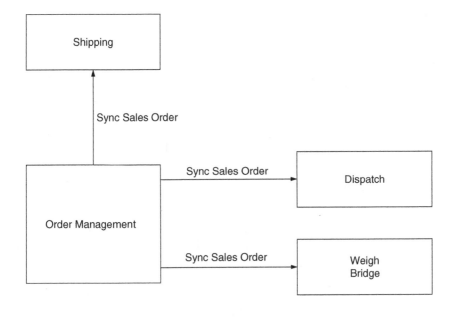

Figure B.44   Context Map 38

communicate to a business application module or system the sending system's representation of SequenceSchedule information. This request can be used as a response to a GetSequenceSchedule request or as a push notification of an event.

SyncSequenceSchedule

The purpose of the SyncSequenceSchedule (Figure B.32) is to enable the exchange of SequenceSchedule information authorizing a sequenced shipment of parts for specific trading partners and addresses. Commonly, the SequenceSchedule is generated by a Work In Process application and transmitted to an Order or Material Planning application.

Shipment

ShowShipment

A ShowShipment (Figure B.13) is a business document that details the intent to transport a specific quantity of material goods from a supplier to a customer or business partner destination.

ShipmentSchedule

GetShipmentSchedule

Commonly, the ShipmentSchedule is generated by a Material Planning application and transmitted to an Order or Material Planning application. The purpose of the GetShipmentSchedule (Figure B.32) is to enable a business applications module to request this ShipmentSchedule (Figure B.45) information from another business application. The response to this BOD is ShowShipmentSchedule.

ShowShipmentSchedule

Commonly, the ShipmentSchedule is generated by a Material Planning application and transmitted to an Order or Material Planning application. The purpose of the ShowShipmentSchedule (Figure B.32) is to communicate to a business application module or system the sending system's

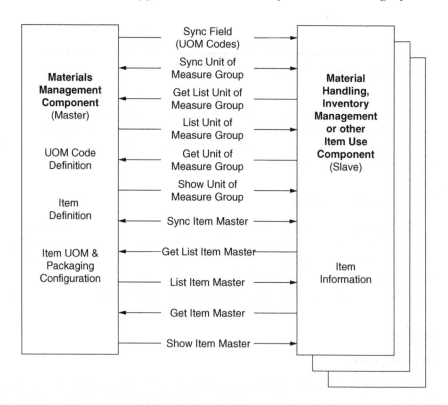

Figure B.45   Context Map 39

representation of ShipmentSchedule information. This request can be used as a response to a GetShipmentSchedule request or as a push notification of an event.

SyncShipmentSchedule

The purpose of the SyncShipmentSchedule (Figure B.32) is to enable the exchange of ShipmentSchedule information, authorizing a shipment quantity and date for specific trading partners and addresses. Commonly, the ShipmentSchedule is generated by a Material Planning application and transmitted to an Order or Material Planning application.

UnitOfMeasureGroup

GetUnitOfMeasureGroup

The purpose of the GetUnitOfMeasureGroup (Figure B.45) is to communicate to a business application component or module a request for an existing UnitOfMeasureGroup to be returned in a ShowUnitOfMeasureGroup.

GetListUnitOfMeasureGroup

The purpose of the GetListUnitOfMeasure (Figure B.45) is to communicate to a business application component or module a request for a summary list of UnitOfMeasureGroups to be returned in a ListUnitOfMeasure.

ListUnitOfMeasureGroup

The purpose of the ListUnitOfMeasureGroup (Figure B.45) is to supply Unit-of-Measure Group summary information to another business application module. This may be the result of a GetListUnitOfMeasureGroup request or initiated by some other business event. When a Receiving application receives this BOD, the information can be used as is or it can be used to initiate a selection of a specific UnitOfMeasureGroup through the GetUnitOfMeasureGroup request. The processing is designed to provide multiple occurrences of summary data.

ShowUnitOfMeasureGroup

The purpose of the ShowUnitOfMeasureGroup (Figure B.45) is to supply Unit-of-Measure Group relationship information to another business application module. This request can be issued as a response to a GetUnitOfMeasureGroup request or as the result of some other business event.

SyncUnitOfMeasureGroup

The purpose of the SyncUnitOfMeasureGroup (Figure B.45) is to supply a set of Unit-Of-Measure relationships to another business application module. This BOD addresses the need for applications to exchange item-independent, alternative UOM information beyond the stocking UOM.

WIPConfirm

GetWIPConfirm

The purpose of the GetWIPConfirm (Figure B.46) is to enable the requesting of data necessary to perform a confirmation of the movement of WIP (Work In Progress).

ShowWIPConfirm

The purpose of the ShowWIPConfirm (Figure B.46) is to respond to a request for the data necessary to perform a confirmation of the movement of WIP (Work In Progress).

UpdateWIPConfirm

The purpose of the UpdateWIPConfirm (Figure B.46) is to confirm receipt of WIP (Work In Process) materials.

WIPMerge

ProcessWIPMerge

The purpose of the ProcessWIPMerge (Figure B.41) is to notify a Manufacturing application of the creation of a single production lot from multiple production lots of a product being made on a production order.

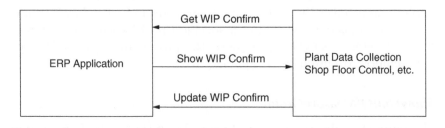

Figure B.46   Context Map 40

The business environment most likely to require this capability is a lot-based, discrete manufacturing scenario. This BOD communicates the originating lots, the resulting lot, lot quantities, and the processing step at which this event occurred, along with the time at which this event occurred.

WIPMove

ProcessWIPMove

The purpose of the ProcessWIPMove (Figure B.41) is to notify a Manufacturing application of the progression through the production processing steps or operations of a product being made on a production order. The business environments most likely to require this capability include any type of manufacturing scenario. This BOD communicates which processing step the product is coming from and which step it is being moved to, along with the quantity moving and the time this event occurred. This BOD assumes that the applications involved in this business scenario will have already synchronized the production item and its BOM/Routing information.

WIPRecover

ProcessWIPRecover

The purpose of the ProcessWIPRecover (Figure B.41) is to notify a Manufacturing application of the creation of usable production materials from material previously considered unsuitable for production use. This is most often likely to represent a return to production of scrap material. The business environments most likely to require this capability include any type of manufacturing scenario. This BOD communicates what is being recovered, the quantity being recovered, and the processing step at which the recovered material is to reenter the production process, along with the time at which this event occurred.

WIPSplit

ProcessWIPSplit

The purpose of the ProcessWIPSplit (Figure B.41) is to notify a Manufacturing application of the creation of multiple production lots from a single production lot of a product being made on a production order. The business environment most likely to require this capability is a lot-based, discrete manufacturing scenario. This BOD communicates the originating lot, the resulting lots, their quantities, and the processing step at which this event occurred, along with the time at which this event occurred.

WIPStatus

GetWIPStatus

The purpose of the GetWIPStatus (Figure B.41) is to notify a Manufacturing application of the progress of a production order at a point in time. The business environments most likely to require this capability include any type of manufacturing scenario where BODs for individual manufacturing transactions and events are not utilized. This BOD communicates what quantities of end product reside at which processing steps, along with the time this snapshot view was taken. The response to this BOD is ShowWIPStatus (Figure B.41).

ShowWIPStatus

The purpose of the ShowWIPStatus (Figure B.41) is to notify a Manufacturing application of the progress of a production order at a point in time. The business environments most likely to require this capability include any type of manufacturing scenario where BODs for individual manufacturing transactions and events are not utilized. This BOD communicates what quantities of end product reside at which processing steps, along with the time this snapshot view was taken.

NOTE

1. About Open Applications Group, http://www.openapplications.org/(19 Nov. 2003).

Appendix C

GLOSSARY

Activity: Activities are a group of tasks in a workplan that has similar purpose of effort or design.

Advanced Software Development (ASD): An interactive approach to software development designed for projects requiring fast turn-around, changing needs, and uncertainty. In ASD, resources are continuously learning and geared for constant change, reevaluation, and strong collaboration among developers, testers, and customers.

Agile Approach:A software development approach that focuses on simplified code, frequent testing, and delivering functionality interactively. The focus of Agile is on developing components of functionality versus large systems.

Application Architecture: The domain of the electronic bits of an organization's assets that primarily focuses on the software supporting the systems. This discipline's focus is on the interaction of applications and their components throughout the enterprise.

Approach: The technique or process of how the resources of an organization will build or modify a system.

Architecture: The discipline of optimizing major components of specific technology and managing the evolution of these components.

Artifact: Artifacts are those diagrams and documents that resources create to capture design concepts for implementation. Unlike a deliverable, an artifact is not generally bounded by a project and is usually the result of specific functional responsibilities by resources in the organization.

Business Process Reengineering (BPR): An approach that examines, rethinks, and redesigns the processes of an organization. The main goal of BPR is to achieve dramatic results in areas of importance to customers and other stakeholders. BPR is commonly associated with dramatic or radical overhauls of existing business processes and uses technology to achieve improved results.

Center of Excellence (COE):COE is a group of resources that shares a common body of expertise that supports a large portion of an organization. Typically, these organizations are centrally located.

Capability Maturity Model® (CMM): A technique that determines the effectiveness (or maturity) of the development life cycle within an organization.

Component: A subset of a system that improves understanding of complex systems.

Conceptual Architecture: This is the middle realm of LEA that captures high-level views that encapsulate key systems and subsystems, including their relationship to the enterprise and other systems. This system view helps decompose the enterprise into smaller systems that more readily help coordinate efforts between IT and business on technology.

Commercial-off-the-Shelf (COTS): Vendor packages that are generally software solutions providing specific functionality useful to business.

Decomposition: The process of breaking down complex systems into simpler components.

Deliverable: A tangible document or event that is produced by projects to demonstrate progress. Deliverables tend to be one-time products versus artifacts that have multiple usages.

Diagram: A graphical representation of a conceptual idea for communicating to various resources.

Encapsulation: The hiding of component design to avoid too much detail that is irrelevant for usage.

Enterprise Architecture: How systems and their components interact and their relationships to other systems and their components, and the principles governing the design and evolution of all the systems.

Execution Architecture: The last realm of LEA that provides a view from a project perspective, giving an approach for the deployment and maintenance of technology. Execution Architecture describes balancing the right amount of detail for increasing a project's success.

Extreme Programming (XP): Ann agile approach that includes a set of best practices as identified by Kent Beck.

Feature-Driven Development (FDD): A short-iteration process approach for software development projects driven by functional needs.

Framework: The overarching structure that focuses on all significant systems within an organization and provides a simplified view of the complex entities and processes that comprise the components of these systems.

Information Architecture: Focuses on interactions with the systems throughout the enterprise. The key view of this discipline is on the processes and flows supporting interactions with employees, customers, business partners, and external systems.

Lean Management: Emphasizes getting the right things to the right place at the right time, while minimizing waste and being open to change. Lean management accomplishes this through reduction of planning and creating more flexible production processes, which results in products and services that are made-to-order.

Lightweight Enterprise Architecture (LEA): An enterprise architectural framework that uses a minimal set of artifacts to best evolve the technical landscape within an organization.

Methodology: Provides the governance model and manages the activities and tasks for the life cycle of projects.

Milestone: A key event that shows major progress in a project.

Model: A graphical representation of an actual or intended system for communicating to various resources.

Object-Oriented (O-O): O-O builds on the concept of an "object," which is an abstraction of data structures. These objects are encapsulated with a set of routines, called "methods," that are the only source to operate on the data. This allows the interface of objects to be well defined and facilitates easier code development if the interface remains the same.

Prototyping: From an approach perspective, prototyping is a technique of validating ideas and is usually thrown out after design. From a methodology standpoint, prototyping is an iterative process that successful iterations build upon to achieve the final product.

Rapid Application Development (RAD): A software technique designed to yield faster development cycles and better results using recent advances in software tools. In addition, RAD employs the principles of collaborative requirements, prototyping, software reuse, and less formality in the life cycle.

Resources: The human capital, assets, and facilities in an enterprise.

Rational Unified Process® (RUP): An object-oriented software development methodology built upon the systematic use of the Unified Modeling Language (UML). RUP has four distinct phases of development, each organized into a number of separate iterations that must satisfy defined criteria before proceeding to the next phase.

Systems Development Life Cycle (SDLC): A structured approach to system development, created to manage all the processes involved, from an initial planning through maintenance and support of the final product.

Spiral Methodology: A software life-cycle method that uses incremental development, based on the waterfall model for each step, with the aim of reducing risk. In the spiral method, developers define and implement features in order of decreasing priority, thus addressing significant challenges and major functionality first.

Stage: As used in the context of project management, a stage is a series of activities that represents a significant effort and usually results in the realization of a major milestone.

Strategic Architecture: The first realm of LEA that provides the enterprise view of technology and sets the measures and guidelines for the successful stewardship of the systems in the organization.

System: Systems are the collection of resources and procedures to accomplish a set of specific functions.

Task: The lowest form of effort in a workplan (see Work Breakdown) that represents a unit of work that is assignable to specific resources.

Technical Architecture: Provides the physical assets to support the applications deployed in the enterprise. In addition, Technical Architecture governs and evolves the facilities of the enterprise to support the resources identified by Information Architecture. These are the assets like servers, storage devices, and network equipment. In addition, they include the data center facilities and all the peripheral equipment, such as generators, power conditioners, and backup units.

Total Quality Management (TQM):TQM focuses on the best optimization of a current system to achieve better products and services for consumers. TQM places emphasis on continuous, incremental improvement of processes to achieve the best system.

Unified Modeling Language (UML): A standard notation for the modeling of real-world objects as a first step in developing an object-oriented software project. The notation is the collaboration of several industry experts and is the accepted standard of the Object Management Group (OMG).

Vertical Solution:A vendor package that provides functionality specific to an industry.

Waterfall Model: Commonly describes a development methodology that is linear and sequential. Once a development phase is completed, the development proceeds to the next phase and does not reiterate any previous phase. This view allows for better departmentalization and managerial control.

Work Breakdown Structure (WBS): A hierarchical representation of effort for a project that time and resources can be applied. A WBS is often referred to as a workplan.

Lightweight
Enterprise
Architectures

Other CRC/Auerbach Publications in Software Development, Software Engineering, and Project Management

INDEX

R

T

T - #0096 - 101024 - C0 - 234/156/19 [21] - CB - 9780849321146 - Gloss Lamination